The Internet Handbook for Canadian Lawyers

Third Edition

The Internet Handbook for Canadian Lawyers

Third Edition

M. DREW JACKSON, BA LLB
TIMOTHY L. TAYLOR, BA MBA

CARSWELL
Thomson Professional Publishing

Canadian Cataloguing in Publication Data

Jackson, M. Drew, 1962 –
   The Internet handbook for Canadian lawyers

3rd ed.
Includes index.
ISBN 0-459-23908-2

1. Internet (Computer network) – Handbooks, manuals, etc.
2. Law – Canada – Computer network resources. 3. Law – Computer network resources.

I. Taylor, Timothy L., 1963 – . II. Title.

TK5105.875.I57J33 2000   025.06'34   C00-932638-3

 The paper used in this publication meets the minimum requirements of American National Standard for Information Sciences – Permanence of Paper for Printed Library Material, ANSI Z39.48-1984.

 **CARSWELL**
Thomson Professional Publishing

One Corporate Plaza, 2075 Kennedy Road, Scarborough, Ontario M1T 3V4
Customer Relations:
Toronto 1-416-609-3800
Elsewhere in Canada/U.S. 1-800-387-5164
Fax 1-416-298-5904

About the Authors

M. Drew Jackson is the Manager, New Media for the Continuing Legal Education Society of BC, where he is responsible for CLE of BC's Internet-based offerings.

Email: *djackson@cle.bc.ca*

Timothy Taylor is a Vancouver writer. His work has appeared in *Saturday Night*, *Canadian Lawyer*, and other publications.

Acknowledgements

For Daphne, Zoë, & Téa.

For Jane.

TABLE OF CONTENTS

6 THE WEB: ITS RESOURCES

7 THE WEB: FINDING TOOLS

LIST OF FIGURES

1 WHY THE INTERNET MATTERS

WHY IS THE INTERNET SUCH A BIG DEAL?

WHAT CAN THE INTERNET DO FOR MY LAW PRACTICE?

WHAT IS THIS BOOK?

The Internet is hardly new. Indeed it was 30 years old in 1999 for those who are counting. But for its first 15 years (at least) it was something of a fringe affair: an on-line community of researchers, academics, hackers and computer enthusiasts who met and exchanged ideas in a place not quite overlapping the rest of popular culture or society. It took a working knowledge of the computer language UNIX to navigate the Internet, for one thing. And even the idea of a computer network in itself was just beginning to gain familiarity among end users—those of us who are non-technical, who use computers in service of other pursuits. Not much about the Internet in those days made it easily accessible or even necessarily useful to the average layperson. Or to the lawyer for that matter, or to any professional with an interest in legal information.

Since then, there has been a sea change in popular perceptions of the Internet. The Internet has suddenly become part of our everyday life. Email and the World Wide Web have revolutionized the way we communicate, the way we access information, the way we conduct business. Most clients now expect, even demand, that their lawyers be accessible through email. The web gives us unprecedented access to information, leaving some of us reeling from information overload while making others feel more empowered as consumers and as professionals. Internet (or dot com) companies have led an unprecedented escalation in the world's stock markets.

> The Internet is said to be both over-hyped and undervalued. Ask any signed-up member of the "digirati," and you will be told that the Internet is the most transforming invention in human history. It has the capacity to change everything—the way we work, the way we learn and play, even, maybe, the way we sleep or have sex. What is more, it is doing so at far greater speed than the other great disruptive technologies of the 20th century, such as electricity, the telephone and the car.
>
> –*The Economist*, 26 June 1999

There can be no doubt: the Internet is a significant innovation and it's here to stay. The Internet is a tool that can make you more productive, more accessible, and more connected, but only if you know how to use it effectively and how to integrate it into your professional life seamlessly and efficiently.

With the third edition of this book, we have tried to reflect this reality. We have provided more step-by-step guidance for the new user, and for the experienced user we have expanded and updated coverage of such topics as web finding tools, web legal resources, and Internet legal issues. We hope to help make your forays onto the Internet as productive as they can be.

WHY IS THE INTERNET SUCH A BIG DEAL?

The Internet is a new medium that is transforming the way we do things. That, in a nutshell, is why it's so important. To break this thought down somewhat, you might say there are three principal reasons why the Internet has grown so quickly and promises to have such a large impact on our professional and personal lives.

1. The Internet is not just a static resource; it's an interactive medium.

The Internet is a medium that allows users to do more than merely consume information supplied by others. Unlike media such as TV and radio, the Internet allows users to also *supply* information, to *interact*. And the interaction is not limited (as in the case of telephone or fax) to one-to-one communication, but can be one-to-many or many-to-many. This flexibility has resulted in a dizzying array of offerings: on the Internet, you can buy books, read newspapers, debate politics, trade stock, bid in auctions. The Internet is a new place to find information, to be entertained, to converse, to do business; in short, a powerful and flexible new medium.

2. As the Internet grows and gets easier to use, it gets much more useful.

The dramatic growth of the Internet is not happening spontaneously. It's a direct response to innovation. Steadily over its lifespan, the Internet community has been developing and experimenting with increasingly sophisticated services to allow the exchange of information more effectively and easily. This is key. Ease-of-use attracts users. Tricky systems may attract the hobbyist and enthusiast, but easy-to-use systems attract the public, which then attracts the providers of information, which

then attracts more of the public, which attracts more information providers, and so on.

The rapid growth of the the World Wide Web itself is a case in point: in early 1994, the web began to attract a lot of attention. It offered pages of information that could be set up quite easily, and could contain text, graphics, sound and moving images. All of this in a familiar point-and-click environment like the Windows or Macintosh interface familiar to many computer users. By July 1994, the web had an estimated 1,000 sites, where information providers (individuals, companies, universities) had established a presence for the express purpose of supporting the visits and enquiries of information consumers. Within two years, by mid-1996, the number of sites on the web had grown to some 250,000. By the end of 1999, over 10 million unique websites were in existence.

This growth was a response to an ease-of-use innovation, probably the greatest yet seen on the Internet (but standby, there will certainly be others). The web generated interest among casual information users, who attracted information providers, whose information products attracted many, many more users.

This is important to the lawyer, and to many others, because of the content boom the emergence of the web has generated. As the Internet community of information consumers and suppliers has grown, the range of information and offerings have broadened enormously—over the web, you can now access news, buy software, do your banking, reserve airline tickets, trade stock, bid in an auction, research law, and discuss issues. Information and resources of interest to lawyers, as we will see at various points throughout this book, have grown exponentially in the last few years. The Internet is becoming a very useful place indeed.

3. The Internet is transforming the way the world does business.

The Internet is having a profound impact on business. The Internet is helping companies to lower costs dramatically across their supply and demand chains, take their customer service into a different league,

---

Internet Vital Statistics

Number of Internet host computers in August 1981: 213[1]

In July 1995: 8.2 million[2]

In January 2000: 72.4 million[3]

Number of regular Internet users, worldwide, at the end of 1995: 44 million[4]

At the end of 1999: 275 million[5]

Percentage of North American Population projected to be regular Internet users in 2005: 71.5 per cent[6]

Number of Canadians over age 18 having Internet access at the end of 1999: 13.5 million[7]

Rank of Canada in Internet users per capita: 7th[8]

Annual cost of a subscription to the print edition of *The Wall Street Journal*: $175[9]

Annual cost of a subscription to the Internet edition of *The Wall Street Journal*: $59[10]

Revenue earned by Amazon.com in 1996: $15 million[11]

Revenue earned by Amazon.com in the first six months of 2000: $1.15 billion[12]

Market capitalization of Amazon.com in mid-2000: $15 billion[13]

Volume of sales generated by the World Wide Web in 1995: $436 million[14]

In 1998: $46 billion[15]

Percentage of retail stock trades taking place on the Internet at the end of 1998: 25 per cent[16]

Bank's cost to process as in-person transaction, in dollars: $1.07[17]

Bank's cost to process an Internet transaction, in dollars: $0.10[18]

Rank of lawyers among 30 occupations in using the Internet: 16[19]

Percentage of senior executives (CEOs, CFOs, and CIOs) who have Internet access: 92 per cent[20]

Percentage of the Internet users in the United States who are women: over 50 per cent[21]

Percentage of users who find the web "indispensable": 92 per cent[22]

---

enter new markets, create additional revenue streams, and redefine their business relationships. Entirely new companies and business models are emerging in industries ranging from flowers to transportation of goods to bring together buyers and sellers in highly efficient new electronic marketplaces.

Forrester Research argues that e-business in North America is about to reach a threshold from which it will accelerate into "hyper-growth". Inter-company trade of goods over the Internet, it forecasts, will double every year over the next several years, surging from $43 billion in 1998 to $1.3 trillion in 2003. That makes Forrester's forecasts of business-to-consumer e-commerce over the same period—a rise from $8 billion to $108 billion—look positively modest.

Such dramatic change in the way business is done begs for those who are advising business (that is, legal professionals) to pay close attention to the Internet.

CAN THE INTERNET DO SOMETHING FOR MY LAW PRACTICE?

In a word: yes. It can do a lot, in fact. And responding to your retort: "Well, then show me" is the root motivation for this book. We can't describe everything the Internet does, because being a free-flowing information exchange, new transactions are being thought up all the time. But we can point you in a few good directions, and encourage you to think of the Internet as a tool you can use to do at least five specific things.

1. **You can communicate with your professional community.** By this we mean your clients and your colleagues.

2. **You can keep abreast of recent developments in the law or with breaking news of interest to you.** Case summaries, conventional newspapers, financial magazines, and all manner of news outlets are available online to keep you up-to-date.

3. **You can quickly and easily obtain information you need in your practice.** From the text of government bills to court decisions, from corporate filings to medical data, the Internet allows you to retrieve relevant documents and information more quickly and more easily than any other medium.

4. **You can conduct legal research.** Case and statute databases, law journals, and legal publications are available online that can be mined as part of your legal research strategy.

5. **You can market your services.** Regardless of what you may have heard, it's not forbidden to advertise on the Internet. There are places where it is appropriate, however, and places where it is not (as we'll see in The Short Happy Marketing Blitz of Canter and Seigel in Chapter Two).

But enough of this talk. What about if we showed you this in a different way? It's morning, you've just pulled into the office and poured yourself a coffee. You sit down at your desk and turn to your computer screen. It's 7:45 and you have 15 minutes. Let's take this new medium for a test drive and see how far we get.

7:46 You open your email. Your inbox includes two notes from clients. From the subject lines you see that one is confirming your lunch date, while the other is from a client asking you for an update on yesterday's chambers application. You highlight the first note, click reply, and enter the words: "Thanks Jill, see you at noon." You write a short reply to the second client's email, and with a mouse click attach the order that you secured in chambers yesterday.

7:48 You click "send mail" and move on to the rest of your email. Also in your email inbox are several notes from the mailing lists you subscribe to. You browse these quickly. Two notes are responses to your request of yesterday for recommendations of a DNA expert. You send a thank you email to both writers.

7:52 You exit the email reader and open up your World Wide Web browser. You go to the Supreme Court of Canada website and browse through the list of cases handed down yesterday. You see that one case relates to a file going to trial next month. In only a few seconds, you have downloaded a copy of the case to your computer and attached a copy to an email message you send to a colleague who is assisting you on the upcoming trial.

7:56 You have a note to yourself to check on yesterday's parliament proceedings. The passage of a federal bill is being anxiously anticipated by one of your clients. You go to the Canadian Parliament's website. You select yesterday's debates from the menu, and scroll through the speaker's list. You spot your topic and select it, linking directly to the Hansard transcript of that debate. You save a section of the debate to your computer to send to your client later.

7:59 You still have time to check last night's boxscores before your 8:00 meeting.

WHAT IS THIS BOOK?

Hopefully, you're eager to get going at this point now that we've touched on **why the Internet matters**. You have a sense for why the Internet phenomenon is happening, and how using the Internet can be an ongoing asset to your practice of law, your access to the information you need, and to your investigation of Canadian legal matters generally.

The rest of the book builds from this point forward, providing a step-by-step treatment of Internet concepts and user's guidance, important for the busy professional. This is a non-technical treatment, although some technical features are reviewed. It is primarily a practitioner's book, a book for users.

The chapters of the book flow one from an-other, as shown in the chart on the next page.

Chapter Two builds from the introduction by providing a structural **overview of the Internet**. This overview is for those who are new to the Internet, or those who want a well-rounded Internet education. It offers you a sense of how the Internet fits to-gether as a network, how computers on the Internet relate to one another, and what services are offered to help you use the place. Finally, this overview takes in the questions of culture: how peculiar is life on the Internet? What do you need to be aware of?

The next six chapters take off from this point in a detailed exploration of how you can use the Internet. Some of the ground covered here is technical, but you will al-ways be presented with a layperson's dis-cussion of these areas. These chapters cover a vital series of issues, as we move together towards uncovering the real riches of the Internet.

In **Chapter Three**, we address **how to ac-tually get connected to the Internet**, such as the hardware required for the basic connection, types of connections and their cost implications, and security concerns arising from the public nature of the Internet.

In **Chapters Four** and **Five**, we examine the two primary Internet services: **Email** and the **World Wide Web** respectively, re-viewing what can each service do, how you access them, and what software is involved.

Chapter Six launches us into a tour of what **resources** are available on the web, hitting the highlights of what you can put to use in your practice. We'll first look at the wealth of Canadian legal material on-line: cases and tribunal rulings, statutes and legislative proceedings; government policies and documents; bar association materials and resources made available by law firms; and much more. From there, we move on to consider the outstanding access the In-ternet offers to factual resources and to in-ternational legal materials, as well as to business, media, and just plain fun resources.

Chapter Seven is where we suggest how you can **find what you're looking for** online. We recommend the best search tools and show you how to get the most out of them, and we review the steps in-volved in funding specific types of infor-mation, from people to case law.

Chapter Eight provides coverage of the **discussion groups** available online: re-sources that allow you to interact and share information with other users.

Chapters Three through Eight complete our consideration of how to get on the Internet, work its services and find the resources that are useful to you.

Turning our attention from finding and us-ing information, **Chapter Nine** explores how you might **use the Internet to sup-ply information**. Topics include how to set up a website; how to use Internet tools to distribute information internally within your organization; and an introduction to extranets, an emerging way to share information with clients over the Internet.

Chapter Ten looks at the Internet from a different perspective of interest to lawyers, reviewing the **legal issues emerging from the Internet** phenomenon, and exploring the question: "What can I as a lawyer do for the Internet?"

The **Appendix**, finally, offers the **Legal Resources Directory**, a comprehensive annotated listing of information resources on the Internet relating to Canadian law. The Directory strives to be your yellow pages to this new place, and includes address information to guide you to any site you're looking for.

The Bird's Eye View

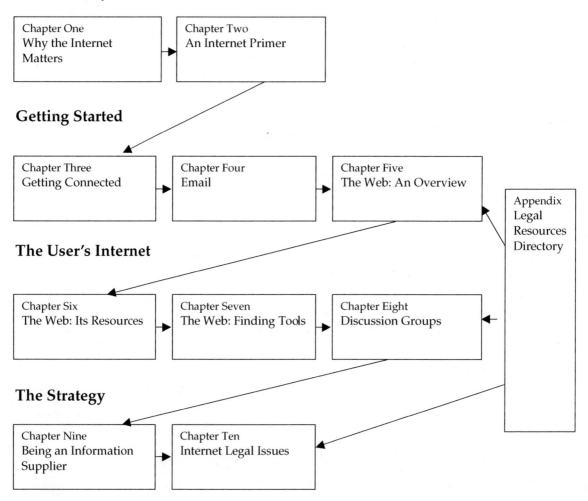

Chapter One Why the Internet Matters	Chapter Two An Internet Primer

Getting Started

Chapter Three Getting Connected	Chapter Four Email	Chapter Five The Web: An Overview

Appendix
Legal
Resources
Directory

The User's Internet

Chapter Six The Web: Its Resources	Chapter Seven The Web: Finding Tools	Chapter Eight Discussion Groups

The Strategy

Chapter Nine Being an Information Supplier	Chapter Ten Internet Legal Issues

END NOTES

1, 2, 3. Internet Domain Survey, Internet Software Consortium (http://www.isc.org/).

4, 5, 6. Computer Industry Almanac (http://www.c-i-a.com/).

7. ComQUEST Research (http://www.comquest.ca/).

8. Computer Industry Almanac (http://www.c-i-a.com/).

9, 10. *The Wall Street Journal* (http://www.wsj.com/).

11, 12, 13. Amazon.com (http://www.amazon.com/).

14, 15. ActivMedia (http://www.activmedia.com/)

16. *The Wall Street Journal* (28 January 1999).

17, 18. Wells Fargo Bank, cited in *ComputerWorld* (5 January 1998).

19. RelevantKnowledge, cited in *The Wall Street Journal* (15 September 1998).

20. Andersen Consulting survey, June 1999 (http://www.ac.com).

21. "It's a Woman's World Wide Web" in Jupiter Communications and Media Metrix (August 2000) (http://www.mediametrix.com).

22. CVU's 10th WWW User Survey, October 1998, Georgia Institute of Technology (http://www.cc.gatech.edu/gvu/user_surveys/).

2 AN INTERNET PRIMER

For many, the Internet is now familiar enough that there's no need to start from the beginning. For those who are new to the Internet, however, or those who want a well-rounded Internet education, this chapter is for you.

Imagine you're approaching Dublin in an airplane, about to begin a visit to what the European press has recently been calling "the hippest city in Europe." Your travelling companion has never been to Ireland before and is craning her neck near the tiny window, trying to get some sense of what lies ahead. Her choice had been Paris all along. You won the toss. And now the airplane circles southward, and Howth, Dublin Harbour, and the beautiful, urbane and eloquent City of Dublin itself unroll dramatically to the west, shrouded in a light Celtic mist, full of promise and magic and Guinness. You are entranced.

Then your friend turns to you and says sceptically: "So what exactly *is* this place all about?"

How can you answer such a big question? So you ponder, and then you say: "Well in order to adequately answer that question I will have to break my response into constituent pieces as follows":

1. **The lay of the land:** how the city fits together. From Howth to Dalkey, from the mouth of the River Liffey to Phoenix Park.

2. **The services:** how you make everything work. Cabbies and trains, librarians and shopkeepers, your man the barkeep at McDaids.

3. **The main attractions:** parks, cafés, libraries, Joycean stuff and, of course, pubs.

4. **Culture:** the Dublin way. How to blend in and not look like a tourist.

Your point in all this being that the only way to make sense of a new place is to appreciate its structure and style, the sights and services it has to offer. Ultimately, you must get on the ground and explore, but initially, it helps to get a bit of perspective, a bird's-eye view.

Understanding the Internet is a similar undertaking. In this chapter, we're going to give you the same kind of primer you might have given your travelling companion, providing perspective on a big, new place by looking at its basic pieces:

1. **The lay of the land:** how the computer network called the Internet is structured. The sites, the connections between sites, and the protocols that make it work.

2. **The services:** how to make use of all this and get quickly from place to place. Email, the World Wide Web, and other technologies that allow you to access and share information on the Internet.

3. **The main attractions:** what you can actually see on the Internet. Law (cases, legislation, tribunal rulings), government documents, libraries, bar associations, other lawyers, international law, companies, clients, newspapers, magazines...and much more.

4. **Netiquette:** the Internet way. How to blend in and not look like a tourist.

THE LAY OF THE LAND – INTERNET STRUCTURE

One of the most confusing things about getting plugged into a new place, a new city, even a new job, is you have to start assembling from scratch your own mental map of how everything fits together. For the first while you wander around half-lost and in denial.

Then, after a while you find yourself understanding the spatial relationships between different things without even thinking about it. So you're reading the *Irish Times* one day and an article about Dublin mentions the famous Customs House, and you automatically think: "Just off the Liffey River, down Eden Quay from the O'Connell Street Bridge."

It's like navigating your own mental topographical map.

Bad news. This does not translate perfectly to the Internet, which is notoriously difficult to map.

So how do you get the sense of the way things fit together? Some actually argue that you don't need to. Since the Internet is a vast, shifting data cloud (these folks might say) why bother trying to get your head around it? Just wander and explore and let it flow over you.

Well, this approach may be very Zen but it's not for everybody. For one thing, you want to get plugged in with a minimum of confusion. You want to make a good, timely decision about which kind of Internet connection is best for you. Also, you want to minimize the wandering-around-totally-lost period. The Internet has to work for you not vice versa, or it's a bottomless, time-sucking pit.

LANs & WANs, Very Briefly . . .

The Internet works like a meta-version of the kind of computer network running in law firms all over the country. With firm networks, the typical starting point is the visionary idea that stand-alone computers would be more powerful if they were linked together. Not because 23 personal computers make one larger computer collectively, but because if they are linked together they can share data (provided they talk the same language). This allows flexibility, synergy, and faster communications.

So, everybody gets onside, and you link all the computers together. In fact you hardwire them together using communications cables and a network router that stands in the middle and directs traffic. You install some kind of central, mother-ship computer (called a file server) to act as a repository of common files and other data for everyone to use. And if you've gotten this far in networking your computers in the firm, you've created what is called a LAN, or Local Area Network.

Now take it one step further. Say you want to link your LAN to the LAN in your branch office. You accomplish this by making the link from your LAN to the branch office LAN over a phone line. And if you then want to establish links from your LAN to people working from home, no problem. You'll need more phone lines, but the phone company will accommodate. You set up a server that answers phone calls, one that understands remote transmissions from far away places. And once all this is up and running—a network incorporating your firm, your branch office, and a handful of lawyers working at home—you have created what systems people call a Wide Area Network, or a WAN.

Now that you've learned these two new acronyms, LAN and WAN, please forget them immediately. We were only making a point: the Internet is something like the ultimate WAN. It relies on a trunk system of interconnected phone lines to link networks with other networks, individual computers with other individual computers. As long as these linked computers are using the same set of rules, they can communicate and work together.

Indeed, these are essentially the three easy pieces of any network:

Sites: places, nodes, locations...people call them different things
Relationships: links between those sites, lines of communication
and a **Protocol:** the uniform set of rules that holds everything together.

This goes for networks of any kind. For example, your law firm itself is a network of sorts. Not the computer network *in* your firm, but the firm itself. It has:

Sites: individual people—partners, associates, staff, articling students, legal researchers
Relationships: lawyers to staff, mentors to students, partners to partners
and a **Protocol:** in fact, probably a *set* of protocols governing everything from how lawyers solicit business to office attire.

It's worthwhile thinking about the Internet as a creature of precisely this simplicity. In the case of the Internet, however:

Sites: computers or computer files at businesses, universities, government offices, and homes—each site having a precise address called an URL
Relationships: phone line links between those sites, over which computers communicate, often as hosts and terminals, and servers and clients
and a **Protocol:** in fact a set of protocols called TCP/IP, which dictates how computers exchange data and how people contact other people on the Internet.

Structurally speaking, the Internet is a network with sites, relationships and protocols. Let's now look at each of these components in turn.

SITES

The important thing about the Internet is that it consists of thousands and thousands of computers with publicly accessible data. Sharing information, after all, is what networks are all about. To make sense out of it all and actually find anything, you need an addressing system. No surprise. Even Dublin has addresses, although McDaids is "in Harry St. off Grafton," not exactly a Global Positioning System read-out. (Indeed, Dublin's addressing system is known technically as "cab-driver-dependent.")

Happily, almost everything on the Internet has a very precise address called a **Uniform Resource Locator**, or URL. This goes for an individual emailbox, an article from *The Economist*, or a photograph of M. Emmet Walsh available in the University of Washington graphics archive.

Learning the rudiments of the URL addressing system will make your entire life much easier, and so we explore these more fully in How to Decipher a Web Address in Chapter Five (The Web: An Overview). At this point, simply understand that the URL tells you two things: (1) the kind of data at the site in question, and (2) who is making the data available on the Internet.

RELATIONSHIPS BETWEEN COMPUTERS

Two of the most important relationships that govern how computers on the Internet communicate are the Host-Terminal and Client-Server relationships.

Hosts & Terminals

If you're not on a network, your computer is devoted to serving you alone. When you type commands on the keyboard, it consults data held in its own storage compartments, or it manipulates the data you give it using its own computing power and software. When you're not typing commands your devoted silicon chip worker sits there patiently and hums.

This luxury is not possible for a host computer that is expected to serve many people at the same time. An Internet host computer might be a mainframe sitting in air-conditioned comfort in a telecommunications giant's server park. Or it might be a computer not much bigger than your PC. It might be intended to handle 100 guests a day, or 10,000, or 1 million. In order to fulfill its hostly obligations, the host computer must simply be big enough to deal with all its users simultaneously, without being driven to its knees.

In computer-speak, the guest of a host computer is a *terminal*. More precisely, a terminal is the computer each guest communicates through. Although the guest user might be logged in using a PC—a machine capable of storing data and executing commands in its own right—its relationship to the host computer after login is that of a dumb terminal, a network end-point existing only to input commands and wait for the host's response.

On the Internet, the host-terminal relationship is integral. Data is largely available on host machines and in order to retrieve it, you and your computer must become a terminal to the right host, in the right way. In fact, the host-terminal relationship is so common on the Internet that almost *any* computer accessible as a site on the Internet is called a *host*.

Clients & Servers

The motive behind all of this is sharing data so that computers working together on the network can be more powerful than computers operating in isolation. The host-terminal relationship is designed to help make this possible. The *client-server* relationship also plays a role.

Clients and *servers*, however, are not hardware but software. The server software manages a body of data (graphics, news articles, papal decrees ... it could be almost anything), while client software is designed to get the data and return it to the user. *Server software* (as you have already guessed) is resident on a host computer of some kind. *Client software*, on the other hand, is resident on a user-computer, operated typically by someone who is seeking data. This is the essence of the client-server relationship: a two-way software interaction that connects a data provider with a data user.

If you're going to mine the Internet for data, then, you are clearly going to need a piece of client software. Prior to the emergence of the World Wide Web, you actually needed different clients depending on the kind of data you were after. A great deal of what is on the Internet now can be retrieved with web client software (typically

called a web browser), although you can still use clients designed to work with a particular type of data to access that material if you prefer. (See Chapter Five for a discussion of working with web browser software.)

Similar to the host-terminal relationship, the prevalence of the client-server relationship has resulted in a naming convention you should be familiar with. Virtually any computer on the Internet that provides information for public access is known as a *server* in itself. More precisely, computers are referred to as web servers, or mail servers, or news servers depending on what Internet *service* they provide.

THE MOTHER PROTOCOL – TCP/IP

Sharing data is a great idea, of course, but if independent institutions all over the world put up servers with public data on them, how is it possible that all the servers and clients and hosts and terminals could possibly be speaking the same language? Didn't the Tower of Babel networking initiative end badly?

This is where the TCP/IP protocol comes in, to act as a common language. TCP/IP is actually a set of protocols that governs every operation performed on the Internet. It takes its name from:

1. TCP – Transmission Control Protocol

2. IP – Internet Protocol

TCP governs how data is sent and received by two different computers. TCP does this by breaking up the data of one transmission into pieces called packets. TCP then addresses and numbers these packets, and sends them out onto the Internet towards their destination.

While in transit, IP looks after the packets. It sends each packet the fastest way, even sending packets from a single transmission by different routes if necessary. IP avoids heavy traffic and diverts packets around computers that are down. It even mingles the packets of different transmissions along the same routes, making transmission times faster for everybody.

As the packets of one transmission begin to arrive at the destination computer, TCP picks up the ball again. It sorts the arriving packets into the proper order. If any are missing, it has these retransmitted. TCP then delivers the reassembled transmission to the destination computer for processing.

TCP/IP is a tough set of protocols. It stands up in heavy traffic and stickhandles around computers gone down on the network. In fact, it was designed to keep on ticking during a nuclear war, so this shouldn't be a surprise. Even though it's never been field tested under ICBM attack, network computers go down daily for other reasons and the Internet stays on its feet. You have to hand it to the original designers, the Internet protocols are really robust. That said, the Internet's explosive growth has placed strains on the network that hint at problems to come (see the sidebar, The Internet: Too Successful for its Own Good?).

INTERNET SERVICES

The Internet has to work for you, not vice versa. To make this happen you have to understand how to access resources using the various Internet services. In theory, the Internet is composed of a range of services, each of which offers access to a particular kind of information resource. For example, you can use a different Internet service depending on whether the data you are concerned with is an email message, an archived newspaper article, a library catalogue entry, or a posting to a particular discussion group. This structure of different Internet services and different kinds of data resources has evolved naturally over the Internet's lifespan, with Internet services typically succeeding and supplanting one another over time as new data resources became popularized. When text was predominant (five years ago) the Internet service gopher was considered the state-of-the-art service. Now that users have come to expect a fully graphical Internet experience (complete with text, pictures, audio clips and moving images) the stand-out Internet service has become the World Wide Web, which nicely accommodates all these kinds of data resources.

In fact, the more sophisticated the service, the greater the range of data types and media it can support. Thus the World Wide Web affords seamless access to most of the other services, and has become in a way the single dominant Internet service.

Chapter Four (Email) and Chapter Five (The Web: An Overview) offer a full discussion of the two main Internet services:

A Brief History of the Internet

In the beginning (1969) there was the United States Department of Defense, which begat ARPANET, a hard-wired military network built on the TCP/IP protocol and specifically intended to withstand partial collapse due to nuclear war. In the event the other side took out one computer, or even ten, TCP/IP was designed to complete its transmission by finding alternate routes.

ARPANET begat NSFNet in the 1980s, which linked in a handful of American universities and which refocused the network on research and academic matters. NSFNet begat the interest of other American universities, which built more permanent links to NSFNet. This begat worldwide interest in other academic communities, which begat NetNorth and CDNNet in Canada, which begat CA*net, linked directly into NSFNet at various points across Canada, and which tied together each of the regional nets in each of Canada's provinces into one Internet whole.

And this begat public attention, which begat the arrival of commercial service providers who built their permanent links to the universities and turned to the great information-hungry public and said:

"Come, enter the Internet through us."

Thus giving rise to the global telecommunications giants, the AOL-Time Warners and BCE-CTVs, and the rush to return the world's telecommunications networks to regular broadcast programming. But that's another story entirely.

The Internet: Too Successful for its Own Good?

The Internet has grown at a rate far beyond the wildest dreams of those who designed the network's TCP/IP protocol. Millions of users now send transmissions over the Internet daily, and newer services that transmit video and voice hog finite bandwidth in the overall telecommunications system. Delays, breakdowns, and occasionally glacial transmission rates are part of everyday life online.

Because of such realities, many large companies are setting up their own private TCP/IP networks to exchange data. A group of leading American research universities, several of which were key architects of the Internet itself, are in the process of developing "Internet II," dedicated to academic traffic and free of commercial users, much as the Internet itself was just a few years ago. The United States government is backing such a separate Internet for higher education and advanced research applications, and is also making plans of its own to build a "Next Generation Internet," which would be hundreds of times faster than today's Internet.

Talk of the Internet's accelerating decline ignores the reality that the network is less congested than it was a few years ago. The Internet's backbone networks are now run by private companies, many of which are expanding their capacity aggressively. And when you ask the folks who built the Internet, they say that given the amount of growth during the past five years, it's amazing how well the network is holding up.

1. **The web.** The World Wide Web, or the web, is the leading Internet service, so much so that many think of the web and the Internet as one and the same thing. The web is a figurative web of linked multimedia documents containing combinations of text, graphics, sound and moving images. More practically, it is a revolutionary way to access and share information.

2. **Email.** Email is the central communications service on the Internet. There are other ways to communicate with other users but email is by far the most flexible and popular. Correspondence can be exchanged with any other Internet user anywhere in the world quickly and at a relatively low cost.

There are also several other Internet services, many of which were stand-alone Internet services in their day. The data to which they provide access can now more easily be retrieved directly via the web. Examples include:

Newsgroups. Newsgroups are venues for lively discussion along highly topical lines. Discussions range from computers to hobbies, from the sciences to the arts, from trademarks to torts law. In a sense they work like electronic bulletin boards. Participants post their messages where everyone can read them and respond. See Chapter Eight (Discussion Groups) for further coverage of web-based discussion groups of this kind.

Mailing lists. Mailing lists similarly provide forums for topical discussions, via email messages sent to a common address.

Mailing lists actually work by taking advantage of the email infrastructure in place. They are automated information sources that circulate the messages of participants to a pre-set list of email subscribers. See Chapter Eight (Discussion Groups) for further coverage of email mailing lists.

Telnet. Telnet is a granddaddy Internet service, the basic protocol that allows you to login to a remote host computer as a terminal. Once logged on through telnet, you can operate the host machine in the way it was intended: exploring an online catalogue for example. It has now been supplanted almost entirely by the web.

File Transfer Protocol ("FTP") is an Internet service that allows you to visit a remote host computer and take data and other public files home with you. In its day, FTP was the primary way of accomplishing file transfers from remote computers to your own. With the explosion of the web, however, FTP sessions (the process of the download) are most often done through web pages. In other words, the use of this Internet service remains common, but it has become less visible to the end user.

Gopher is a more sophisticated information retrieval service built on thousands of linked menus maintained by universities and other institutions. The menus provide access to a range of resources including text, graphics and links to resources available via other services such as FTP and telnet. Gopher was in many respects the prototype for the web itself and has been effectively replaced by the web's more sophisticated capabilities.

Internet Relay Chat allows you to engage in real time on-screen conversations with people. Again, this service has been largely subsumed into the web experience.

THE MAIN ATTRACTIONS – INTERNET RESOURCES

At its root, the Internet is about the information, the interaction, and the transactions that it makes available to users. These are its resources, the reasons for this book. The services above are merely the means to access information, interact with others, and perform transactions on the Internet. There is now an enormous range of activity on the Internet of interest to the lawyer. Here is just a taste of what you can expect to find and use.

1. **Courts and Tribunals.** Courts and administrative tribunals are obvious sources of material that lawyers use in their practice, and the Internet offers a new way to get at cases and tribunal rulings. No longer is it necessary to journey to the library or use a commercial online service to get a copy of, say, a Supreme Court of Canada case handed down last week, or a ruling issued by the CRTC.

2. **Government.** Federal and provincial governments have embraced the Inter-net as a way to distribute their material at reduced cost and to a wider audience. Lawyers are among the many beneficiaries. It's never been easier to get statutes, legislative proceedings, government policies and rulings, budgets, Ministry reports, and other government documents.

3. **Law-related associations.** Bar associations, law societies, continuing legal education societies, and other law-related associations are also online, providing information and resources to the legal community. Lawyers on the Internet will find bar association materials, legal discussion groups, law society newsletters, law reform commission reports, CLE materials, and collections of documents prepared by law-related non-profits.

4. **Lawyers.** Most law firms now have websites. Many firms are not only promoting themselves with their Internet sites, but are also providing useful content for clients and others, including listings of Internet legal resources and articles on various legal issues.

5. **Law schools.** Law schools are also alive to the way in which the Internet can deliver information to a wide range of people at a modest cost. Law journals, the archives of law institutes and law school library catalogues are among the many resources available from law schools on the Internet.

6. **Business and finance.** The business world and financial markets have embraced the Internet. The volume of cor-

porate and market data on the Internet is simply staggering. The challenge is no longer in gaining access to material, but rather in making sense of it all.

For further discussion of Internet resources, see Chapter Six (The Web: Its Resources), Chapter Seven (The Web: Finding Tools), and Chapter Eight (Discussion Groups).

INTERNET CULTURE AND NETIQUETTE

There has been a lot of writing about how different Internet culture is from mainstream society. A common theme in this writing is that online veterans resent the intrusion of newcomers. Much of this is by now very dated, and might well have been overstated in the first place.

It *is* true that the roots of the Internet lie jointly in the research, academic and computer hacker communities. This polyglot online universe developed a quasi-anarchist, *laissez-faire* culture precisely because of the unique mix of people who called it home. But the boom of the web in the past few years has led to an unprecedented influx of outsiders from completely different backgrounds, and this kind of growth has simply forced Internet veterans to deal with new dynamics. If you sign up today and take your first foray out onto the Internet in the morning, you will be in the

company of thousands of others in the same position, checking out the sites for the first time.

With these words of encouragement in mind, there should be no doubt that the research/academic/hacker origins of the Internet have left their mark on the place. Nobody should take that first foray out into the online world without first appreciating two strongly held principles, which will be evident wherever you turn:

1. The sanctity of freedom of speech

2. The common property nature of information

These two principles represent a good deal of what people are talking about when they talk about Internet culture.

You should also be aware, however, that the founding Internet community is distrustful of central authority, and this is reflected in how these two principles are enforced. Given that the Internet information resources are common property, the network is controlled directly by no one. It is a shared public space (literally a commons) and in order to remain independent of central authorities, it has of necessity become a self-regulating environment. A lot of shoulder rubbing and jostling takes place, and with this comes a certain amount of friction. But the Internet takes care of its own.

No single case better captures the interplay of our two basic principles and the self-regulating nature of the Internet than the legendary case of Canter and Seigel (versus almost everyone else on the Net). The fact that the two individuals involved were lawyers is of additional interest. Although the events in question happened in 1994, by their behaviour and attitudes, Canter and Seigel set the standard not only for how not to advertise on the Internet, but they also undoubtedly raised the standards by which the online activities of lawyers are judged to this day.

As such, The Short Happy Marketing Blitz of Canter and Seigel deserves a very special place in the volumes of Internet Lore.

THE SHORT HAPPY MARKETING BLITZ OF CANTER & SEIGEL

Laurence Canter and Martha Seigel were immigration lawyers in Arizona who became infamous in April 1994 when they tried a new marketing technique. To promote their services to those who might want help entering one of the United States Department of Immigration Greencard Lotteries, Canter and Seigel decided to advertise on the Internet.

This wasn't a revolutionary marketing strategy by any means. In fact, the Internet already offered a few different options to the marketer. The World Wide Web was still in its infancy as a popular medium but numerous companies had established web pages. Among the newsgroups (online bulletin board-like discussions), there had been areas devoted to advertising for several years. They served as online classified ads, with some popular groups specifically devoted to computer equipment, for example, or (yes indeed) professional services.

Instead of either of these options, Canter and Seigel chose to advertise on newsgroups in a big way. Not posting just to, say, the newsgroups devoted to legal matters. Not just to newsgroups devoted to advertising professional services. Rather, Canter and Seigel posted the same promotional message to every newsgroup then in existence – some *six thousand newsgroups*. To be sure, they got their message in front of people who actually wanted help entering the Greencard Lottery. Of course their posting also showed up in the middle of completely unrelated discussions about everything from cats to the space shuttle.

Canter and Seigel, unwittingly or otherwise, had perpetrated one of the earliest wide scale *spams* in the history of the Internet.

> **spam** 1. (v.) to send an unsolicited usually commercial email to a large number of addresses. 2. (v.) to post the same message to a wide number of newsgroups without considering the suitability of the posting to the discussion in progress. 3. (n.) such an email or a newsgroup posting. 4. (n.) a tinned meat product made mainly from ham (*sp*iced h*am*).

Spamming is a cardinal Internet Sin.

Spamming is freeloading. When you advertise in a magazine or on TV, you pay for it. You pay for the right to appear before the message recipient. When you advertise on the Internet, this is not the case. It's worth noting that fax ads are illegal in quite a few jurisdictions because of the costs they impose on the recipient without the recipient's consent. Internet citizens felt Canter and Seigel had violated their rights as re-cipients in a similar way. And the impres-sion of freeloading can only have been ex-acerbated when Martha Seigel boasted to the computer writer K.K. Campbell that their posting made them over $100,000 in additional revenues.

Spamming is a traffic violation. If there were six groups to which the Canter and Seigel posting was truly suited, then their marketing strategy imposed one thousand times the necessary traffic on the Internet. To generate so much unnecessary traffic for personal gain was to bring about the Trag-edy of the Commons (an economic paradox wherein rapacious competitive activity causes the annihilation of a commonly owned resource). No one can be certain that widespread spamming would drive the Internet to its knees, but those concerned about protecting this unique common property resource are not interested in finding out.

The reaction to Canter and Seigel's spam was immediate. Canter and Seigel were snowed with emailed objections, even email "bombs" containing hundreds of blank pages. Their Internet Service Provider collapsed under the crush of traffic, and closed Canter and Seigel's account. The firm's move to a larger provider might have been the end of it, were it not for Laurence Canter's public statement that he and his partner would spam again as they pleased. Fearing the worst, their new service pro-vider pre-emptively closed their account.

In May 1994, a month following their orig-inal offence, the unrepentant Canter and Seigel announced their intention to publish a book on Internet marketing for use by other businesses and law firms. They set up a website called Cybersell advertising their intention to become Internet marketing specialists.

Homegrown attempts at censure contin-ued. The Canter and Seigel offices were purportedly swamped by fax and email bombs, tying up the firm's computers for hours at a time. Later that summer, Nor-wegian hacker Arnt Gulbrandsen issued a Cancelbot program that could be used to automatically erase Canter and Seigel post-ings from a server. A university student named Joel Furr proposed to release a line of T-shirts bearing the slogan "Green Card Lawyers: Spamming the Globe." Canter threatened to sue. Offers from all over the Internet poured into Furr's emailbox re-garding financial and *pro bono* legal assis-tance in the event that Canter pursued his action.

Canter and Seigel were, to say the very least, *persona non grata* on the Internet. In the space of six months, they had managed to offend a very large community by ignor-ing its basic cultural conventions. Detrac-tors argued that they had endangered the common property nature of the Internet through their profit-motivated abuse of In-ternet posting guidelines. They had threat-ened to sue into silence those who opposed them. And, they had threatened to con-tinue spamming. The response of Internet citizens, on the other hand, had been pre-cisely in keeping with the cultural norms of the place. Internet citizens had acted im-mediately, they had acted to restrict the offending parties' access to the common resource, and they had acted without consulting a central authority.

SOME BASIC GUIDELINES

Canter and Seigel were not censured for advertising on the Internet but because they showed disrespect for the basic principles of free speech and common property that underlie the Internet. If you remember their case, you've gone a long way towards understanding Internet culture.

In fact, you really need to know only a few guidelines to prepare for your first visit to this new place. But bear in mind that no single list of Internet "rules" can exist. The Internet is simply too freewheeling to accept a single code of conduct written in any central place. The following are some simple, broad principles that reflect the kinds of conventions that have developed to make Internet life more efficient and enjoyable for all.

Advertise in the appropriate place. The fastest growing, most graphically oriented part of the Internet (the web) is open for business and advertising. This does not contradict Internet culture, because the visitors to a website do so voluntarily. You are not interrupting an unrelated discussion with your marketing message, nor are you foisting the cost of your advertisement on an unwilling recipient.

Do your bit to minimize traffic. The Internet is actually many networks linked together, so your transmission to a distant location will represent traffic on potentially a whole range of other computers and networks. This is a big part of the reason why spamming is considered such an egregious offence; it overloads the circuits. So be concise with email signature lines. Post messages only to the appropriate discussions. Also, many popular sites are "mirrored" or duplicated at different points around the Internet. If you're trying to contact such a site always use the location closest to you geographically. It minimizes the distance your transmission has to travel and cuts down on traffic.

Use caution posting public messages. When you participate in an online discussion or post a message to a mailing list, remember that your words may be read by thousands of people. Diplomacy is the watchword. If someone does take offence to something you post, ignore the response if you can. Responding to the angry response is like the "third-man-in" during a hockey fight. More often than not, the benches clear.

Find the FAQ. The Internet is chock full of information about itself (it's a highly self-referential medium). Much of this information is available on Frequently Asked Questions lists (FAQs). These are great resources for the new user. There are scores of FAQs that will guide you step-by-step through whatever Internet function you're trying to figure out.

Six Steps to Net Sanity

Or: Reasons Why Visiting the Internet is Like Your First Visit to Dublin

1. If you get a sense for the lay of the land, you will get around much more easily.

Maps are handy, but a basic understanding of your surroundings is much better. (An understanding of North and South and which way the trains run, for example.) Understanding the basics of how the Internet hangs together will allow you to connect to it more easily, and explore more efficiently. If you do get lost, and you probably will, you'll always be able to find your way home.

2. If you know what you're looking for, you will find it faster.

Serendipity is a good thing, but you'll get more done if you know what you're after when you set out in the morning. (Today: the Georgian doors of Fitzwilliam Square.) Your excursions will be more directed, your time more efficiently spent. If you find this retentive, remember that the Net can be a time-pit if you are unwary. Review source lists so you know what the Net has to offer. Then plan your searches carefully.

3. Knowing the basic lingo is more than enough.

Know enough to communicate, but don't worry about the really technical stuff. The more users on the Net, the more vernacular the discussions become. Know enough to function. (Don't worry about *Pionta eile, le do thoil* on your first visit. Just ask for a pint.)

4. Stories about bizarre local mannerisms are exaggerations.

It's not hard to fit in if you stay cool. Even if you're a complete tourist no one will bite your head off. Of course, if you completely ignore local customs you can run into trouble anywhere. Cordiality and respect for local conventions demonstrate that you have a clue.

5. Regarding your personal security, caution is prudent, paranoia isn't.

It's always a good idea to avoid dark alleys in a new place, but a bulletproof vest is clearly unnecessary. On the Net, there are security concerns and there are viruses to think about. Neither of these should be more than a passing concern if you take certain simple precautions (see A Word on Security in Chapter Three).

6. You must get out there and explore on your own.

You have to nose around a bit on your own. Visit some sites. Talk to people. Listen to discussions and add your thoughts with confidence. You'll find out a lot more by doing that for a few days than reading ten books. (No Baedeker ever prepared anyone for the pleasure of reading the *Times* on a busy Saturday afternoon in Bewelly's Café, but if you go there, you'll soon see why the locals do.)

3 GETTING CONNECTED

Let's hit the ground running. You want to get connected to the Internet—how do you go about it? There are now a host of connection options available to access the Internet, ranging from a dial-up modem and phone line to plugging in via the cable TV network. High-speed Internet access is now a reality for many, with new technologies coming on fast and providers seemingly merging and multiplying every month. Acronyms abound: ISDN, ADSL, ISP, Kbps. This chapter attempts to bring some order to the connectivity puzzle, breaking down the undertaking of getting connected to the Internet into five pieces:

1. **Hardware.** What basic equipment do I need? Tell me what I need to know about modems (but no more please).

2. **Plugging in.** What are the different ways I can connect to the Internet? What are the strengths and weaknesses of dial-up modems, ISDN lines, ADSL technology, cable modems, leased lines, and satellite technologies? What are the relative costs? How can I maximize my bandwidth? What is bandwidth anyway?

3. **Software.** What software do I need to access the Internet?

4. **Getting started.** What is involved in actually connecting to the Internet for the first time?

5. **Security.** What are the real security risks in accessing a global network of public computers?

HARDWARE

To access the Internet, you (of course) need a computer. Your other hardware needs will depend on the way you connect to the Internet. If you plug in to the Internet via a dial-up modem, you need a phone line and an analog modem. If you plug in via an Integrated Service Digital Network (ISDN) line, you need something called an ISDN terminal adapter instead of an analog modem, and possibly a new phone line. For cable Internet access, you need a cable line, a cable modem, and a network card. And so on. There are certain essential elements, however, no matter what your method for connecting to the Internet:

1. **Computer.** The computing power you need to use the Internet is not great. An early Pentium computer (old enough that they haven't been on the market for several years) can easily perform basic tasks. Even a 486 can do a serviceable job providing you aren't accessing the most densely graphic parts of the World Wide Web, which typically take longer to load up and are therefore best suited to faster machines. If you want to take advantage of all the new capabilities of the Internet, however, speed and multimedia capabilities are definitely useful. In this regard your needs will be met with a basic Pentium II or III desktop system with Windows 95/98 and 32 MB of RAM, or a Macintosh of the equivalent level. You will be happier with 64 MB or even 128 MB of RAM, and of course performance will improve with a faster processor as well.

2. **Connection line (phone line or equivalent).** To use the Internet, you need some kind of connection line that allows you to plug in to the network. This can take the form of a regular phone line that doubles as a voice phone line, a dedicated phone line that you lease from a telephone company, a cable line that also provides your cable TV access, or even a satellite dish. In the section below on Plugging In, the discussion of the connection options includes more on what form the connection line will take for each option.

3. **Hardware intermediary between computer and connection line (modem or equivalent).** To complete the connection between your computer and the line that plugs in to the Internet, you need a piece of hardware that can act as an intermediary. For a basic dial-up connection, this piece takes the form of a modem. A modem is a device that allows your computer to send and receive data over ordinary telephone lines. An equivalent but different piece of hardware is involved with other kinds of Internet connections: an ISDN terminal adapter, an ADSL modem, a cable modem, a router (in the case of a leased phone line), or a satellite modem card. In the section below on Plugging In, the discussion of the connection options includes more on what form this hardware intermediary piece will take for each option.

PLUGGING IN

There are now several options available to connect to the Internet:

1. **Dial-up modem.** The most basic way to connect, and still the cheapest for a single user in isolation.

2. **ISDN line.** An increasingly popular way to connect at higher speeds (two to four times faster than using a dial-up modem).

3. **Digital Subscriber Line (ADSL).** The latest trend in high-speed access, faster than ISDN and no longer more expensive, but not available everywhere.

4. **Cable modem.** Touted as providing higher access speed at lower prices than any other method, but availability is limited and security issues are a consideration.

5. **Leased line.** Very fast, dedicated connections (via T1 and T3 lines) that cost more in set up and ongoing charges.

6. **Satellite downlink.** Faster than ISDN, but slower than ADSL or cable, it is the forgotten cousin of high-speed connection options despite being available virtually anywhere.

Each of these options has pros and cons. Some are (much) more expensive than others. Some are (much) faster than others. Some take more effort to install. The following discussion provides a description of each option, its benefits and drawbacks, and the steps involved in setting up your computer to access the Internet in this way. The hope is to help you choose the connection option that's most appropriate to your needs and resources. Bear in mind that this is still an evolving market and it isn't uncommon for the price structure of a given service to change markedly over the course of a year.

DIAL-UP MODEM

Just as the name suggests, accessing the Internet via a dial-up modem provides for temporary access to the Internet, established by "dialing up" an Internet Service Provider (an ISP). It's not much different than making a telephone call. The ISP provides a telephone number into which your modem can dial to gain access to the high-speed digital lines that form the backbone of the Internet. After the connection is made, information can be exchanged, but when you hang up, the connection is severed.

Using a dial-up modem remains the least expensive way for a single user, in isolation, to access the Internet. The main downside is that a dial-up modem connection is slow. Even today's fastest modems provide speeds that are only a fraction of the speeds possible with ADSL, cable, or even ISDN connections. Put another way, a dial-up modem provides the lowest "bandwidth" of any connection option available (see the sidebar, What is Bandwidth Anyway?).

Another drawback with a dial-up modem connection is that you can't use a phone line simultaneously to access the Internet and to do something else, such as have a voice conversation or send a fax. (As we'll see in the discussion of ISDN and ADSL technologies below, those connections allow you to use the same wire simultaneously to, say, send a fax and access the Internet.)

To go about connecting to the Internet using a dial-up modem, here's what you will need.

What is Bandwidth Anyway?

Bandwidth is the capacity that a telecommunications medium has for carrying data, but people use the word synonymously with "speed." What is the bandwidth of that Internet connection? Read: How fast is it downloading pictures of HalBop?

The bandwidth of analog communications is expressed in Hertz (cycles per second). The bandwidth of a digital communications device is expressed in bits per second (bps). Bits are the 0's and 1's at the root of binary coding. One Kbps (kilobits per second) is 1,000 bits per second. One Mbps (megabits per second) is 1 million bits per second. The bottom line with these measures is how fast a given piece of data can be transmitted across the communications link in concern: from a computer through a modem through a phone line through another modem and into a computer again. The "bandwidth" of the telephone line (its carrying capacity) is therefore only one factor in the speed of this transmission, which also depends on modem and processor speeds.

1. **Phone line.** A regular, plain old telephone line.

2. **Modem.** A device that allows your computer to send and receive data over ordinary telephone lines.

3. **Internet Service Provider.** A company that provides you with a phone number that your modem dials to plug in to the Internet.

Phone Line

One of the main advantages of using a dial-up modem to access the Internet is that you can use a regular phone line to plug in to the network. You can use the same phone line to take voice calls and access the Internet, although when you are connected to the Internet, callers will get a busy signal. If you plan to use the Internet often, you will likely want a separate phone line.

Modem

A modem (*mo*dulator-*dem*odulator) is the device that allows your computer to send and receive data over ordinary telephone lines. You will want to buy the fastest modem standard available, which is to say the one with the highest Kbps rating. (Sitting for 5 minutes while a single document loads up can quell enthusiasm and drive up costs.) The current standard is 56 Kbps. If you have a 28.8 Kbps or 33.6 Kbps modem, consider at least three factors if you are considering an upgrade in modem speed:

- How much do you use (or expect to use) the Internet? If it is an important part of your work life, don't cut corners. Choose the fastest, standards-based modem you can afford. A PC Computing study in 1999 found that, when the average business user replaces a 28.8 Kbps modem with a 56 Kbps modem, the savings amount to more than 400 hours a year.

- What services are available in your area, and what does your ISP offer? Your ISP might say it offers 56 Kbps access, but you might like to verify which kind. The V.90 standard is currently the best. Older varieties — such as x2 or K56Flex — are also still offered.

- Be aware that your upstream speeds won't match your downstream speeds. 56 Kbps modems are asymmetrical. You will experience (at least in theory) 56 Kbps speeds in the "downstream" direction, which affects the performance of loading web pages and downloading software. But the "upstream" bandwidth – the data sent from your computer to the Internet (mainly mouse clicks and e-mail messages) – is limited to 33.6 Kbps.

A final note: there are people who will advocate strenuously the merits of internal versus external modems (of course if this is a new debate to you, it's probably the sign of a healthy social life). The external modem is a small box that sits next to your computer, and the internal modem is a card installed inside the machine and out of sight. The respective sides typically base their preference on one of the following:

- *Internal Buffs:* less clutter on the desktop, fewer connecting cables, less expensive.

- *External Buffs:* easier installation (since you don't have to open your computer), pretty lights that blink on the modem box when you connect.

Internet Service Provider

To access the Internet via a dial-up modem connection, you need to set up an account with an Internet Service Provider (an ISP). There has been ongoing, rapid change in the ISP industry. In Canada and the United States there has been significant consolidation of service providers, although there are still many options for the consumer, ranging from small local companies to large national providers such as Sympatico and iStar. Some national providers such as AOL Canada and the Microsoft Network offer not just Internet connectivity but additional content and services, such as their own proprietary information services, web-based e-mail services, and parental controls on Internet access. Such additional services can cost more than simple Internet connectivity, but the marketplace is in such flux that the packages offered by these value added providers (sometimes called "commercial online services") can be very competitive.

To locate an ISP, you can check your local yellow pages and computer newspapers, which will have many ISP advertisements for both national and local companies providing dial-up Internet access. Alternatively, there are sources of ISP information on the Internet itself. The List (http://thelist.internet.com/), the directory (http://www.thedirectory.org/), and CANOE's ISP Directory (http://www.canoe.com/ISPdirectory/) are all excellent ISP catalogues, providing contact numbers and other information by area code or province. One way to access these resources is by trying a trial membership with an ISP, which is a good idea in any event to get an idea of your needs and the provider's level of service.

Most ISPs provide a range of payment options, ranging from a set monthly fee for unlimited access down to a lower monthly fee for access for a certain number of hours, after which hourly usage fees apply. The crucial estimate you must make in selecting a payment option is how much time you think you'll be online weekly or daily. This is a difficult estimate if you're new to the Internet, so you may wish to get a short membership package at first, as short as a month. Make your needs assessment, and sign on for a package that most closely matches your required usage. Then watch your usage closely. If it grows significantly, causing you to incur high monthly usage charges, you may want to upgrade to a more comprehensive package. To give you some guidance in making your choice, we provide the sidebar, An ISP Shopper's Guide, in which we suggest questions to ask the various ISPs you're considering.

ISDN Line

The Integrated Service Digital Network service (ISDN) is an increasingly popular alternative to using an analog modem to dial in to the Internet. ISDN offers the dial-up user an opportunity to access the Internet at speeds of up to 128 Kbps, as well as the ability to use the same line for various purposes simultaneously (i.e., data and fax). While not as fast as either cable modem or ADSL connections (see the sidebar, Speed,

Speed, Speed), ISDN service is more widely available than cable or ADSL, and significantly faster than 56 Kbps modems.

ISDN works by completing a fully digital link between you and your destination (in this case your firm and your Internet Ser-

An ISP Shopper's Guide

Get some detailed information from the Internet Service Providers with whom you're considering setting up an Internet account. The following questions should give you enough information to compare one ISP to another:

Capacity and Customer Service:

1. What is their ratio of modems to users? (A high modems-to-users ratio will mean you'll be less likely to get busy signals.)
2. Do they offer 56 Kbps access? If so, is that access V.90 standard compliant or one of the two proprietary, legacy varieties — x2 or K56Flex? (V.90 compatibility is better.)
3. What is their "backend" connection to the Internet: an ISDN line (128 Kbps), a T1 link (1.5 Mbps), or a T3 link (approx. 45 Mbps)? (A bigger backend is better.)
4. Do they support ISDN connections? ADSL access? (Even if you aren't looking at these high-speed access options now, the flexibility to upgrade in future would be desirable.)
5. Is there local number access to the ISP from other cities, or is it a long distance call?
6. How many customer service representatives do they have?
7. What are the hours of the customer service switchboard?

Internet Services and Accounts:

8. Do they offer LAN accounts? (If it's a network you want to hook up, the connection to your provider will have to work differently, incorporating a network router and special charges.)
9. Do they supply a suite of pre-configured client software?
10. Can you get accounts for multiple email addresses without paying for separate individual accounts?
11. Can you put up a website for no additional cost?
12. Can the ISP get you your own domain name? Can you get your own independently registered domain name (which you could move to another ISP if the need arises)?

Price:

13. Do they offer a trial membership? (Check out a free ISP trial if you can.)
14. What is the monthly rate for unlimited access?
15. Do they offer payment options that for a lower monthly cost provide a certain number of "free" hours? If so, how long can unused free time be "banked" for future use? What is the hourly rate once your free time is used up?

vice Provider). Most of the world's telephony infrastructure is digital with the exception of the final leg running from your local phone switch into your office (or house as the case may be). This section of the phone grid is made up of copper wire, and ISDN provides a means to squeeze digital capacity transmission (128 Kbps) down this copper. It does this by using two 64 Kbps bearer (B) channels for voice, data, and fax calls, either independently or linked together into one wide 128 Kbps digital connection.

The roll out of ISDN has been ongoing across Canada for the past couple of years, so you need to check with your local telephone company to determine availability in your area.

If ISDN service is available in your area, here is what's involved in setting up an ISDN connection:

1. **Find an ISP that supports ISDN.** To access the Internet over an ISDN line, your Internet Service Provider must support ISDN connections. Many of the larger ISPs (for example, Sympatico, UUNET, and AT&T Canada) and some of the smaller companies now offer ISDN service.

2. **If necessary, have an ISDN line installed by your telephone company.** While some offices and homes may need to be re-wired for ISDN, many will not. The copper twisted pair wiring that currently provides standard analog telephone service can be successfully used for ISDN. However, with the increasingly popularity of multiple lines, you may not have spare wiring available for your ISDN service. Therefore, installing an additional line for the ISDN service may be necessary.

3. **Get an ISDN terminal adapter.** An ISDN connection requires a different piece of hardware than the modem used with an analog dial-up connection. The ISDN equivalent of a modem is called a terminal adapter. (Technically, there is no such thing as an ISDN modem, since digital signals don't have to be modulated and demodulated.) There are two types of ISDN terminal adapters: internal and external. External adapters are stand-alone devices that connect through a COM port on the back of your computer. Internal ISDN adapters are ISA cards that you install inside your computer. Prices for an ISDN terminal adapter range from approximately $200 and up.

Usage costs for ISDN service generally range between $60 to $100 per month, depending on your area and usage patterns.

Note that ISDN lines can support small LANs (Local Area Networks). To allow computers on a LAN to access the Internet via an ISDN connection, you will need to install an ISDN router. Because ISDN routers use Ethernet connections (typically 10 Mbps), they can take full advantage of ISDN's speed. Many of the most popular ISDN routers also support analog voice, modem, or fax applications, as well as sophisticated network management capabilities. ISDN routers are typically more than twice as expensive as terminal adapters, but they are often worth the money since they allow multiple computers on a small LAN to leverage your ISDN investment.

DIGITAL SUBSCRIBER LINE (ADSL)

The latest trend in high-speed Internet access is DSL (Digital Subscriber Line). DSL is a high-speed data service that works over copper telephone lines and is typically offered by telephone companies. There are a host of versions and flavours of DSL, which has led to the common designation of "xDSL" when referring to this type of technology in general.

The most common service is ADSL, for Asymmetric Digital Subscriber Line. It is asymmetrical because it provides different

Speed, Speed, Speed

So much talk about speed. Just how fast are the various options of connecting to the Internet? Here are the vital statistics you'll hear people throwing around, from the various modem standards (some now very old), to the hottest, fastest, biggest data pipeline available. To keep it realistic, costs are also shown (averages that may vary by area):

Connection option	Speed	Hardware cost	Usage cost
Your old obsolete modem	28.8 Kbps	$200 three years ago	$40/month (regular phone line + ISP charges)
Your not-quite-as-old obsolete modem	33.3 Kbps	$350 two years ago	$40/month (regular phone line + ISP charges)
Current modem standard	56 Kbps	$100	$40/month (regular phone line + ISP charges)
ISDN line	64–128 Kbps	$200 + installation	$60–$100/month
Satellite downlink	400 Kbps	$500–$1,000 (including installation)	$20–$100/month
ADSL line (basic)	384 Kbps	$300 + installation	$40–$80/month
ADSL line (high-speed)	1.5 Mbps	$300 + installation	$100–$200/month
Cable modem	500 Kbps–2.5 Mbps	$100–$200 (including installation)	$40–$60/month
T1 line	1.5 Mbps	$2,000+	$500–$1,500/month
T3 line	45 Mbps	$2,000+	$1,500/month+

bandwidths in the upstream and down-stream directions, giving the user a much bigger "pipe" in the downstream direction. ADSL can support downstream bandwidths of up to 8 Mbps and upstream bandwidths of 1.5 Mbps, meaning Internet access at 50 to 150 times faster than with a dial-up modem. (By comparison, a T-1 connection also provides 1.5 Mbps.)

Besides higher bandwidth, another key advantage with ADSL access over dial-up access is that you get an "always-on" connection for your monthly fee.

The real beauty of DSL technology, however, is that it works on existing POTS lines—Plain Old Telephone Service—which allows the phone companies to provide this service without costly installation of higher-grade cable. DSL uses a different part of the frequency spectrum than analog voice signals, so it can work in conjunction with your standard analog POTS service, sharing the same pair of wires. This may seem counter-intuitive, but that is one of the real strengths of this technology—it can piggy-back right on top of your existing phone line, without even disturbing that service. You can even use your analog portion of the phone line as a modem or fax line, while simultaneously using the data portion for your DSL access.

The drawback with ADSL access is that it isn't available to everyone. ADSL service is being rolled out quickly in many areas in Canada, but you will want to call your local telephone company to find out if you have DSL access as an option in your area.

If ADSL access is available in your area, here is what's involved in setting up an ADSL line:

1. **Find an ISP that supports ADSL.** Getting started with ADSL Internet access is quite a bit different than with a regular dial-up ISP. You will either be dealing with your local telephone company—the provider of the ADSL service—or an ADSL-equipped ISP who will coordinate with the phone company. In many cases the telephone companies offering the ADSL services are also getting into the ISP business, and they may handle both aspects of the service for you. This can simplify billing and service considerations.

2. **Have an ADSL phone line installed.** With traditional ADSL services, a technician will install a splitter at your telephone line point-of-presence. This device will split out the standard analog voice line that gets wired to your telephone jacks, and the data line that gets connected to an ADSL modem.

3. **Install an ADSL modem.** An ADSL modem is a significantly different beast that your traditional analog modem. You will need to connect the ADSL modem to an Ethernet network (NIC) card in your computer. Today, ADSL modems are external devices that accept the data line from the telephone company, and provide a 10-baseT Ethernet interface to connect to your computer. (Expect to see internal ADSL modems very soon.) Many computers today

come with built-in Ethernet capability, but don't worry if yours doesn't. The cost and installation of the network card is generally included by the DSL provider. If you are not dealing with your local telephone company, you will most likely need two separate installation visits to get it all going. First the ISP will arrange for the telephone company to turn on the DSL line and install the splitter at your home, then a technician will come and install your ADSL modem on this line, and possibly the network card in your computer. Whatever the specific arrangements your ADSL provider makes with you, rest assured they will be much more involved in setting up your connection than a standard dial-up Internet Service Provider.

Costs for DSL services vary more than ISDN connections or cable modem services, although this area has recently been getting more competitive. There has been a strong effort to get monthly costs down below the $50 mark, which conventional wisdom says is necessary for widespread acceptance. DSL providers typically offer several different pricing/bandwidth options. Today, you may pay anywhere from $39 to $80 a month for a basic ADSL service that provides 384 Kbps downstream and 128 Kbps upstream. For higher bandwidth options the price obviously climbs. A typical 1.5 Mbps downstream/384 Kbps upstream connection will be in the $100–200 range.

Of course there are installation and set-up fees as well. These also vary greatly, and are often waived or reduced for one-year com-

mitments. Typically, installation fees range from $200–$400.

CABLE MODEMS

ADSL is not the only technology that promises high-speed Internet access. The cable TV network is being touted as providing higher access speed at lower prices than any other method of connecting to the Internet. The same wire that brings cable TV service into your home or office is capable of providing Internet access at speeds more than one hundred times faster than dial-up modem access. While availability is still rather limited, this is changing rapidly. The cable companies are in the process of installing and upgrading equipment to offer this service, and now you might have this option in your area.

Access to the Internet via the cable TV network is possible with a "cable modem," a device that connects to your cable feed and to an Ethernet network card in your computer. A cable modem is a true modem (*mo*dulator-*dem*odulator), but it is a much different device than a dial-up modem. Today's cable modems are external devices that connect to a network card in your computer and support much higher speeds than dial-up devices. That is because the cable TV network and the coaxial cable that brings it into your home or office are capable of very high data transmission rates. In the downstream direction (from the Internet to the computer), network speeds can be anywhere up to 27 Mbps, an aggregate amount of bandwidth that is shared by users. Few computers will be capable of connecting at such high speeds, so a more realistic number is 1 to 3 Mbps. In the upstream direction (from your computer to the Internet), speeds can be up to 10 Mbps. However, most cable modem producers have selected a more optimum speed between 500 Kbps and 2.5 Mbps.

Another significant advantage to using a cable modem is that the connection to the Internet is a full-time connection that does not require you to dial out to connect and as a result does not tie up the telephone line.

There are some drawbacks with cable modem access. In accessing the Internet through the cable TV network, your computer is essentially being put on a Local Area Network (LAN) with other users in your area. As with any LAN, the performance degrades as usage increases. Other users in your area share the same data "pipe" you are using, so if everyone is downloading at the same time your performance will suffer. Perhaps a more disturbing issue is that of network security. One of the main purposes of a LAN is to allow file sharing among the computers on the LAN. This LAN feature doesn't work well with cable Internet access, however, as you no doubt don't want others in your area accessing your files. There have been widely reported incidents of this type of breach, where a cable modem user can access files on another user's computer in his or her area who inadvertently had their file-sharing settings turned on. It's a very good idea to make sure you don't have file sharing allowed on your computer if you are going to get cable modem access (see the sidebar, Cable Modem User Tip).

Another limitation to cable modem access is that it isn't yet available everywhere. The major cable companies like Shaw, Rogers Cablesystems, and Videotron are rolling out Internet access services across the country. You will need to ask your local cable company whether you can get Internet access from them.

If cable modem Internet access is available in your area, here is what's involved in setting up a connection.

1. **Establish an account with a cable provider.** Your cable provider will send a technician to install a splitter onto

---

Cable Modem User Tip

A cable modem user can access files on another user's computer in his or her area who inadvertently has their file sharing settings turned on. If you access the Internet via a cable modem, you will want to make sure that you don't have file sharing allowed on your computer. To disable file sharing on a computer running Windows 95/98, open the Control Panel window and:

1. Select the item called "Network."
2. Click on the "Configuration" tab.
3. Click on "File and Print Sharing" in the lower part of the window, and make sure the button beside "I want to be able to give others access to my files" is not selected.
4. Click "OK" twice.

Now your files will not be visible to anyone else who happens to be on the same LAN as you.

your existing cable, which allows you to connect to the Internet while still using this wire for your cable TV access as well. There is no problem using the Internet connection and watching cable TV at the same time.

2. **Install a cable modem.** The cable company will also arrange for a cable modem installation. A cable modem is a modem in the true sense of the word; it *mo*dulates and *dem*odulates signals. But the similarity with a dial-up modem ends there because cable modems are practically an order of magnitude more complicated than their telephone counterparts. Cable modems can be part modem, part tuner, part encryption/decryption device, part bridge, part router, part network interface card, and part Ethernet hub.

3. **Install a network card.** The cable modem connects to your computer via an Ethernet network card. The network card is usually provided by the cable company. Your computer must have an available slot for the Ethernet card.

The cost to have a cable modem installed typically ranges from $100 to $200, depending on your cable provider and the city in which you live. Cable providers are typically charging $40 to $60 per month for an Internet service package that includes software, unlimited Internet access, specialized content, and a cable modem rental.

Note that a cable modem can provide Internet access to multiple computers, assuming they are connected via a Local Area Network (LAN). Cable modems typically have an Ethernet output, so they can connect to the LAN with a standard Ethernet hub or router. Each computer must have an assigned IP address, for which cable providers typically charge $5 to $10 a month per computer.

LEASED LINE

Another option for high-speed Internet access is to lease a dedicated high capacity phone line from a telephone company. These are dedicated, full time connections that are "on" 24 hours a day, 7 days a week.

A T1 line, which can provide a high level of service for a large to medium-size organization, has a capacity of 1.5 Mbps, or roughly 12 times faster than an ISDN connection. T3 lines, which make up the Internet's backbone, and might be leased by very large organizations, have a 45 Mbps capacity.

However, as you are no doubt already beginning to suspect, these powerful connections aren't cheap. There are set up costs and substantial monthly fees. Installation costs range from $500 to $2,000, and monthly usage costs range from $500 to $1,500 and up. Note that for a dedicated connection, you'll also need a router at your office end of the line that channels transmissions from local computers out to the Internet itself. In some cases, the phone company line lease package will include this router. In other cases, you'll have to buy one yourself and set it up. The cost to purchase and install a router will be in the $2,000 range.

You will also need a server at your location to handle the Internet services you want to offer: for example, a mail server to handle incoming and outgoing mail to the Internet, and a web server if you want to put up a web page advertising your firm or providing other information (see Chapter Nine for a detailed discussion of setting up a site on the World Wide Web).

As with any kind of Internet connection, security is a concern with a dedicated line. Since the dedicated connection is open day and night, your server and the machines attached to it are vulnerable to intrusion. A firewall is mandatory. We discuss how to set one up later in this chapter.

SATELLITE DOWNLINK

Yet another option for accessing the Internet at higher speeds is satellite downlink technology. Information arriving from the Internet is delivered via satellite to a small satellite dish, less than two feet in diameter. Requests for information are sent via a standard analog modem and connection through an ISP. The satellite dish is connected to your computer via a special type of network card and satellite receiver installed in the computer.

It may be hard to imagine that bouncing your requested pages 22,200 miles up to the Hughes satellite and back down again would make for faster access, but the 400 Kbps you can receive data at is almost eight times faster than today's fastest analog telephone modems, and three times faster than ISDN. However, it is not as fast as today's cable modems or DSL services, which both can provide over megabits of bandwidth.

Sort of the forgotten cousin of the current family of high-speed Internet access methods, satellite technology has one strong advantage over cable modems and DSL—accessibility. While the cable companies and telephone companies are struggling to upgrade their facilities to support these other technologies, the infrastructure exists today to provide 400 Kbps downstream bandwidth to almost anyone with a 21-inch satellite dish.

To get satellite Internet access virtually anywhere, you need a place to mount the dish with a clear view of the southern sky (if you're in North America), and a fairly basic Windows-based computer. You'll also have to buy a satellite downlink package, like the DirecPC Personal Edition which includes the 21-inch satellite dish, PCI satellite modem card, software, and documentation. Typical costs for such a package are about $500 to $1,000, including installation. Monthly charges for access range from $20 to $100 depending on usage.

SOFTWARE

A critical piece of the puzzle in getting connected to the Internet is getting the appropriate software on your system.

A key piece of software that you will need for a dial-up connection is the communications package that lets your computer talk to the Internet in its own language, TCP/IP. Recent versions of the most popular operating systems build such a package right into the system. Dial-up Networking is the component of Windows95/98 that performs this function. For recent versions of the Macintosh operating system, the communications piece is located in the TCP/IP Control Panel. There are also many stand-alone communications packages, such as Trumpet Winsock. See the section, Getting Started below for a discussion of how to configure and use the communications piece to connect to the Internet.

Your remaining software needs depend on the services you want to make use of on the Internet. As email and the World Wide Web are the two critical services for the professional user, you will want to obtain email and web software. See Chapter Four (Email) and Chapter Five (The Web: An Overview) for a discussion of some of the leading programs in each category.

As for actually getting your hands on Internet software, recent versions of the most popular operating systems come with web client software, also known as a web browser, built in. Alternatively, you can assemble a full suite of Internet software at no cost by downloading free programs off the Internet itself (sites such as ZDNet, at http://www.zdnet.com, feature massive collections of software programs available for download). This can be time consuming, however, as you must not only find and download the software, but you must also manually set each client program to work with an appropriate server. This involves tracking down the right addresses and entering them in the set-up areas of each software program. A lot of ISPs offer a pre-configured suite of clients to work

with their own server, and make these available to new users.

GETTING STARTED

You've selected your method of connecting to the Internet, established an account with a provider, installed the necessary hardware (for example, an analog modem or a cable modem), and installed Internet software on your computer. Now you want to actually connect for the first time. The connectivity option you choose (dial-up modem, ISDN, cable, etc.), your operating system, and the client software you choose will determine the exact look and feel of your session. The following is a brief, generic description of how to establish your first connection using a dial-up modem and Windows 95/98:

1. **Get the necessary access information from your ISP.** Ensure that you have in hand several pieces of information that you should get from your ISP when you sign up for an account: your user name and password, the dial-up access number for your ISP, the ISP's host name and domain name, and the ISP's Domain Name System (DNS) server address.

2. **Install (if necessary) and configure your communications package.** In order to use the networking capabilities in Windows 95/98, two components

must be installed: Dial-up Networking and the TCP/IP protocol. Once these components are installed, you need to configure them so that they can dial in to your ISP. See the sidebar, Windows 95/98 Set-up for step-by-step instructions on both of these steps.

3. **Establish the connection with your ISP.** Double-click on the icon you have created that designates your ISP. Click "Connect." Note that once the Dial-up Networking is properly configured, it will retain your user name and password information so that they do not require manual re-entry each login. This software then connects with your ISP, using the Internet's own protocols, and allows you to maintain a temporary (but unique) IP address for the duration of your current session.

4. **Activate the clients you need.** The connection you have established using Dial-up Networking remains open throughout your Internet session, as it maintains the pipeline to the ISP and through the ISP to the Internet itself. But you won't have to do anything with this connection until you want to sign off, so you can minimize it on your screen or leave it running in the background as you wish. To actually use the Internet services, you have to activate the appropriate client. To use the web, for example, you would open a web browser like Netscape Communicator or Microsoft's Internet Explorer at this point. Chapter Four (Email) and Chapter Five (The Web: An Overview) give detailed instructions on how to use these services and clients.

5. **Sign off.** Close all the service-related clients. Select "Disconnect" on the Dial-up Networking dialogue box. You are now unconnected and no longer on the Internet.

A WORD ON SECURITY

Participating in the Internet phenomenon has some risks, there's no denying this, but it would be a mistake to let this prevent you from proceeding. The risks to the average Internet user are the same kinds as those for a traveller in a new city. The traveller knows a tiny fraction of what there is to know about the place and any local could conceivably take advantage of this.

It should be reassuring to know, however, that most security problems on the Internet result from the activity of garden variety delinquents, not sophisticated criminals. Since they are rarely up to much beyond random mischief making, a massive defence plan is not typically necessary. The way to combat the risks is to stay calm, become familiar with the issues, and to use a common sense protection strategy.

VIRUSES

Viruses have a high profile, probably not because of the damage they have caused over the years, but because the notion of a computer getting "sick" with a virus is very

Windows 95/98 Setup

Windows 95/98 comes with its own networking capabilities and does not require Trumpet Winsock or a similar communications package to connect to the Internet, as did previous versions of the Windows operating system. In order to use the networking capabilities in Windows 95/98, however, two components must be installed: Dial-up Networking and the TCP/IP protocol.

Checking to ensure Dial-up Networking is ready to go

1. Open the item "My Computer" on your desktop. If Dial-up Networking is installed there will be a folder here called Dial-up Networking (alongside icons for each of the drives on your computer, and a folder each for the Control Panel and Printers). If there isn't a Dial-up Networking folder, then you must activate it and install the TCP/IP protocol. Both of these components are included with the system disk and can be activated and installed from the Control Panel.
2. To activate Dial-up Networking, open the Control Panel and double-click "Add/Remove Programs." Select "Windows Setup," "Communications," "Details," then "Dial-up Networking."
3. To install the TCP/IP protocol, open the Control Panel and double-click "Network." Select "Add," "Protocol," "Microsoft," then "TCP-IP."

Configuring your connection to your ISP

1. Ensure that you have in hand several pieces of information that you should get from your ISP when you sign up for an account: your user name and password, the dial-up access number for your ISP, the ISP's host name and domain name, and the ISP's Domain Name System (DNS) server address.
2. Open the item "My Computer" on your desktop.
3. Double-click the "Dial-up Networking" folder to open it.
4. Double-click the item "Make New Connection." This will bring up the New Connection Wizard, which walks you through the process of creating a connection icon for your ISP. For example, you will be prompted to enter the ISP's dial-up access number, your modem type, and other information.
5. Once the connection icon has been created, you can drag it to any part of the desktop you wish, where it need only be clicked to activate the connection process.
6. As a final step, you will need to configure Dial-up Networking with the details of the ISP's server (for example its DNS entry or host address). This is done by right-clicking on the new connection icon you have made, and selecting "Properties." This brings up a dialogue box from which Server Type information can be configured.

Note that your ISP customer service department should walk new users through the Windows 95/98 set-up procedures.

sci-fi material indeed. People love this kind of stuff.

Practically speaking a virus is three things:

1. **It is a program.** Someone writes it, and someone has to run it in order for it to do its work. Like any program, there is a programmer and then a user (although an unwitting user).

2. **It is a replicating program.** Once it is "run," a virus duplicates itself at the first opportunity. When the copy is run, it too will duplicate itself, and so on.

3. **It is damaging.** The effects may be minor or major, but they are never positive. When a virus program is run, it does arbitrary things within your system without your permission. Data is fragile, so arbitrary activity within your system is always bad news.

The Main Breeds

We will describe three breeds of virus in this section. The *Boot Infector* and the *Program Infector* are the originals and still the most common. There is also a third relatively new (but rapidly growing) breed of virus that is written in the programming language of another program. The very first of this breed were written in the macro language of Microsoft Word, and to simplify matters we'll call this whole class of viruses *Macro Viruses*.

The *boot infector* works because of two basic principles of the personal computer. First, every disk has a boot sector. This goes for hard disks and floppy disks. Second, whenever your computer is powered up, it looks

first to the boot sector where it finds a set of instructions on what to do. This set of instructions is called the Master Boot Record. In addition to this, if you boot your computer with a disk in the floppy drive, your computer will typically look to the boot sector of the floppy disk before looking to the boot sector of the hard disk.

Here's where the boot infector virus has its opening. A floppy disk infected with the boot virus has a bit of viral code written into its boot sector. If you try to start your computer with an infected disk in the floppy drive, your computer looks to the floppy disk boot sector first and activates the virus hiding there. Once activated, the boot infector virus copies itself over to the boot sector of your hard disk. Sometimes it will re-copy the Master Boot Record that was in the hard disk boot sector to another part of the hard disk. Sometimes it will overwrite the Master Boot Record entirely and replace it with its own version.

In either case, your computer is now infected. Every time you start it up, the virus in the hard disk boot sector will be loaded into your computer's memory. And once in your computer's memory, every time you read a disk in your floppy drive, the virus will copy itself to the boot sector of that disk. This is one potent little bug. Imagine the number of disks that go in and out of your floppy drive, and exchanged with others in your office in a single afternoon, let alone in a year. One copy of a boot infector virus can become one hundred in very little time at all.

Program infectors are slightly less common, but just as potent when they're on the loose. Instead of infecting the boot sector of your hard drive, a program infector virus is carried in an application: your word processor or your spread sheet program for example. Within the program, the bit of viral code that does the damage will be found in one of the program's executable components, for example the .EXE file (which kicks off the program when you first ask it to start up). You catch a program infector virus by starting the infected program, it's that simple. Every time an infected program is started, the virus code in the .EXE file is loaded into the active memory of the computer that started it. If a second program is started while the first is running, the viral code in memory then copies to the .EXE file of the second application. All the applications on your machine can be infected this way as you work with one and then another.

Note that program infectors can be sent by email. You will not catch one by simply opening an email note (experts seem to agree that no such virus exists at the moment). However, emails may carry attachments. Attachments may be programs (.EXE files). So ... beware of unsolicited emails bearing gift attachments. Beware also of strange emails bearing hypertext links to other places on the Internet. There have been recent cases of email containing dummy links which, when clicked, execute viral code.

There is a reason why the transmission of a virus in this fashion is called a Trojan Horse.

Macro viruses are a third kind of virus worth knowing about. These viruses infect documents, not executable programs or floppy disks and this fact alone makes the macro virus breed a dangerous one. People (that means people in your firm) are typically much freer about exchanging files such as Word or Excel files, than they are about exchanging programs.

In the wild, Microsoft Word, Microsoft Excel, and Lotus AmiPro macro viruses have been observed running free, but theoretically any piece of software incorporating macro languages could be used to incubate a macro virus. By some estimates, the number of macro viruses soared to over 2,000 different breeds through 1998 and 1999, many of which were created (and passed through) Microsoft Word.

Word macro viruses are typically spread through Word document templates. Templates are shells of commonly used documents—business form letters, for example, or standard contracts. Since these templates can carry macros within them, they may be used to transport viral macro code written in a macro language such as WordBasic. The virus will be executed when an infected template is opened, whereupon the rogue macro will conduct whatever operation it has been written to carry out. Typically, the virus will also attempt to infect Word's global document template, NORMAL.DOT. If it succeeds in this, every document you subsequently create in that copy of Word will also be infected (it will have the rogue macro attached to it). Thereafter, other systems which open your infected documents with Word will also be infected. Their NORMAL.DOT template will then be infected and their new documents will have the virus. And so on.

Like program infectors, macro viruses can be exchanged by email. The same caution, therefore, should govern your acceptance of email attachments (documents or spread sheets) as it does your acceptance of programs. If the attachment is opened without being scanned first, you might unwittingly release a macro virus into your system.

Virus Symptoms

Viruses can in theory be programmed to do a lot of different things, from annoying to very damaging. Once you have a piece of renegade coding in your boot sector, the computer will load it into memory every time you boot up. If the code prevents access to certain parts of your disk, for example, or even formats your entire disk, well then you've had a very bad day.

Please be reassured, however, by the fact that most virus creators are not in the game to destroy your system. They are indulging, in many cases, in the computer programming equivalent of graffiti. Every time their virus passes to a new computer, they've spray painted their name on the side of another house. The replication is the end in itself, because for the virus programmer, his reputation spreads with the virus program. The programmer may even achieve something like fame, in time. You'll notice this when you read the anti-virus literature, where you'll quickly start to recognize the names that have entered the pantheon: the Melissa virus, the Form virus, the Natas virus, Michelangelo and Stoned, just to name a handful.

Having said this, the virus typically does something to make its presence known

(there could hardly be any satisfaction in writing viral code that no one ever noticed). And what the virus does is never helpful. There are viruses that disable your computer for a single day or for the same day every year. There are viruses that disable certain programs or parts of your system or parts of your disk. There are viruses that simply slow your system down by using up memory, or which generate repeated error messages. Viruses can cause system crashes, disk space shortages, strange clicking noises from your keyboard or bizarre graphics that sweep unexpectedly across your screen.

Macro viruses have their own unique symptoms which, as we described above, are essentially macro routines over which you have no control. The macro routine might shift the location of words within the document (think of your contract templates here), or merely insert strange words somewhere on the page ("Wazzu" is one real-life example, a word that rarely fits smoothly into business correspondence). Other more sophisticated macro viruses will insert a line or two of text at the end of every document, at the time of printing or faxing. The macro virus "Nuclear," for example, inserts the words "STOP ALL FRENCH NUCLEAR TESTING IN THE PACIFIC." Added in the seconds just before printing, such "payloads" are easy to miss (and are potentially embarrassing).

Protection Strategies

Your main weapon in the war against viruses is the virus scanner, which works on the same principle as America's Most Wanted. Once a piece of viral code is identified, the scanner memorizes it and adds it to an internal "most wanted" poster. Now, when you borrow a piece of software you want to check for viruses, you simply turn on the scanner and aim it at the software in concern. The scanner reviews the software, line by line, looking for any code that matches any of the viruses in its rogue's gallery. The same scanning principle applies to a strange floppy you've picked up, or to a document you've borrowed.

The key with scanners is that the internal wanted poster must be up-to-date. New viruses are being dreamed up all the time, most of which you never have to worry about. But some virus programmers will succeed in writing codes that spread the world over. These you want to know about, which is why the scanning software must be updated periodically.

Once you have your scanning software in place, you should develop a regular pattern of usage: a Virus Scanning Policy, in other words. This kind of internal policy is going to be a trade off at some level. It would be best to scan every diskette that comes into the firm, but this simply isn't always practical. Just like with biological viruses, your firm will have to balance the desire for perfect health against the cost and inconvenience of living life in a bubble.

Even with a regular policy, however, you might as well accept that there is no way to be absolutely water tight. Based on the way the common viruses spread your main attention should be focused on a couple of major areas: the programs that are used on your system, the diskettes that are passed

around for common usage, and the documents you receive from outside the firm (assuming you've satisfied yourself that you are not already infected). If you managed to keep all the programs and diskettes in your office virus-free and avoided taking in strange documents, you would have greatly eliminated the virus risk. With this in mind, some basic rules should suffice:

1. Buy a good virus scanner and use it regularly to check new programs and disks in the workplace.

2. Develop a Virus Scanning Policy. Establish a common procedure for any software downloaded from public online sources, for any new diskette, and for any unsolicited document coming into the firm.

3. Restrict the use of non-approved computer programs in the firm; *i.e.*, someone's favourite graphics program brought from home.

4. Scan every new program purchased by your firm. Viruses have been known to appear in new software as well.

5. Delete all unsolicited email attachments. Do not follow any unsolicited hypertext links sent to you via email.

6. Review online sources of information on viruses. There is a growing community of virus watchers and experts, many of whom are involved in the virus scanner business. The websites of such companies as F-Secure Corporation (at http://www.f-secure.com/) provide extensive archives of known vi-

ruses and symptoms, and normally offer options for the download or purchase of scanners (see the sidebar on Virus Information Resources).

PRIVACY

The structure of the Internet lends itself to a loss of privacy if you are unwary. There are two kinds of predators: people who snoop, and people who trespass. Both present a potentially serious risk, but both can also be countered.

Snooping is possible because of how information on the Internet is sent from one place to the other. You'll recall from the discussion of the TCP/IP protocol in Chapter Two (An Internet Primer) that when a transmission crosses the Internet, it's broken into packets that bounce from computer to computer on the way to their destination. At any of the computers these packets pass through, it is conceivable that a person who controls that system might intercept, copy and read the transmission.

Trespassing, on the other hand, is possible primarily if you have a dedicated connection to the Internet. Given such a connection, a hacker can swim upstream (as it were) from the great Internet ocean into your peaceful little backwater, and do whatever trespassers do. Anyone who has a dedicated Internet connection (one that is "open" 7 days a week, 24 hours a day) has

---

Virus Information Resources

Without devoting yourself to it full-time, it might be impossible to stay on top of all the viruses out there. Good news: your panel of experts is already in place. For starters try any one of:

F-Secure Corporation. F-Secure, which develops anti-virus, data security, and cryptography software, features on their website information on thousands of viruses: names, aliases, symptoms, how they are spread, defences, and techniques for de-infecting your system.

http://www.f-secure.com/

McAfee.com's Anti-virus Centre. Comprehensive virus news, clean-up instructions, glossary, and detailed descriptions of over 50,000 viruses. From the provider of one of the leading anti-virus programs, McAfee's VirusScan.

http://www.mcafee.com/centers/antivirus/

Symantec AntiVirus Research Center. Information, news, and research papers on viruses from the provider of the popular Norton AntiVirus products.

http://www.symantec.com/avcenter/index.html

Vmyths.com. A good antidote for the paralysis that might be induced by reading too much about viruses and their dangers. There are, in fact, a lot of virus myths and urban legends out there. This website specializes in cataloguing them all and putting viruses in a realistic, non-sensational light.

http://vmyths.com/

to be aware of this and build the appropriate barriers to manage the access of outsiders.

Using Encryption Programs to Stop Snoopers

Encryption is coding, in the secret agent sense. Encryption programs can scramble a message such that only a single designated recipient can unscramble it. For many things that you may do on the Internet, using an encryption program is not truly necessary. Do you really care if someone finds out that you searched for a John Irving book on the Amazon.com website? For other things, however, encryption programs are either highly advisable or essential: using Internet email for sensitive client correspondence, for example, or submitting a credit card number into an order form on a website.

Encryption technology is gradually being incorporated right into the most common Internet software programs. Recent releases of the major web browser programs incorporate encryption to allow you to securely exchange sensitive information (such as credit card numbers) with websites that are designed to support a secure connection. Some email software programs (such as Eudora Pro and Netscape Messenger) include built-in encryption, allowing you to send and receive secure email with a click of the mouse. For those email programs that don't have built-in encryption, there are encryption plug-in programs such as Network Associates' PGP Personal Privacy or InvisiMail Deluxe. These programs seamlessly integrate into many of the major email programs, and make secure Internet email a real possibility for any Internet user.

These programs, like most modern encryption programs, work on something called the public-key system. When you originally download and activate the encryption program, it creates two keys for you. One is your private key, and the other is your public key. Everyone with a public-key encryption program has their own unique set of two keys. Any two people with an encryption program can send encrypted messages to each other as long as they have exchanged their public keys. The following are the five basic steps to secure communications with a public-key encryption program:

1. Give out your public key to your intended recipients. Think of it as giving out your phone number; it isn't secret in itself. You can send it by email to the people you want to have it. You can also post your public key to your firm's website.

2. Collect the public keys from all the people to whom you might like to send encrypted correspondence. In time, if you get in the habit of doing this, you'll have an electronic key-chain of public keys.

3. Select the public key (from your key-chain) of the person to whom you want to send an encrypted note.

4. Encode the message using the recipient's public key *and your private key*.

5. Send the message.

You are now a secret agent. When your recipient gets the encrypted message they will:

1. Select your public key from their own key-chain.

2. Decode the message using your public key *and their private key*.

3. Read the message.

Each message encrypted in this way can only have one sender and one recipient, which is the genius of the public-key system. No one other than the sender and the recipient will have the correct combination of keys.

Using Encryption Programs to Apply Digital Signatures

An encryption program can also act as an electronic or digital signature. Say you're sending unencoded messages to various people, and posting messages to web discussion groups and email listservs. Without a signature, there is really no way for the reader to be sure the postings are from you and not someone masquerading as you. In the non-electronic world, of course, we would employ the low-tech solution called a signature. In the electronic world, we would use encryption programs to append an *electronic* signature to the document. The electronic signature is a small block of encrypted text attached at the bottom of the document. The signature is encrypted with your private key, but without any specific public key (no recipient is specified). Anyone with your public key can decrypt this block of text to confirm that the message is yours.

Using Firewalls to Stop Trespassers

A firewall, literally speaking, is what they used to call the floorboards of your car be-tween the pedals and the engine compartment. The firewall gave the driver access to the engine via the pedals, but in the event the engine blew up it kept the fire out. Handy thing that firewall.

The need for a computer version of this device arises from the fact that many companies wish to set up a host computer on the Internet that provides information to the Internet public, and they also wish to attach their internal network to the Inter-

---

Cryptography Resources

For further reading on cryptography (the art of creating and using disguises for messages), to stay abreast of the issues, or to download encryption software, try one of the following:

Network Associates' PGP Home. Information and downloads relating to the popular PGP series of encryption programs.

http://www.pgp.com/

The International PGP Home Page. News, information, and support relating to the freeware version of PGP.

http://www.pgpi.org/

Cryptography Research. News, research papers, and links relating to issues in cryptography and data security.

http://www.cryptography.com/

CERT Coordination Center. A research center at Carnegie Mellon University specializing in security vulnerability issues.

http://www.cert.org/

net so that their employees can access the Internet as consumers of information, exchangers of email, etc. If you decide to do this, however, you need to be assured that you can access the Internet effectively and do the things you want to do, but not have traffic come off the Internet and climb up into the parts of your office network that you do not want to share. Host computers are accessible to anyone wandering around the Internet. Since your host computer has an IP address, a would-be trespasser can (to simplify somewhat) make note of the address and pay you a visit. If you have a network in your office which is connected to the host computer, the data on this network is also exposed. Client files, correspondence, personnel appraisal forms, etc.

Consider a firewall mandatory if you're contemplating setting up an Internet host computer, to which private firm, eyes-only parts of your network will be attached. If you don't set one up, you may as well leave your office unlocked. In essence, the firewall lets you access the Internet in the way that you want to, but keeps the trespassers out. Firewalls are not off-the-shelf items, however. The technical design of this barrier needs to be handled by a systems security expert. Still, you should understand them conceptually in order to make good managerial decisions with respect to the security of your network.

The firewall works by being a chokepoint. All Internet transmissions in and out of your network pass through the firewall. In practice, the firewall is often a dedicated stand-alone computer. The dedicated computer is linked to the Internet; your network and its computers are protected behind the firewall. If you have decided you also wish to provide some information to the Internet public, then you will set up a server near the firewall. The firewall will then act as the access control point, allowing only authorized transmissions to get through.

The firewall also serves as an Internet traffic log book. Since every Internet transmission ideally passes through the firewall, it can be used to keep an exact accounting of all transmissions entering and leaving your network. This can be vital information for your system administrator, who can consult the log of activity in the firewall to determine traffic levels, or to find out if anyone has tried to break into the system.

The firewall cannot be the only item on your security agenda. You can build the best firewall in the world to keep out trespassers and still lose data in other ways. If you have other access points into the network, the firewall can be circumvented. If you don't have a uniform confidentiality standard in the firm, data can wander out the door on a floppy disk, or over the phone if someone is careless in conversation. A firewall also does not, in itself, protect you from viruses. You can have a virus scanner built into a firewall, but even that won't take care of all your virus scanning needs since programs and files will come into your network from all kinds of sources, not just through the firewall.

Firewall design is a trade-off between absolute rigorous security and practicality of use. The tighter the controls exerted by the firewall, the more restricted traffic can become. At a certain level of security, the firewall may become apparent (and possibly annoying) to the user. The way to approach the firewall design process is to answer the essential questions:

1. What exactly do I want out of this? Fort Knox security or some basic assurance with respect to my most sensitive network areas?

2. Which traffic do I want strictly controlled, and which can I afford to let go?

3. What is the downside if a trespasser gets into this part of the network, or that part? Are there some natural partitions I should be building?

4. How much money can I really spend on this?

Out of this list of questions, in conjunction with a systems security person, you should begin to get a sense of the kind of firewall that you really need.

A final note: if you have data that you consider extremely sensitive, data that you literally could not afford to lose, you might consider whether that kind of material should be anywhere near the Internet. To be absolutely sure that Internet trespassers don't get at it, consider storing such data on an isolated network, or computer, safely offline.

4 EMAIL

Email is the essential service offered by Internet access, some might say the skeleton of the system. If someone has Internet access, they almost certainly have email. At little or no cost, they can rapidly send and receive electronic messages to anyone else in the Internet world, which is to say, almost anywhere in the geographic world too. This is true for individual users or organizations. A company with an internal email system, like that offered by the Microsoft Office suite, can open a gateway to the Internet and begin exchanging mail with other organizations and individuals on the network. In this way, the Internet's email infrastructure is inclusive.

Although the World Wide Web is more glamourous, email is the Internet's most valuable service for lawyers. Email is a tremendously powerful and cost-effective communications tool. Most clients now expect, even demand, that their lawyers be accessible through this new medium. A business card that doesn't have an email address suddenly looks dated, from an earlier era.

This chapter begins with a discussion of why email has so quickly become a key communications medium, then provides a user's guide to selecting and using email software, and concludes with a discussion of some of the security issues to which email gives rise.

WHY EMAIL MATTERS

Email matters because it is powerful and cheap. It allows for swift, flexible communication at virtually no cost. Email can be sent as swiftly as you can make a phone call, allows you to be terse and to the point without seeming rude, permits you to send as long a message as you want (for no additional cost), and lets you attach a document that contains the information underlying the exchange. To fax or courier a 50 page document from Toronto to Vancouver can cost $10 to $50. To email the same document costs pennies, and (if desired) the document can arrive in a format that the recipient *can readily revise* and send back with the same efficiency.

While email is not right for every type of exchange, here are the potential benefits it can offer over other types of communication.

Speed. Email is easy to send and receive. Even a modest typist can compose and send a (short) email in a matter of seconds, less time than it can take to place a phone call. And once an email is sent, its passage across the Internet is virtually instantaneous. Your recipient will receive your correspondence within seconds, and incoming correspondence will arrive in your emailbox with the same expediency.

Costs. Email is cheap. Chapter Three (Getting Connected) discusses the costs of the different options of connecting to the Internet, but long distance rates do not apply under any of these scenarios. Since you can attach documents to email messages, it's the equivalent of a courier in some situations, but much more cost effective.

Efficiency. Most of us are familiar with the annoying game of phone tag. Voice mail systems don't always seem to help. Email circumvents some of the problems by allowing you to deliver the content of your message fully, regardless of whether your recipient is actually available at that moment. In most email programs your outbox will retain a copy of the correspondence that can be kept on your computer, printed or deleted as you wish.

Document exchange. When you send an email you are not limited to the text you type into your email message. You can attach documents to an email, including documents prepared using a word processor or any other software program. Your recipient then not only gets a copy of your document but a copy that he or she can easily revise if desired. This is particularly valuable in the case of drafting agreements or other legal documents. You can email a copy of the document to the client or a colleague for review, and they can make changes right in the text of the document and email it back to you. You can then use the revision comparison feature of your word processor to see what changes they have made, and finalize the document in a fraction of the time you would have spent otherwise.

Competitive advantage. Email doesn't replace verbal contact, of course, but by opening a new channel of communication between you and your clients it creates a competitive advantage. Communication continues smoothly regardless whether ei-

ther of you are immediately available. It also proceeds without the formality, the cost, and the delay of written correspondence. The link this establishes between you and a client in the course of a file can greatly effect how the client chooses counsel in future. The client might well be inclined to approach you first for assistance if the patterns of communication are already well established and proven efficient.

Firm benefits. Some of these same advantages can be realized within the firm as well. Email is a convenient memorandum system, particularly for circulating a single memo to more than one person in the firm. It's also an efficient, cost-effective way to get the firm newsletter on everyone's desk. By permitting routine office communication to take place in this electronic form, email cuts paper and copying costs significantly. In firms with national operations, communication between cities can be achieved more reliably and less expensively than via the phone system. Finally, email can be useful for contacting a busy system administrator in the event of technical problems or questions. Your question goes into the administrator's emailbox who can respond with a personal note, or in the case of common problems, through a single note sent to multiple users.

User's Guide to Email

If you're like most lawyers, you will probably spend more time working with your email software than with any other Internet application. As a result, you'll be best off selecting a powerful and easy to use email program, and learning how to use it.

Email Software Programs

The good news is that there's no shortage of Internet email programs. The bad news is that, as with many things to do with the Internet, the options seem dizzying at times. There are rich, full-featured programs such as Microsoft Outlook and Eudora Pro that offer many features beyond the ability to send and receive email (such as integrated contact management, rich text formatting options, and the ability to filter incoming email messages). There are email programs that come bundled together with the popular web browsers, such as Outlook Express (bundled with Microsoft's Internet Explorer browser) and Netscape Messenger (bundled with the Netscape Communicator suite of programs). Online services like AOL have their own proprietary email programs. To further complicate matters, a more recent development is web-based email, which involves accessing your email through a web browser rather than a separate email program. Hotmail (from Microsoft) and Yahoo! Mail are two of many entrants in this category.

Considerations to keep in mind in selecting an email program include:

How easy is it to use the program's address book? An address book stores the email addresses and contact information of your regular correspondents. This can save a great deal of time, providing the address book is easy to use. Can the address book import an address automatically, without you having to retype it? Does it have shortcuts allowing you to select addressees quickly?

How easy is it to sort and retrieve old messages? Many email users find themselves using their email programs as a key repository for correspondence. This only works if the email program allows you easily to create and organize folders, move messages between folders, and find messages later.

Email's Impact on Client Expectations

The speed of email has increased the pace of business. Because email is such a rapid means of communication, clients who are using email will likely expect faster responses. As a general rule, the client who sends you a letter by post likely expects a response in a week; the client who tries to reach you by phone or fax expects a response in a day; and the client who contacts you by email expects a response in a matter of hours. One way to handle this business reality is to get in the habit of sending an email acknowledging that you received a client's email and letting them know when you will have time to fully address their inquiry.

Will the program automatically sort incoming messages? For those who receive a lot of email, more sophisticated message management features, such as filters, can be critical. Essentially, they monitor incoming email based on a range of criteria—text within a message, who sent it, what account it was sent from, the file size, and so on—and perform specific actions, such as sorting e-mail into folders, forwarding it, or automatically replying using message templates.

Does the program have word processing-like features? Programs that have built-in spell checkers and allow you to format an email like you would a word processing document permit you to create more professional, richer emails. With the proliferation of email, it will become increasingly important that email correspondence be as polished as traditional correspondence.

Does the program have built-in encryption or permit the integration of a strong encryption program? Most email programs do not yet have encryption built in. However, some are better than others at integrating encryption plug-in programs such as Network Associates' PGP Personal Privacy or InvisiMail Deluxe. Anything that makes it easier to exchange email securely is a good thing, so be sure to note what encryption plug-ins are supported by the email programs you are considering.

HOW TO DECIPHER AN EMAIL ADDRESS

Making effective use of Internet email is made much easier by understanding the basics of the Internet's addressing system.

Every resource on the Internet has a precise address called its Uniform Resource Locator, or URL. The resource in concern could be a single article from the *National Post*, a video clip from the latest Hollywood blockbuster, or an email address.

In the case of an email address, the format of the URL is as follows:

username@domain

For example, **djackson@cle.bc.ca** or **billg@microsoft.com**.

The username is typically either the first initial and last name of the individual in question, or the first name and last initial. For example, **djackson** or **drewj** are likely usernames for Drew Jackson.

The domain is the computer on which the resource in question resides (an individual's emailbox, in the case of an email address). Domain names can take one of two formats:

institution-name.geographic-identifier

OR

institution-name.institution-type

The domains of most Canadian-based resources take the first of these formats: institution-name.geographic-identifier. The institution name is typically the key portion of an organization's name, or the acronym for the organization's name. For example, the Internet institution name for the Continuing Legal Education Society of BC is **cle**. The Internet institution name for McCarthy Tétrault is **mccarthy**.

The geographic identifier for Canada is **.ca**. The geographic identifier for British Columbia is **.bc**. The domain of CLE of BC, accordingly, is **cle.bc.ca**. The domain of McCarthy Tétrault is **mccarthy.ca**.

Common geographic identifiers are:

.au – Australia

.ca – Canada

.de – Germany

.fr – France

.uk – United Kingdom

The domains of most US-based resources, on the other hand, take the other domain format: institution-name.institution-type. The most common institution-type identifiers are:

.com – a commercial entity

.edu – an educational institution

.org – a non-profit organization

.net – other networks

For example, **microsoft.com** and **harvard.edu** are two US-based domains.

WORKING WITH EMAIL MESSAGES

To get you started in working with your email software, we include some descriptions here of several important features. The specific program pictured in the following sections is Netscape Messenger (part of the Netscape Communicator bundle of Internet programs), but most common email packages have the same features. Most even have similar buttons and layouts.

The button bar at the top of the program window provides short cuts to all main program functions. If you want to send a new message, check for incoming messages, reply to a message, forward a message, or delete a message, all of these can be accomplished with the button bar.

If you want to send a new email message, for example, you would click the "New Msg" button. The following window would appear.

Now, you need only:

1. Type in the email address of your recipient in the "To:" line.

2. Tab or cursor to the Subject Line and type in the subject of your message.

3. Tab or cursor to the message window and type your message.

4. Click the "Send" button in the toolbar.

You have just participated in the communications revolution known as email.

Note that with this same simple interface
open on your computer desktop, you can

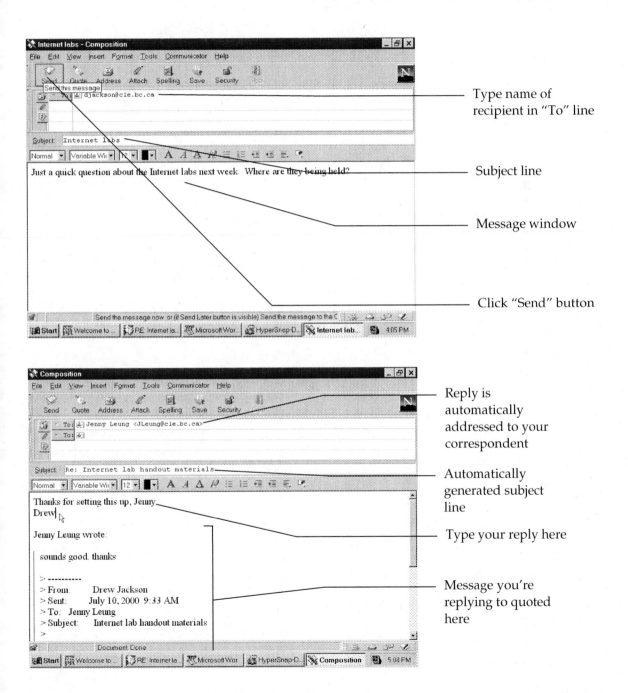

Type name of
recipient in "To" line

Subject line

Message window

Click "Send" button

Reply is
automatically
addressed to your
correspondent

Automatically
generated subject
line

Type your reply here

Message you're
replying to quoted
here

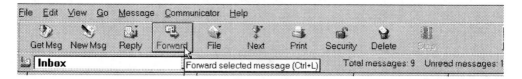

also check for incoming messages and reply to these. To check if you have any messages, click the "Get Msg" button in the toolbar. Mail that has been sent to you will be downloaded into your email inbox one at a time (in the event you have dial-up access to the Internet; if you have full-time Internet access, messages will appear in your email inbox as they arrive in your of-fice's network). Double-clicking on a specific message will expand it, so it can be read. If you wish to respond to this open note, click the "Reply" button in the tool bar and another window will open.

You might also wish to forward a message you have received, or a message you have written, to a third party. This is done by

What's All This at the Top of my Email Message?

To: Timothy Taylor ⟨ttaylor@home.com⟩
Date: Thu, 9 Mar 2000 11:14:27 -0700
From: M. Drew Jackson ⟨djackson@cle.bc.ca⟩
Subject: Have you finished the Third edition yet?
⟨message body follows⟩

This is the infamous email header. Looks like scrambled eggs, doesn't it? You can actually glean some useful information from it. This particular header is from the Eudora Pro email program and depending on your software and your preference, this information can appear in a different order or not at all. There is, however, essential information in each of the "To," "From," "Date" and "Subject" lines.

"To" and "From" are self-explanatory.

The "Date" line tells you when the message was sent. Note that time is given in your local time using a 24-hour clock (where 3:00 PM = 1500 hours). The "-0700" notation following the time situates your local time zone relative to Greenwich Mean Time; i.e., GMT -0700 hours if the message is arriving in Vancouver, as above.

The "Subject" line is used by the writer to alert you to the message contents before you read the message body. This is important because your email in-basket is normally arranged as a list of messages and their respective subject lines. A descriptive subject line allows the reader to pick out important correspondence quickly based on topic and urgency.

Other information that may appear in the header includes the names of any persons who have been cc-ed on the message, whether the message has been designated important by the sender, and whether there is an attachment to the message.

highlighting the message in question in your email in or outbox (wherever the message happens to be) and clicking the "Forward" button.

A mail composition window will open. And just as it did when you opened a new message window, you need only enter an address and add whatever additional message you wish, then click the "Send" button.

USING AN ADDRESS BOOK

In the discussion above, we refer several times to entering the email address of a recipient. In practice, this process can be automated by using your Address Book. The Address Book stores information about

---

Using a Signature Block

Any good email software program will allow you to automatically attach a description of you and your firm, along with contact information, at the bottom of your outgoing email messages. This "signature block" saves you the trouble of typing this information in with each message, and serves the same function as law firm letterhead in print correspondence.

While there is no fixed limit, generally signature blocks should not be longer than four or five lines. Most Internet users now refrain from the elaborate "sig blocks" used by some early Internet users: clever expressions, jokes, or ASCII art (keystrokes that form a pattern on the screen) that could stretch a signature block to a dozen or more lines.

---

your correspondents, and helps you quickly address your various email messages.

First, you have to add entries to your Address Book. To pull up the address book, you select "Address Book" from the Communicator drop-down menu. The following window appears:

To create an address "card" for a correspondent, click the "New Card" button; type the name, email address, and other contact information of your correspondent into the card; and click "OK."

Now, when you wish to send a message to this person, you simply:

1. Open your Address Book.

2. Select the name of your correspondent.

3. Click New Msg on the toolbar.

An automatically addressed message window will open. Type your note and send.

The address book also allows you to create mailing lists, which are very useful if you need to send a message or a document to many people at once. When the Address Book is open, you will find a "New List" button on the toolbar. Click this to bring up the mailing list dialog.

WORKING WITH ATTACHMENTS

Attachments are files that are sent along with an email message. The file can be a word processor document, a web page, a spreadsheet, a program or virtually any other kind of filed data.

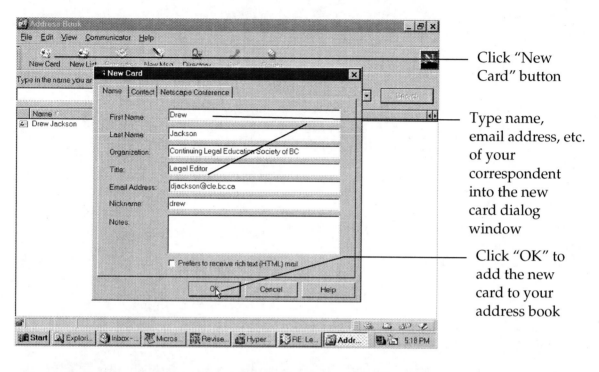

Click "New Card" button

Type name, email address, etc. of your correspondent into the new card dialog window

Click "OK" to add the new card to your address book

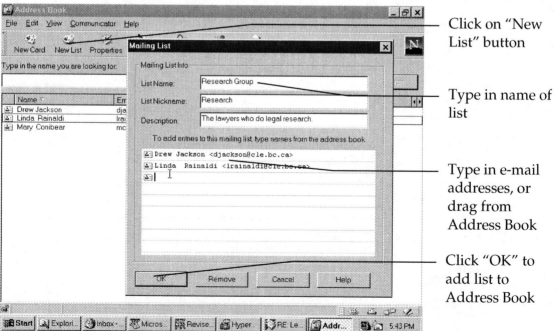

Click on "New List" button

Type in name of list

Type in e-mail addresses, or drag from Address Book

Click "OK" to add list to Address Book

You attach a file to a message while the message window is open.

Note that once attached, the file's name will appear on the Attachments List of the email message. Click send, and the email message with its attachment will be sent to your recipient.

Of course, you may also receive attachments from time to time. When you receive an email message with an attached file, most email programs will indicate that there is an attachment by displaying a paper clip icon beside the subject line of the email. At the bottom of the message, meanwhile, there will be a link to the document as well as information about the file. Clicking the link will open the application that the file can be read with (your word processor or your web browser etc.).

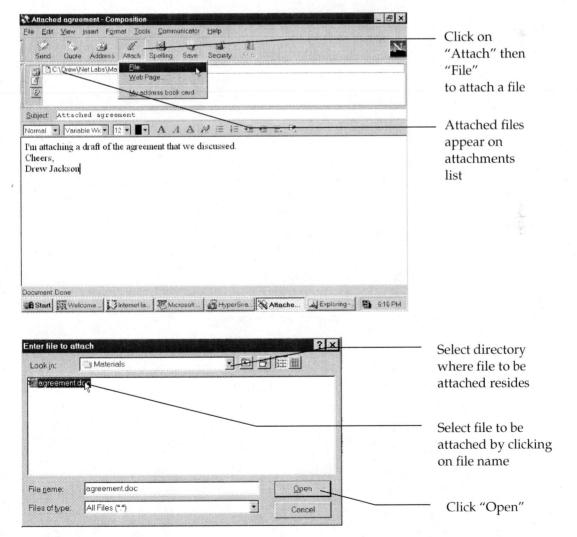

Click on "Attach" then "File" to attach a file

Attached files appear on attachments list

Select directory where file to be attached resides

Select file to be attached by clicking on file name

Click "Open"

When dealing with attachments, note that if you or your recipient does not have a good email software program, you may encounter difficulties with the format of the attachment. An attachment can only be sent by email if it is converted to text format by one of various methods. In good email programs, this happens automatically behind the scenes without you even realizing it. If your recipient can't open your attachment, it may be because one of your email programs could not handle one of the converting methods (alternatively, it may be because they don't have the appropriate software application on their computer, such as Microsoft Word if you sent them a Word document).

The three methods commonly used to convert attachment files to text format are MIME (Multipurpose Internet Mail Ex-

tensions), UUENCODE (Unix to Unix Encoding), and BinHex (Binary to Hexidecimal). If your recipient is having trouble with your attachment, first try sending the attached file in MIME (the most common conversion method with newer software), then UUENCODE. Try BinHex first with recipients who are using Macintosh computers.

Virus Alert!

This is a good place to note the discussion of viruses in the section on Security in Chapter Three. Some viruses can be passed through email attachments. It is very important to have a Virus Scanning Policy in place that considers how incoming attachments will be handled by your firm. This might even go so far as requiring the deletion of all (unopened) attachments from sources unknown.

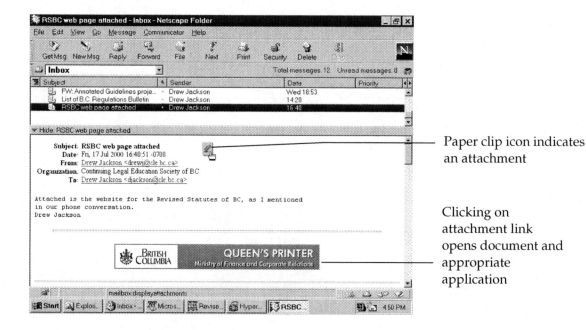

Paper clip icon indicates an attachment

Clicking on attachment link opens document and appropriate application

EMAIL ETIQUETTE

Email is different enough from other forms of communication that unique conventions have developed around its use. For the most part, these are useful guidelines that respond to the misunderstandings possible with high-speed written communications. Use common sense, it will be your best guide.

1. **Don't use capital letters.** IT IS THE WRITTEN EQUIVALENT OF SHOUTING.

2. **Try to limit the length of your email.** Most email programs allow you to "quote" the message you are responding to by copying parts of the message into your response. This is a good feature to use so long as you quote only passages that are relevant to your response. Including the entire message thread leading up to your response adds to Internet traffic and makes your note harder to read.

3. **Be careful with irony and other kinds of humour.** The sharpest witticism can often fall flat in print, or worse, offend. If you absolutely can't resist the temptation, and you're writing to someone you don't know very well, you might consider punctuating your aside with one of several common abbreviations or symbols. Internet users call the symbols emoticons (*emotional constructs*). They're used to remind the reader of intended humour or other emotion.

Silly Emoticons You May Encounter ... (look at them sideways)

:-)	Happy or just joking
:-(	Sad or disappointed
;-)	Wink, get it?
#-)	I'm severely hungover
:-P	Sticking out my tongue
:-@	Yelling, upset etc.
:-O	Shocked
⟨g⟩	Grin

Abbreviations You May Have to Interpret

BRB	be right back
BTW	by the way
FAQ	frequently asked question
FYI	for your information
IMHO	in my humble opinion
OS	operating system
LOL	laugh out loud
RTFM	read the f-----g manual
WRT	with respect to

EMAIL SECURITY ISSUES

The benefits of email do not come without some cost. New users should be aware of the unique problems that email is heir to.

First among these, in the minds of many people, are the concerns surrounding the security of email messages you send and receive. Just as phone lines can be tapped, email can be intercepted in transit. At any of the computers through which your email message passes as it travels across the Internet, it is conceivable that the transmission could be intercepted and read. As is discussed more fully in the Security section in Chapter Three, encryption technology offers a solution. Encryption programs can scramble a message such that only a single designated recipient can unscramble it.

Some email software programs (such as Eudora Pro and Netscape Messenger) include built-in encryption, allowing you to send and receive secure email with a click of the mouse. For those email programs that don't have built-in encryption, there are encryption plug-in programs such as Network Associates' PGP Personal Privacy or InvisiMail Deluxe. These programs seamlessly integrate into many of the major email programs. See Chapter Three for a discussion of how these programs work to allow you to send encrypted messages or apply a digital signature (when you aren't concerned with keeping the message private but want to verify that it was you who sent it).

Another area of concern with email is the security of your Internet account. In 1999, a security hole was uncovered in Hotmail, Microsoft's web-based email service, which allowed hackers submitting a command in the proper format to access any valid email account. Microsoft moved to plug the hole soon after it was revealed. But the fact that a major provider like Microsoft could be exposed caused the web-based email market to noticeably sag afterwards.

Hackers have also been known to steal passwords, but the way they do this is not always particularly sophisticated. There are high-tech (extremely uncommon) cases in which hackers have electronically "eavesdropped" as users type in their passwords. More infamous by far are the stories of hackers diving in dumpsters behind targeted offices looking for passwords on old Post-it notes. This doesn't mean that the occurrence is either frequent or likely in your case. Simple rules are your best bet to combat the remote possibility that your firm will be targeted. Adhering to these rules will greatly improve the security of your email:

1. Never choose an obvious password, for example "password," or any password taking the format <mypartner>, <mymom> or <mydog>.

2. If possible, make your email password different than your system password.

3. Change both your passwords often, at least once a month.

Under certain circumstances, viruses can also be a concern using email. As is discussed more fully in the section on Security in Chapter Three, programs and documents can arrive in your firm attached to email messages. Both can contain viruses (word processor, spreadsheet, and other documents can contain macro viruses). If you are exchanging programs and text files with other people, especially people you don't

know very well, then you must take the
precautions of developing a Virus Scanning
Policy—in other words, common procedures for how to deal with new software,
floppy disks, and documents that are received by your firm (see Chapter Three for
further details).

5 THE WEB: AN OVERVIEW

The World Wide Web (hereinafter the web) is the most glamourous and fastest growing service on the Internet. It's the part of the Internet that is most responsible for the media fascination with the Internet, the drama surrounding high tech stocks being played out in markets around the world, and for the pronouncements that the Internet is the most transforming invention in human history.

The web may be over-hyped. It may be over-valued. But there's no doubt it's an important new technology. The web is a radically powerful, easy-to-use medium to exchange information across a broad range of forms. Over the web, you can now access news, buy software, do your banking, watch a TV broadcast, listen to music, trade stock, bid in an auction, research law, discuss issues. And new uses of the web are being thought up seemingly every day.

This chapter is intended to introduce you to the web and give you a start in making use of what it offers. Chapter Six (The Web: Its Resources) and Chapter Seven (The Web: Finding Tools) explore in more detail what you can do on the web, and how you can find your way around.

A BRIEF ACCOUNT OF THE WEB REVOLUTION

Hypertext is a way to link and access information of various kinds as a web of nodes in which the user can browse at will. It provides a single user-interface to large classes of information (reports, notes, data-bases, computer documentation and on-line help). We propose a simple scheme incorporating servers already available at CERN...

A program which provides access to the hypertext world we call a browser...

—Tim Berners-Lee and R. Cailliau "World Wide Web: Proposal for a HyperText Project" 12 November 1990, CERN

The web was birthed in 1990 at CERN (European Laboratory for Particle Physics) located in Geneva, Switzerland. It was intended to provide a simple, standardized interface for retrieving and publishing data by various researchers. Like archiving systems that preceded it, the web was designed to make the Internet easy to use for both seekers and providers of information.

Older Internet services such as gopher and something called WAIS were also motivated by the desire to facilitate information publishing and retrieval. The web protocols developed by CERN, however, added some powerful capabilities to the mix, capabilities that set the stage for the web to grow into *the* dominant Internet service in just a few years. Think of the web as being based on four essentials: the easily published web page, the hypertext link, the combination of media forms, and the interactive element.

THE EASILY PUBLISHED WEB PAGE

The web page is the basic document that carries web data, the information currency of the medium if you will. Anyone with access to a server can put up a web page. The page can be as short as a résumé, or it can be as long as the full text of NAFTA. Content is driven almost entirely by the party with the information. The innovation in this lies in how straightforward the publishing process has become. Web pages are written with a set of codes called HyperText Markup Language (HTML). HTML editors (software programs that allow you to create web pages) have quickly matured into flexible and relatively intuitive programs, no more difficult to use than word processors were five years ago. More significantly, though, the popular word processors now have HTML capabilities built in, so you can put together a web-publishable page in the time it takes to type the thing. This accessibility is a primary reason for the web's explosive growth. There are pages put up by everyone from General Motors to your nephew. Figure 5.1 is but one example, the homepage of Yahoo! (http://www.yahoo.com), a popular web "portal" (a portal is a website that offers a broad array of resources and services to attract a large audience).

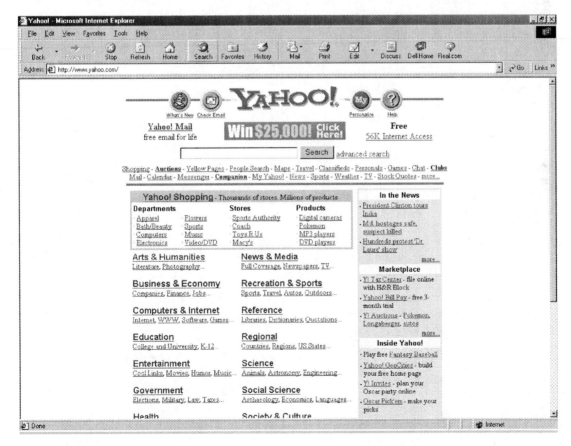

Figure 5.1. Yahoo!

THE HYPERTEXT LINK

Make note of the highlighted (underlined) words. These are the web's second great innovation: hypertext. It's actually not an entirely new concept. When you jump from a highlighted word to further topical detail in the Windows Help facility, you are also using a kind of hypertext. But in the web's case, this concept is put to use on a grand scale. The "author" of any web page, on any server, anywhere, can link their page to virtually any other page, on any server, anywhere. HTML allows this through the use of hypertext links. Links, as they are known, appear as highlighted, underlined words or as icons. When you select a link by clicking on it with your mouse, your web browser finds and retrieves the page to which the link has been established. In Figure 5.1, by clicking your mouse on "Arts & Humanities" on the Yahoo! greeting page, your web browser is instructed to retrieve another page at the Yahoo! site, this page containing a listing of subtopics that fall under the main heading "Arts & Humanities" (Yahoo! is at its core a directory of sites on the web, organized into a series of topics and subtopics that you can navigate through to find websites of interest). The actual coding for the link appears as follows, wrapping itself around the destination URL:

<A HREF = "http://www.yahoo.com/Arts">**Arts & Humanities**</A>

You don't have to worry about the coding details; as we said, HTML is already a transparent operation in the popular word processors. But understanding the structure of the hypertext link does tell you something. Virtually any location on the Internet with an URL (which is to say, a Uniform Resource Locator, the term for an address on the Internet; more on the Internet's addressing scheme below), is linkable, regardless of the kind of resource it actually is. This is crucial to the web's innovative force because a link from a web page can point not just to another web page, but to any kind of Internet resource: to an email address, to a document file to download, to an audio file, and so on.

MULTIMEDIA

The idea that a web page can link to an audio file hints at the third web essential: multimedia. Pages in the conventional publishing world contain text and pictures. Web pages can contain any media at all: text, graphics, sound, and moving images. Anything that can be binary encoded can be transmitted on the Internet and embedded in pages on the web. Multimedia itself is not new, but the web provides for some innovative ways to present this material broadly. Over the web, you can now watch TV broadcasts, listen to music, view movie trailers, or tune in to streaming video of live events. At the CBC website (http://cbc.ca/), for example, you can watch the latest of Newsworld's hourly newscasts or dozens of other TV programs, or listen to any number of radio programs. Multimedia is a large part of the reason for the web's explosive growth and the expansive talk of its revolutionary capabilities.

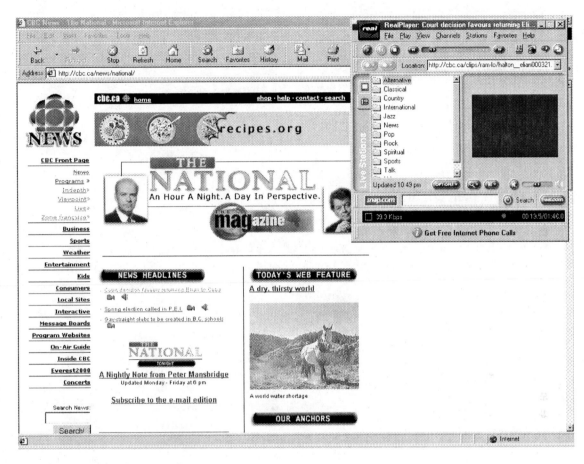

Figure 5.2. *CBC's "The National"*

THE INTERACTIVE ELEMENT

The web has also greatly narrowed the gap between the information supplier and consumer. This is the product both of technological breakthroughs in the form of new client software, and of the evolution of ideas that preceded the web. As it has matured, the model of the Internet has steadily shifted away from an archival system, where static deposits of data are mined by a user, to something more like an information exchange, where data users and data providers actually meet—a place where information transactions take place.

Consider a simple example of this aspect of the web. Using a link encoded with a "mailto:" URL, HTML allows the user to communicate (via email) with the publisher of a web page, directly from the page being viewed. This creates a meaningful, immediate feedback loop between information providers and information consumers.

More sophisticated examples of this interactive element abound. At online auction sites like eBay (http://www.ebay.com), you can submit bids for items being auctioned off by other users of the site. At travel sites like Travelocity (http://www.travelocity.ca/), you can check the cost of flights and hotel rooms and make your own reservations online, using their incredibly sophisticated database of travel offerings. Online communities like the investor community site Raging Bull (http://www.ragingbull.com/) allow you to participate in thousands of ongoing discussions with others interested in like topics.

It is this interactive quality of the web, more than any other, that sets it apart from previous Internet services and defines the web as a powerful new medium. The other essentials are important—the ease of publishing on the web, the web's multimedia capabilities, and the fact that users can easily link to related information—but it is the web's ability to allow for information exchanges and in particular transactions to take place that is primarily responsible for the web's tremendous popularity.

There is no doubt this innovative medium will continue to grow. In the larger context, the web is still so young and dynamic that it's impossible to get a sharp fix on where it might end up. But it's already clear that the web is a real phenomenon, a real innovation in popular communication patterns and capabilities.

USER'S INTRODUCTION TO THE WEB

If you're accessing the web for the first time or are a relatively new user, this section is designed to give you an introduction to the software involved and how to use it.

WEB SOFTWARE PROGRAMS

To access the web, you need to have a web client software program, known more commonly as a web browser, installed on your computer. There are really two principal choices when it comes to a web browser: Microsoft's Internet Explorer or AOL's Netscape Communicator. The two programs have been involved in a titanic struggle for years now, competing on features, user interface design, and distribution mechanisms. The result for the user is that both programs have converged in many areas. Both are free (and in fact at least one will come pre-installed on any new computer you buy). They have a generally similar look and feel, with similar toolbars and pull-down menus. They have comparable feature sets. And both incorporate or integrate with a range of other programs, such as email software, web page editors, and other collaboration tools.

The main difference between the two programs may be the different paths the two competing software companies have taken in their attempts to dominate the browser market. With recent versions of its Internet

The Ubiquitous URL Address

The notion of electronic addressing is so engrained in Internet culture and practice that it is uncommon to encounter the word "address" used in the familiar streets and avenues context. Address means either your email address, your website, or the URL of some other information of note. Your street mail address, in fact, is almost *persona nongrata* on the Internet, where it will be referred to (if at all) as your snail mail address.

Explorer, Microsoft has effectively merged the web browser and the operating system. An integral component of the Windows shell, Internet Explorer is now the browser for both local and web content.

In Netscape's vision, the browser suite is not simply a tool for navigating the web, but the client side of an enterprise-wide, cross-platform architecture for exchanging information both within a company and outside it. This vision has been clouded somewhat by AOL's purchase of Netscape in 1999. AOL has continued to develop the Netscape browser, but recent versions have been focused more on supporting AOL's expansive new media empire than on enhancing the browser's functionality as a workplace tool.

With a recent version of either web browser, however, you'll be well equipped to begin exploring the web. For more information on the leading browsers, and to download recent versions of the software, check their respective websites: http://www.microsoft.com/ for Internet Explorer, and http://home.netscape.com/ for Netscape Communicator.

HOW TO DECIPHER A WEB ADDRESS

A key step to feeling comfortable navigating through the countless sites on the web is to have some ability to decipher a web address. Every page on the web, and in fact every site or resource on the Internet, has a precise address called its **Uniform Resource Locator**, or URL. The resource in concern could be an emailbox, a single article from *The Globe and Mail*, or a video broadcast on the CNNfn Financial Network website.

Each URL tells you two things: (1) the service you can use to find and retrieve the resource in question, and (2) the location of the resource.

URLs take the following essential format:

service://location information

First, the service information. Each Internet service has a unique URL service code as follows:

World Wide Web = **http**
email = **mailto**
FTP = **ftp**
news = **news**

Second, location information. By location we mean the location of the computer on which the resource in question resides. The heart of the location information in a URL is the *domain name*. Most organizations that provide information over the web obtain their own domain name. Domain names can take one of two formats:

institution-name.geographic-identifier
OR
institution-name.institution-type

The domain names of many Canadian-based organizations take the first of these formats: institution-name.geographic-identifier. The institution name is typically the key portion of an organization's name, or the acronym for the organization's name. For example, the Internet institution name for the Canadian Broadcasting Corporation is **cbc**. The Internet institution name for the Ontario Court of Appeal is **ontariocourts**. The geographic identifier for Canada is **.ca**. The domain name of CBC, accordingly, is **cbc.ca**. The domain name of the Ontario Court of Appeal is **ontariocourts.on.ca**.

Common geographic identifiers are:

.au – Australia
.ca – Canada
.de – Germany
.fr – France
.uk – United Kingdom

The domain names of most US-based resources, on the other hand, typically take the other domain format: institution-name.institution-type. The most common institution-type identifiers are:

.com – a commercial entity
.edu – an educational institution
.org – a non-profit organization
.net – other networks

The domain name of the New York Times, for example, is **nytimes.com**. The domain name of the American Bar Association is **abanet.org**.

To further complicate matters, there are Canadian resources that take this institution-type domain format. The Globe & Mail's domain, for example, is **globeandmail.com**. The domain of the Canadian Bar Association is **cba.org**.

Beyond the domain name, the balance of the location information indicates a precise address for a particular page on the site in question.

Let's put all this together in the form of an example.

http://www.globeandmail.com/
TopNational/20000318/UCHREN.html

Here, **http://** tells you that the service of the resource is the World Wide Web. The **www.** reinforces that we're looking at a web resource (note that this is a highly common but not mandatory part of a web address). The **globeandmail.com** tells you that the domain is a computer at *The Globe and Mail*. And **TopNational/20000318/UCHREN.html** is the precise address for a particular article on the site.

MOVING AROUND IN YOUR WEB BROWSER

To get you started in working with your web browser, we include some descriptions here of several important functions. The specific program pictured in the following sections is Internet Explorer, but for those using Netscape Communicator or another browser, the functions will be available in those programs, using very similar (and possibly even the same) commands and steps.

What Happens When We Run Out of Domain Names?

Given the dizzying rush to register domain names under the existing .com, .net, and .org "top level domains," the question arises: what happens when we run out of domain names? In recent years, a number of plans have been proposed to create new top level domains, such as .firm, .store, .law, and .arts. Some companies have even taken orders for them. Finally, in July 2000, ICANN (Internet Corporation for Assigned Names and Numbers), which administers the domain name system, outlined a plan to add new top level domains in a "measured and responsible manner." Specifics of the new "TLDs" were to be announced in late 2000.

The rationale behind ICANN's use of language like "responsible" and "measured" is that not everyone agrees that new top level domains are a good thing. Those in favour argue that new top level domains are technically easy to create, will help relieve perceived scarcities in existing name spaces, and are consistent with a general push towards consumer choice and diversity of options. Those opposed point to greater possibilities for consumer confusion, the risk of increased trademark infringement, cybersquatting, and cyberpiracy.

For recent developments on this issue, see ICANN's website at http://www.icann.org/.

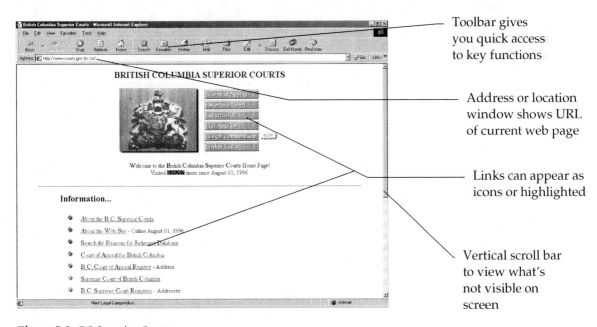

- Toolbar gives you quick access to key functions
- Address or location window shows URL of current web page
- Links can appear as icons or highlighted
- Vertical scroll bar to view what's not visible on screen

Figure 5.3. BC Superior Courts

As with any graphical software program, the key functions in your web browser are placed in a toolbar for quick access. From the Internet Explorer toolbar, for example, you can go backwards or forwards, print a page, go directly to a designated Home page, or call up your favourites (sites that you "bookmark" in order to make return visits).

One way to open a web page is to type its address into the address or location window. To do this, double-click (by clicking the left mouse button twice in quick succession) anywhere in the address window. Type in the URL (the address) of the web page you want to open, and press the ENTER key on your keyboard.

If you click on any of the links offered, your browser will take you to the location that is linked. This could be a related page on the same site or a page on an entirely different site on the web. In this way, you can link from page to page across the Internet. This is what people sometimes call "surfing" or, for some, "drilling down."

Of course, linking page to page can get you lost fairly quickly if you aren't keeping track of where you have been. Often, after drilling down through a number of links, you will decide that you want to return to the original page where you started. Thankfully, the browser keeps track of where you've been and backtracking is easy.

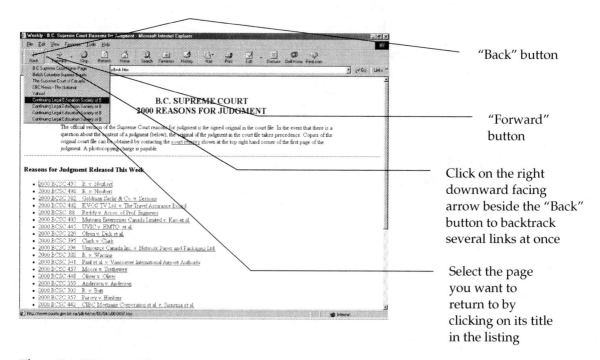

"Back" button

"Forward" button

Click on the right downward facing arrow beside the "Back" button to backtrack several links at once

Select the page you want to return to by clicking on its title in the listing

Figure 5.4. *BC Supreme Court*

Simply click on the "Back" button to go to the last page you visited. Click the "Back" button again to backtrack another step, and so on. The "Forward" button will advance you a step along the link track you have made.

If you want to skip backwards or forwards several steps at once, you can do so by clicking on the small right downward facing arrow beside the "Back" button. Note that the titles of pages you have visited in the current session are listed in reverse order (the first page you visited is at the bottom of the list—or may be off the list if you have visited more than ten pages in the current session). Clicking on the title of the page you want to return to will take you directly to that page.

Keeping What You Find on the Web

When you find a web page that you want to keep or take a copy of, there are several options available to you. You can print the page, save the page to your computer, or cut and paste a portion of the page into another application such as a word processing file.

The print option is straightforward. Simply click the "Print" button in your web browser's toolbar. The page presently on your screen will print.

There may be times, though, when you want an electronic copy of a web page rather than a print copy. For example, you

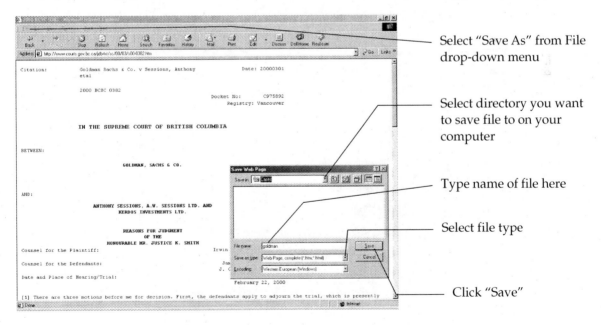

Figure 5.5. BC Supreme Court judgment

may want to adjust the formatting of a document to include in a document brief, or to prepare an "electronic brief." In such cases, you will want to save the page to your computer.

To do so:

1. Select "Save As" from the "File" drop-down menu.

2. In the "Save As" dialog window that appears, select the directory on your computer where you want to save the file to.

3. Type the name of the file in the "File name:" box.

4. Select the file type you want to save the page as (.txt or .html, for example).

5. Click "Save."

If you want to work with a small piece of information from a web page, for example to copy a paragraph into a document you are preparing, then an effective technique can be to copy from the web page and paste into your word processor. To copy a portion of a web page and paste it into a word processing file:

1. Highlight the selection you want to copy by clicking with your mouse at the beginning of the selection, holding the mouse down and dragging the mouse to the end of the selection, and then releasing the mouse. The selection should be highlighted in blue.

2. Select "Copy" from the "Edit" drop-down menu.

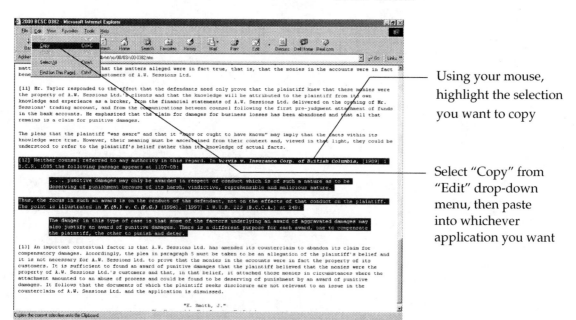

Using your mouse, highlight the selection you want to copy

Select "Copy" from "Edit" drop-down menu, then paste into whichever application you want

Figure 5.6. BC Supreme Court judgment, cont'd

3. Open the application you want to paste the selection into (in this case, your word processing software).

4. Select "Paste" from the "Edit" drop-down menu in the other application.

PDF: When Your Browser Isn't Enough

There are many documents accessible via the web published in a format called Portable Document Format (PDF) that you can't view or use with a simple web browser. PDF makes it easy for information providers to publish documents on the Internet so they look exactly like their paper counterparts. Forms are often made available in PDF format, as are highly formatted reports and newsletters. You will recognize PDF documents as ending in the extension **.pdf**.

In order to work with PDF documents, you need a web browser plug-in called the Adobe Acrobat Reader. You can download the free Acrobat Reader from the Adobe website at http://www.adobe.com/products/acrobat/main.html. You will be led step-by-step through the straightforward installation by the Acrobat software. Once installed, the next time you click on a PDF file, the Acrobat plug-in will open automatically within your web browser, and display the document.

USING FAVOURITES TO REMEMBER WHERE YOU'VE BEEN

One of your immediate concerns navigating the web is simply remembering where you found the good stuff. Favourites (or Bookmarks in Netscape Communicator) help solve this problem. When you find a web page you think you'll want to visit again, add the page to your favourites list. To do this:

1. Ensure the page you want to add to your list is open on your screen.

2. Click on the "Favourites" button in the toolbar.

3. Click "Add" in the Favourites window that appears on the left side of your screen.

4. Note that the title of the page is added to the bottom of your favourites list.

In time, given the number of pages you might wish to visit again, you will find you need a means of organizing a growing list of favourites. This is where favourites folders come in. These folders are like other folders on your computer desktop; they allow you to cluster related favourites together within separate folders. In Internet Explorer, you can create, organize, and delete favourites folders by clicking on the Favourites button in the toolbar and:

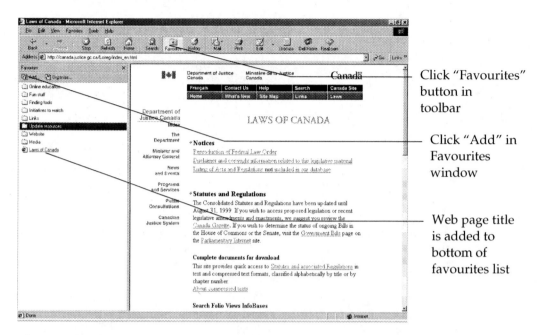

Figure 5.7. *Department of Justice – Laws of Canada*

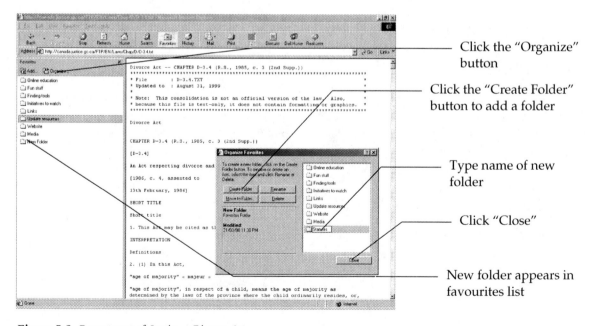

Figure 5.8. *Department of Justice – Divorce Act*

1. In the Favourites window that appears on the left side of your screen, click on the "Organize" button.

2. In the Organize Favourites dialog window, click on the "Create Folder" button to create a new folder.

3. Type in the name of the new favourites folder.

4. Click "Close."

5. Note that the new folder will appear in the favourites list with a file folder icon beside it.

When you encounter a useful page at some point later, you can then add the page directly into the appropriate folder.

USING WEB FINDING TOOLS TO MAKE YOUR EXCURSIONS EFFICIENT

The web is a data cloud. There is no up and down once you're in it. No sideways really either, no specific entrance or exit. You can pick a location on any site anywhere on the web to begin your exploration. From there you can follow links offered by the various pages you encounter. At times this can work just fine. Some days, serendipity seems to smile on you as you drill down excitedly through layers and layers of a given topic, uncovering information and related topics that sites have linked into their pages. But other days this approach can be pretty aimless, even pointless. In general, the disorganized user will rely on raw luck and plenty of free time to find relevant information.

Fortunately, there are techniques and tools that you can use to help you find your way around efficiently. Chapter Seven (The Web: Finding Tools) provides a more detailed discussion of web search techniques and tools, but this introduction is intended to get the new user started.

First, a few words about terminology. Broadly speaking, there are two kinds of finding tools: search engines and directories. A *search engine* works by allowing you to type a word or a string of words into a form. The engine will then grind away searching and return to you with the results. The results are presented in the form of a list, where each item on the list is a hypertext link itself, usually accompanied by a description of what lies at the far end of the link. In other words: once you've got your search results, you can begin exploring directly from the results page to evaluate the success of your search.

Note that there is some syntax involved in creating complex searches—for example, "(airbag and injury) but not decapitation." This syntax includes the use of search operators to give your search more accuracy than just typing in a series of words. Typically, a help section at the search engine site will provide instructions on how to use the search engine, including how to compose a complex query. In Chapter Seven, we look at search syntax and strategy in further detail.

Directories are somewhat different than search engines, but at the end of the day they are trying to provide the same service: to help you find what you're looking for in a large body of information. The technique is different, however. Directories compile and organize links in some kind of logical structure (normally topical, but geographic is common as well). In this respect, directories are more like your standard library catalogue. You go in, you click on "laws," you click on "criminal law," you click on "sentencing," and so on until you "drill down" to sites or information relevant to your search.

If they have a weakness, the drawback of directories is that you are relying on the directory designer to come up with some rational Dewey decimal alternative to provide for the diversity of subject matter on the web. Some argue this is next to impossible, and that you're better off trusting a robot (as in the case of the search engines) to simply go out there and bring back links to

pages that contain relevant keywords. In the end, you will develop your own preference. There are many search engines and many directories out there. You'll like some better than others because of the directory structure, the search syntax, or even the layout of the search page.

As for actually using finding tools, there are many search engines and directories that allow you to search over large parts of the web (no one search tool covers the entire web, as it is simply growing too quickly for any one tool to map comprehensively). One of the easiest ways to search over the web as a whole (although not the most sophisticated) is to use the built-in web search facility in your web browser. Here is how you might use this facility in Internet

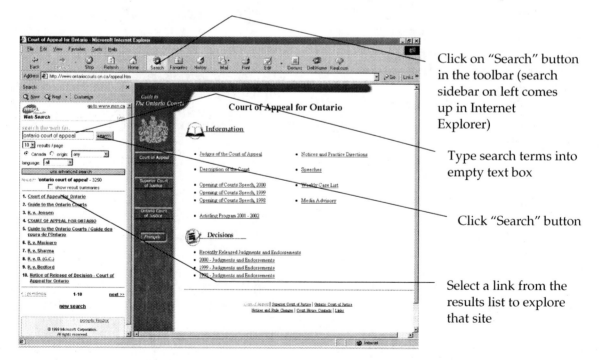

Click on "Search" button in the toolbar (search sidebar on left comes up in Internet Explorer)

Type search terms into empty text box

Click "Search" button

Select a link from the results list to explore that site

Figure 5.9. Ontario Court of Appeal

Explorer to search for the website of the Ontario Court of Appeal:

1. Click on the "Search" button in the browser's toolbar.

2. This will open up a search window on the left part of the screen that allows you to search over the web using a leading web-wide search tool.

3. Type your search terms into the empty text box.

4. Click the "Search" or "Go Get It!" button to begin your search.

Alternatively, you can begin a web-wide search by going to the site of one of the many search engines and directories that allow you to (in theory at least) search over

the web as a whole. Some of the leading web-wide search tools include Yahoo! (http://www.yahoo.com), Alta Vista (http://www.altavista.com), and HotBot (http://hotbot.lycos.com/). Here is how you might use HotBot to search for the website of the Ontario Court of Appeal:

1. Go to HotBot (or your search tool of choice) by typing in the web address or selecting it from your favourites list.

2. Type your search terms into the empty text box.

3. Select your search options (look for all or any of the words, select a date range, etc.)

4. Click the "Search" button to begin your search.

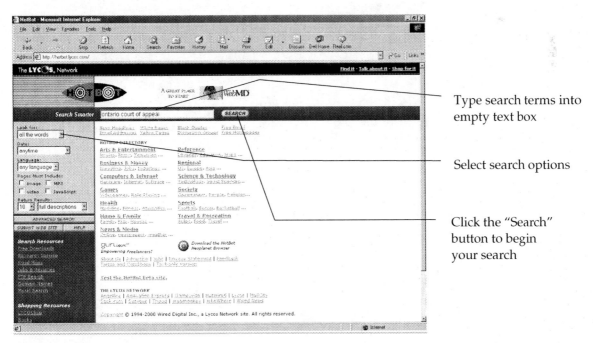

Type search terms into empty text box

Select search options

Click the "Search" button to begin your search

Figure 5.10. HotBot

Finally, also keep in mind that the better websites have their own search engines that allow you to search over the contents of that site. You will often see a search button or link somewhere in the site's navigation. If you click on that link, you will bring up the search form allowing you to search over that site. Opposite is one example of using such a search form at the Department of Justice website.

See Chapter Seven (The Web: Finding Tools) for a fuller discussion of using search tools, including site-specific search engines.

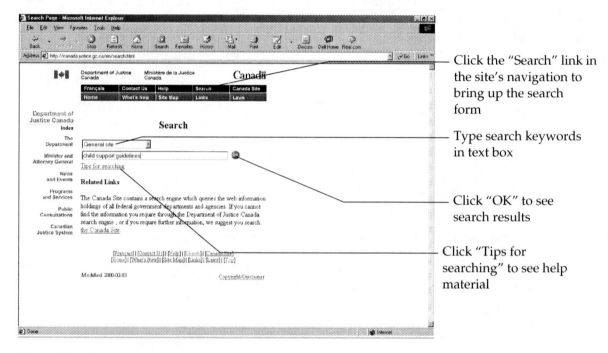

Figure 5.11. Department of Justice – Search page

6 THE WEB: ITS RESOURCES

LAWS
LEGISLATION
CASE LAW
TRIBUNAL RULINGS

BENCH & BAR
LAWYERS
PROFESSIONAL ASSOCIATIONS
JUDGES

GOVERNMENT

BUSINESS & FINANCE
BUSINESS & COMPANIES
MARKETS

FACTUAL RESOURCES
PEOPLE
EXPERTS
REFERENCE

UNITED STATES & INTERNATIONAL RESOURCES

NEWS & MEDIA

It's hard to believe that as recently as a few years ago, the Internet held little interest for the legal professional. That was before the web revolutionized the way we access information. There is now a dizzying array of resources available online that can help make you more productive and efficient in the workplace. Court decisions, statutes, government bills, tribunal rulings, CLE papers, encyclopedias and dictionaries, business and company information: this is information that lawyers use all the time, and tremendous quantities of it are already available on the Internet, and more is sure to come.

This chapter is where we focus in on this wealth of material that you can put to use in your law practice. We'll look at information of interest in seven categories:

1. **Laws.** Legislation, case law, and tribunal rulings.

2. **Bench & bar.** Law firm websites, professional associations, and resources for judges.

3. **Government.** Government policy documents and regulatory material.

4. **Business & finance.** Business news, information about companies, and stock market data.

5. **Factual resources.** The people, experts, and reference material you can access online.

6. **United States & international resources.** Laws and resources from other jurisdictions.

7. **News & media.** The proliferation of media (both serious and fun) on the web.

Keep in mind as we review these offerings that this chapter is not designed to be an exhaustive listing of all the resources available on the Internet. The idea is to give you a flavour for what you will find in your travels, and to offer some pointers on where you might find the best and most relevant material.

The Legal Resources Directory Appendix, on the other hand, *does* aim to be an exhaustive listing of Canadian legal resources on the Internet. Think of it as your yellow pages to this new place. In the Directory, we provide the URL for each resource, and an annotation to alert you to interesting content, so you can pay a visit to any (or all) of the sites that interest you. Also note that in Chapter Seven (The Web: Finding Tools), we suggest ways in which you can find your way around online and use the web to do research.

Two final notes of caution before we begin our exploration of the web's resources:

First, the Internet is a fluid, evolving place. By the time you read this, new sites will have emerged, and others will have changed location. An entirely new trend may have taken the Internet by storm. This chapter reflects the state of the Internet as of the date of publication. In Chapter Seven and in the Legal Resources Directory we recommend sites that can help you find new attractions and developments as they emerge.

Quality Control on the Electronic Frontier

Anyone can post information on the Internet. This publishing freedom has contributed to the staggering content boom online, but it has a serious downside. Many web resources lack the authority and reliability required by legal professionals. We offer here some key steps to determining whether a web resource meets the requisite standard of objectivity, timeliness, accuracy, and authority.

1. **Determine the identity of the source.** The first step is to determine what organization is posting the resource in which you're interested. Consider the objectivity and credibility of the organization. If you're looking at an amending statute posted by a government body, the information is more likely to be accurate and up-to-date than if posted by a public interest group.

2. **Determine the authority of the resource.** Look at the help material on the site to determine whether the posting organization considers the resource to be authoritative. Many court and government sites, for example, will state that the Internet version is not the "official" version of a document.

3. **Determine the currency of the material.** Look closely at how current the resource is. The web creates the illusion that all material posted is up-to-the-minute, but this is rarely the case. Be sure to note the "current-to" date on the page you're interested in, or on the site in general if nothing is posted on the specific page.

Second, no one is in charge of this place we're about to explore. There is no vendor or government that's responsible for organizing the vast body of material available on the Internet, or for filtering out the dubious stuff. For the first-time visitor (even for the veteran) this is an info-metropolis full of surprises. There's a wealth of discoveries to be made in lane-ways and back alleys, although this is not always easy to see when you are first confronted with all the other distractions. For this reason, we suggest ways to help you sift out the good stuff (see the sidebar, Quality Control on the Electronic Frontier).

LAWS

One of the most important uses of the web for a lawyer in Canada is to access the law. Most of Canada's legislation is now on the Internet, and the web represents the fastest and easiest way to get at recent amending legislation. Several important collections of cases are now on the web, led by the Supreme Court of Canada's growing collection of SCC decisions. And the web provides unprecedented access to rulings from administrative tribunals.

Laws of Canada User Tip

Federal statutes and regulations are available in two different formats on the Department of Justice website at http://canada.justice.gc.ca/: a text format for quick reference and easy downloading, and a FolioViews format for searching.

FolioViews is a powerful search tool, but one that takes a bit of practice to become comfortable with (see page 149 for a detailed review of searching a website that uses FolioViews). If you know what statute or regulation you're looking for and want to access it quickly, opt for the text format at the Justice site. To find the text format for a regulation, you can drill down by the title of the statute from which the regulation is associated (for example, the *Divorce Act* if you're looking for the Child Support Guidelines). Alternatively, you can use the search engine for the Justice site as a whole (rather than the Folio engine the searches over the full text of the laws on the site) to type in keywords from the regulation's title. If you're doing the latter, it helps to narrow your search to the Statutes and Regulations on the site.

LEGISLATION

Providing access to legislation is an area where the Internet excels. The Department of Justice website (http://canada.justice.gc.ca/), for example, provides the full text of every federal statute (except, alas, the *Income Tax Act*) and regulation, consolidated to a date within the previous six to nine months. The legislation is available in two different formats: a text format for quick reference and easy downloading, and a FolioViews format for searching. Access to either format is possible from of a "Laws of Canada" page on the Justice Department site.

Most provinces' statutes are also available on the Internet (see the Legal Resources Directory for a complete listing and URLs). For a lucky few provinces (Alberta, Ontario, New Brunswick, Nova Scotia, and all three territories), complete sets of regulations are also online.

One thing you will notice quite quickly as you explore the legislation on the web is that there is no consistent approach to the material. From site to site, you will find that the presentation differs, as do the search tools and syntax, the currency dates, and even whether the material is free or not. (One province, Saskatchewan, has an Internet collection of statutes and regulations that is accessible only for a subscription fee. The more common approach is for a free collection to be available over the web with relatively basic search capabilities, and an enhanced version to be available for a fee either over the web or on CD-ROM.)

This range of approaches to legislative material shouldn't surprise us. In the print world, there are various approaches to presenting a collection of print statutes, with differences in indexing, formatting, and currency dates. As well, the web is so young that site design trends and search capabilities are still evolving rapidly. But what this means for you as a user is that when you dip in to a statute collection on the web for the first time, you will need to pay close attention to several things:

1. **How current is the collection?** In other words, what was the date of the last consolidation? This date will typically be posted in a prominent place on the site.

2. **How do you use the search tool at the site?** Many statute sites use specialized search software called Folio-Views, a powerful search program favoured by legal publishers. Unfortunately, FolioViews is not the most intuitive search program for a user (see the Ontario Statutes, at http://209.195.107.57/en/index.html, pictured in Figure 6.1). See page 149 for a detailed review of searching a website

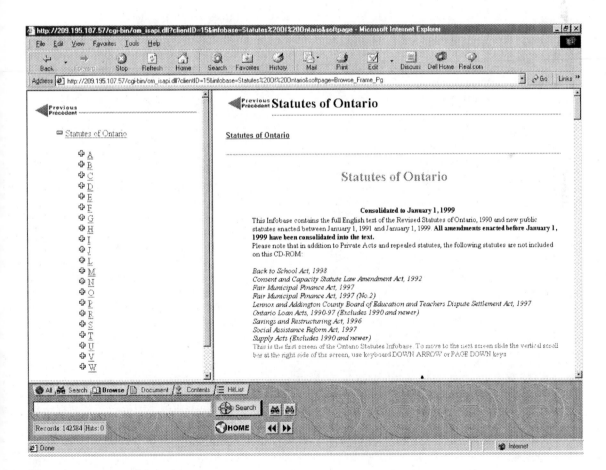

Figure 6.1. Statutes of Ontario

that uses FolioViews. Even if the site is using a more intuitive search engine, be sure to check on what search syntax the engine uses — for example, when you type two words without any "connector" (for example, **child support**), does the search engine treat them as a phrase, as two words that both must appear in a result, or as two words only one of which must appear in the result? Most sites will feature help material on how to use the search tool, including tips and examples.

3. **Is there an enhanced electronic collection that you should be accessing for a fee?** As mentioned above, it is fairly common for a statute collection to be available free over the web with relatively basic search capabilities, and to be available for a fee either over the web or on CD-ROM with more sophisticated search features. The for-pay version will often be more current and offer other enhanced features. In Alberta, for example, you can access a free collection on the web (at http://www.gov.ab.ca/qp/) that offers no searching and is several months out-of-date, or for an annual cost of $230 you can access a web collection that features sophisticated searching and is updated every two weeks. You will want to make a cost-benefit assessment of free versus enhanced access with each statute collection you use.

The issue of the currency (or lack thereof) of a statute collection is eased somewhat by the remarkable access the web now provides to recent amending legislation. Even if a collection is not entirely current, checking for recent bills can be a very quick task on the web. For example, the Parliamentary Internet website (http://www.parl.gc.ca/) features the full text of all government bills and private members bills on the order paper. A listing of bills indicates the stage each bill is at in the legislative process (for example, as passed by the House of Commons), and a single click of the mouse takes you to the text of a bill itself. The bills are formatted much as they are in the printed versions. You can print a bill of interest from the screen, or save it to your computer (or for that matter email it to a colleague or client). A document that would have taken days to obtain previously is now in your hands in moments.

Recent bills from virtually every province are now available on the web (see the Legal Resources Directory for a complete listing and URLs). As with statute material, you will find that the presentation of bills varies from site to site. Most sites offer up bills in HTML (web) format, but some make them available only in PDF format (in which case you'll need the Adobe Acrobat Reader installed on your computer; see page 81 for a discussion of PDF files).

A particularly useful feature on many of the sites providing access to recent bills is a progress of bills page. This page will list all current bills and indicate at what stage in the legislative process the bill is (first reading, third reading, royal assent etc.). Even more valuable are those sites that provide an easy way to determine whether a bill has been brought into force. At the Legislative Assembly of British Columbia site (http://www.legis.gov.bc.ca/), for example, there is a section called "Provisions in Force," which lists all in-force dates for recent bills and references the enactment bringing a bill into force.

Access to Hansard debates is also a common feature on legislative websites. Hansard issues from the House of Commons and the Senate are printed the day following each sitting and are available on the Parliamentary website the next day. You can locate a passage from Hansard by clicking on the date of the debate in a calendar, by browsing through a list of subjects, or by typing keywords into the search form at the Parliamentary site. Note that the site search form allows you to restrict a search to a particular section of the site — Hansard from the House of Commons, for example. Using this feature, you could run a quick search of a bill number that you're inter-

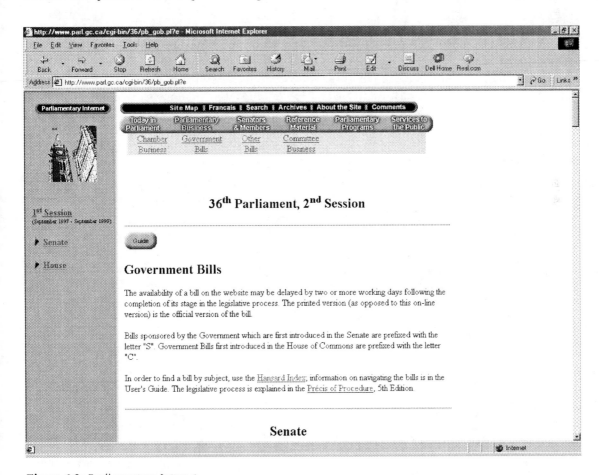

Figure 6.2. Parliamentary Internet

ested in over the Hansard debates and re-trieve the speeches relating to that bill.

This technique is in fact possible with Han-sard debates for any province. The full text of Hansard debates and proceedings from every province's legislative assembly is available at either the main provincial web-site or at the province's legislative assembly site (see the Legal Resources Directory for details and URLs).

CASE LAW

Whereas much of Canada's legislation is now available on the web, the same is not true of the country's case law. The coverage of case law on the web is very thin, and the ability to search over case collections very limited.

The good news, though, is that those case collections that are available over the web show tremendous promise. One of the best resources for lawyers on the Internet, for example, is the Supreme Court of Canada website (http://www.scc-csc.gc.ca/). The site is actually a joint project between the Court and the Centre for Public Law Re-search (CRDP), a pioneering research cen-ter at the University of Montreal. Featured at the Supreme Court site is a collection of full text SCC decisions, with headnotes, dating from 1989. Decisions are loaded the day they are released, so this growing col-lection provides outstanding access to new SCC decisions as they are handed down. Decisions are available in a variety of for-mats, a feature that makes this site very versatile. Any decision can be viewed on

the screen in text or HTML (web) format, or downloaded to your computer in RTF (rich text format, which should open and work with any modern word processing program) or WordPerfect 6.1 for Windows format. If you want to include a copy of an SCC decision in a document brief, down-loading it in one of the latter formats (de-pending on your word processing software) will allow you to print out a version that looks very clean and professional.

The SCC collection can also be used for ba-sic research. You can browse the collection by year and Supreme Court Report volume number or by legal topic (click on the "Search by Concept" link). More effective will likely be to search over the collection by typing keywords into one of the two search forms. There is a simple search form that can be used for basic searches, or a fielded search form for more complex que-ries. The latter allows searches over specific fields such as case name, judge's name, cases cited, or statutes cited. You could, for example, search for decisions with "em-ployment law" in the abstract and Sopinka J. in the judges field. See Chapter Seven (The Web: Finding Tools) for further dis-cussion of using resources like the SCC website to do research.

Other case law collections on the web in-clude sites from the Federal Court of Can-ada, the Alberta Courts, the British Colum-bia Courts, and the Ontario Courts. See the Legal Resources Directory for a full listing and URLs.

As with legislation on the web, you will no-tice that the case collections are all very different from one another. The sites differ in their presentation of the cases, the search tool they use (if they use one at all), and the depth of their coverage. As you begin working with case collections on the web, you will want to make special note of the following:

1. **How comprehensive is the collection?** Does the site post every decision rendered by the court in question? How far back do decisions go?

2. **How do you use the search tool at the site?** Some sites that host case collections don't have a search tool at all, at least for the time being. For those sites that do have a search tool, be sure to check the site's help material to see what search syntax and approach you should use when searching the collection.

3. **Should you be accessing (for pay) a more sophisticated case collection?**

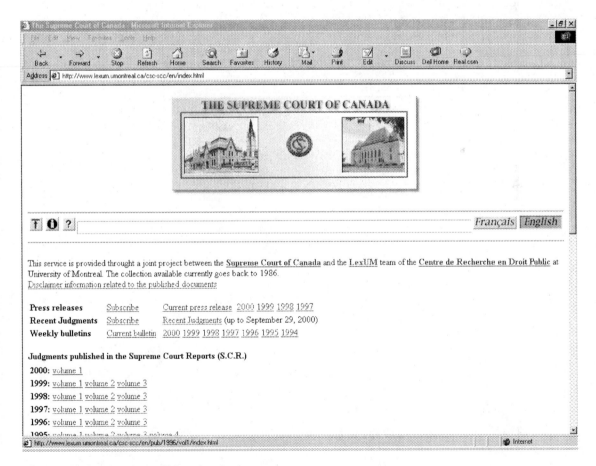

Figure 6.3. Supreme Court of Canada

For quick access to recent decisions, the web can be wonderful. But as a way to research case law, its value is still limited. There are, of course, more sophisticated electronic case collections available. Some are actually available now over the Internet, although not for free. Canada's legal publishers are beginning to provide gateways on the Internet to their subscription-based case collections. QuickLaw and Carswell, for example, allow paying subscribers to access their electronic case services through their websites. (The lines between the "free" Internet and "for pay" commercial services are starting to blur, and this trend is likely to continue in the years ahead as the Internet becomes the primary way for lawyers to access information.) You will want to make continual cost-benefit assessments of whether it is better to access a free, relatively basic website or to use a for-pay, more full featured service.

One final note with case law collections on the web is that virtually all courts that post judgments on the web specify that the Internet version is not the official version. Many state that the official version of the judgment is the signed original in the court file. The only time this is likely to matter is in the event an opposing party raises a question about the content of a judgment. This will no doubt be rare, but it would still be a good idea when using a judgment from the Internet to be aware of the policy of the posting site on this point.

TRIBUNAL RULINGS

An area where the Internet is very strong is in providing access to rulings from ad-ministrative tribunals. Traditionally, obtaining the text of a tribunal ruling was often a challenge. Only the largest tribunals had their decisions published in a reporter system. Even where a reporter existed, it might not be in the firm or local library. More typically, a phone call had to be placed to the tribunal itself and a copy of a decision photocopied by a clerk and faxed or mailed to the firm. The Internet has changed all this.

Take the example of the Canadian Human Rights Tribunal. It makes available at its website (http://www.chrt-tcdp.gc.ca/) the full text of all decisions rendered by the Tribunal since 1990. The decisions are searchable, so finding all recent decisions on age discrimination, for example, can be an extremely quick undertaking.

The website for the Office of the Information and Privacy Commissioner for British Columbia (http://www.oipcbc.org/) goes a step further. The site includes the full text of orders made by the Commissioner under the *Freedom of Information and Protection of Privacy Act* (British Columbia), as well as the full text of the Act itself. In each of the orders, the referenced sections of the Act are linked. A visitor reading an order can click on a linked section and jump right to the text of the section itself. Another click brings them back to the order. In this way, the site exploits the hypertext linking facility of the web, allowing the user to follow a train of thought to retrieve relevant information.

The Canadian Radio-television and Telecommunications Commission (http://

www.crtc.gc.ca/) site goes a step further again. As well as posting the full text of CRTC decisions, notices, and orders (within a day of their release) and having an extensive searchable archive of CRTC rulings, the site provides online forms for licence applications and other matters. The forms can be completed within a web browser and submitted electronically. The use of online forms promises great savings both for users and for site providers, as information can be exchanged very efficiently. There are initiatives underway across Canada to capitalize on this potential, from online land title filings to online court filings. Look for online forms to be an area of significant activity in the next couple of years.

BENCH & BAR

While access to law is a big part of the reason why the web is so valuable for legal professionals, it is by no means the only area where the web has had an impact. The majority of law firms and professional associations now have websites of their own, sites that have changed the way lawyers interact with clients and with each other.

LAWYERS

Like businesses of virtually every stripe, law firms have arrived on the web en masse. Hundreds of Canadian firms have now established their own websites, and law firm sites are getting more sophisticated every year. Early efforts that were more or less

online brochures have given way to a new generation of law firm websites that more fully participate in the web's information exchange and offer extensive content — content that takes many forms, from firm newsletters and publications to hosting online discussions on topical legal issues (see the sidebar, Law Firm Websites: Maturing as the Web Matures).

This content can offer value not just for clients and prospective clients but also for other lawyers using the web. Consider the website of Bereskin & Parr (http://www.bereskinparr.com/), an intellectual property firm. Their stylish site includes excellent overviews of copyright, trademarks, patents, and other areas of intellectual property law. The firm's newsletters are also available at the site, providing discussions of recent cases and legislative developments. Another section provides links to other intellectual property resources online, such as the Canadian Intellectual Property Office, intellectual property legislation at the Department of Justice Canada website, relevant treaties such as the Berne and Paris Conventions, and patent, trademark and copyright offices in other jurisdictions. If you need to advise a client generally on developments in the law relating to domain names, for example, the Bereskin & Parr website would make an excellent starting point.

In the area of family law, Toronto practitioner Joel Miller has developed a remarkably extensive set of resources at his site, the "Family Law Centre" (http://www.familylawcentre.com/). Updates on recent family law cases and legislative changes, CLE papers, Frequently Asked Questions (FAQs) on family law issues, links to sites of interest to family lawyers, and a directory of family law mediators are among the many resources available. He also has one of the more innovative (some would say daring) features on a law firm website — a "chat room" where visitors to the site can discuss family law issues with other similarly inclined visitors.

Boutique firms like Bereskin & Parr and Joel Miller's can offer excellent resources in their area of specialization. But full service firms have by no means been left behind in the rush to the web. Some of the most

stylish and sophisticated law firm websites, in fact, are from some of the larger, full service firms. The smartly designed website of Osler, Hoskin & Harcourt LLP (http://www.osler.com/), for example, features a deep and often updated collection of newsletters and publications on recent developments. The firm's tax department had commentary on the Federal Budget 2000 on the firm's website the day the budget came down, together with links to budget documents elsewhere on the web.

Like many law firms posting valuable information on their websites, Osler is no

Law Firm Websites: Maturing as the Web Matures

The first generation of law firm websites was dominated by "online brochures" — sites that were little more than online versions of the print brochures available in the firms' reception areas. There are still sites of this type, featuring a profile of the firm and its lawyers, some photos of the firm's offices, and some contact information. But most law firms that are serious about being on the web now do much more with their websites.

The better firm sites now feature extensive information for clients and prospective clients. Such sites post updates on recent legal developments, publish firm newsletters and publications, feature special sections for clients with unique information needs, and provide links to resources of interest.

Some sites are going further with this new medium and making use of the web's interactive qualities. Pushor Mitchell (http://www.pushormitchell.com/), a mid-size firm in British Columbia's interior, invites visitors to their website to subscribe to a free legal information email, which provides updates on breaking developments of interest to clients. Colin Singer, a Montreal immigration practitioner, hosts discussion forums on his website (http://www.singer.ca/), where visitors post questions and comments about immigration issues. Campbell, Cohen, another Montreal immigration firm, invites visitors to their site (http://canadavisa.com/) to submit "online assessment forms," in which visitors fill in information about themselves with a view to receiving a professional assessment of their eligibility to immigrate to Canada.

Figure 6.4. Osler, Hoskin & Harcourt LLP [Reprinted with permission from Osler, Hoskin & Harcourt LLP]

doubt aiming to impress clients (current and prospective) that the firm is abreast of current legal issues. But these resources can also be of value for other practitioners. The Internet, after all, was built largely on the concept of "community knowledge" — the idea that users offer their insights and innovations to other users and that everyone will be better off for it.

PROFESSIONAL ASSOCIATIONS

The emergence of the web has given organizations such as law societies, bar associations, and continuing legal education societies an entirely new way to reach their audience, which is excellent news for lawyers. The result is that it has never been so easy to find out about upcoming legal education seminars or to get a copy of the latest Law Society bulletin.

The Canadian Bar Association's website (http://www.cba.org/), for example, provides a painless way to keep up with CBA developments and events. You'll find news about CBA submissions on major legal issues, CBA task force initiatives, schedules for CBA section meetings, and extensive resources from CBA branch locations. The site also includes information about upcoming CLE seminars, and in fact several CLE seminars were delivered over the CBA website in early 2000. Registrants could tune in for 90-minute sessions that took place via conference call, supplemented by slides and interactive elements on the CBA website. Such sessions hold great promise for users and CLE providers, as registrants can participate without leaving their own offices, a tremendous advantage in a country as spread out as Canada.

The Continuing Legal Education Society of BC has been similarly innovative in providing valuable content over its website. The CLE of BC site (http://www.cle.bc.ca/) features news of recent cases taken from its weekly current awareness service, and one of the more extensive collections of links to websites of interest to lawyers.

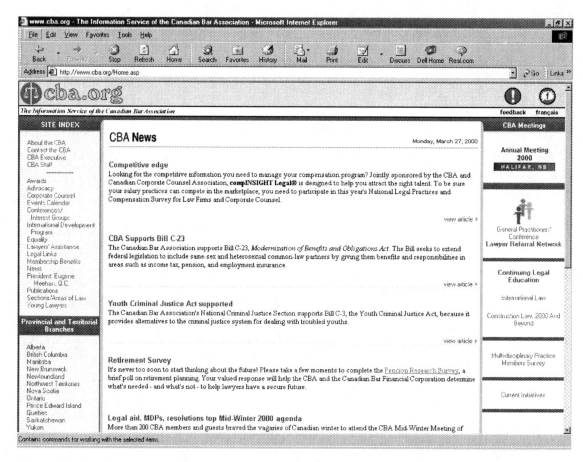

Figure 6.5. Canadian Bar Association

Like bar associations and CLE societies, law societies have much to offer lawyers over their websites. The Law Society of Upper Canada's site (http://www.lsuc.on.ca/), for example, includes such resources as the *Ontario Lawyers Gazette*, Notices to the Profession, practice checklists, CLE materials, and the text of statutes governing the legal profession, the Rules Made under the *Law Society Act*, and the Rules of Professional Conduct. Material that takes up several binders on a lawyer's bookshelf (and we won't even mention the paper costs) now resides on one computer accessible to anyone with an Internet connection.

Keep in mind that other law-related organizations also have content at their websites that offer value for lawyers. Law reform bodies in Alberta, British Columbia, and Nova Scotia all have deep collections of papers and reports that can make your legal research more efficient. And hundreds of legal institutes and non-profit organizations have websites that can be mined for materials on topics from environmental law to civil liberties issues. The Legal Resources Directory provides full details and URLs for such law-related bodies.

JUDGES

As discussed above in the Laws section, several courts now publish their judgments on their own websites. There are also other resources on the Internet that are of note to the judiciary. Sites such as that from the Canadian Judicial Council (http://www.cjc-ccm.gc.ca/) provide access to news and developments of interest to judges. The Judicial Affairs Information Network (JAIN), an information service available to federally appointed judges, is now accessible over the Internet. Even some individual judges have their own websites: Chief Justice Allan McEachern of British Columbia has developed an extensive site (http://www.courts.gov.bc.ca/CJBC/welcome.htm) that includes comments on legal issues and responses to email inquiries from visitors to the site. An introduction states that he launched the site as part of an effort to enhance public understanding about the courts, the judiciary, and the law.

Another initiative spearheaded by Chief Justice McEachern similarly uses the Internet to deliver information about the law to the public. Assisted by a number of colleagues, Chief Justice McEachern wrote "The Compendium of Law and Judges" and posted it on the BC Superior Court's website (http://www.courts.gov.bc.ca/). The Compendium, which includes a general description of the law and the BC judiciary, as well as sections on the *Charter of Rights* and criminal law, attempts to increase public awareness of judicial matters. The initiative was partly a reaction to the treatment of legal matters in the popular press, and the authors chose to distribute it over the Internet in part to make it as widely accessible as possible.

GOVERNMENT

Governments have embraced the Internet. This is excellent news for the legal profession. Government, after all, is the source of much of the information lawyers need to deal with in their practice: statutes, regulations, bills, government policies and rulings, budgets, forms, and Ministry reports. We've seen above in the Laws section how the Internet offers dramatically improved access to statutes and bills. The same is true of other material generated by government.

Consider a few examples at the federal level. Finance Canada's website (http://www.fin.gc.ca/) now provides access to the Federal Budget and related documents at the same time the Minister of Finance is delivering the budget speech in the House of Commons. Revenue Canada's website (http://www.ccra-adrc.gc.ca/) provides tax guides and forms, and such key publications as advance income tax rulings (ATRs), income tax information circulars (ICs), income tax interpretation bulletins (ITs), GST technical information bulletins, and GST notices. Citizenship and Immigration Canada's site (http://www.cic.gc.ca/) features application kits and forms, policy documents and fact sheets, and Ministry Manuals and Operational Memoranda for Citizenship Policy, Legislation, Port of Entry Processing, and more.

Similar examples abound at the provincial and municipal levels as well. The Legal Resources Directory provides a full listing of government sites and URLs, but suffice to say that the Internet has been a boon for access to government documents.

Another area where the Internet is having a significant impact is in providing access to

databases of information controlled by governments that historically have required specialized software to access and have cost money to search. Consider these four examples:

1. **Office of the Superintendent of Bankruptcy's Insolvency Name Search** (https://strategis.ic.gc.ca/sc_mrksv/bankrupt/engdoc/superint.html). This database contains records of all bankruptcies and proposals filed in Canada from 1978 to date, as well as a record of all private and court appointed receiverships filed in Canada from 1993 to date. All petitions registered in the Office of the Superintendent of Bankruptcy are also included. Searches can be run by estate name or information, or by an estate ID.

2. **Canadian Intellectual Property Office's Canadian Patent Database** (http://patents1.ic.gc.ca/intro-e.html). This database allows users to access more than 75 years of patent descriptions and images, as well as search, retrieve and study more than 1.4 million patent documents. Searches can be done using keywords, patent document numbers, or by such fields as title, inventor, owner, and date.

3. **Corporations Directorate's Federal Corporations Data Online** (http://strategis.ic.gc.ca/cgi-bin/newcorp-bin/corpns_se). This database allows access to data on any federal company incorporated under the *Canada Business Cor-*

porations Act. Corporate data available includes a listing of directors, annual report filings, financial data, and affiliate information. Searches can be run by corporate name or corporation number.

4. **Canadian Environmental Assessment Agency's Federal Environmental Assessment Index** (http://www.ceaa.gc.ca/registry/registry_e.htm). This master list of all environmental assessments carried out under the *Canadian Environmental Assessment Act* can be searched by keyword, location, lead department, or ecozone.

These databases are powerful, very easy to use, and provide information that can be easily printed or downloaded to your computer. And unlike electronic databases in the pre-Internet era, they're free. This kind of increased (and less expensive) access to data is one of the reasons why the Inter-

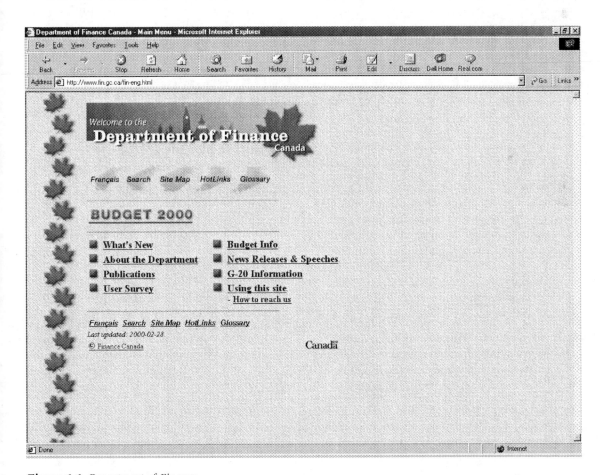

Figure 6.6. Department of Finance

net is already a critical tool for legal professionals.

Another way in which government is using the Internet that will impact lawyers is to allow for online document filing. The Corporations Directorate, for example, now has an "Electronic Filing Centre" (at http://strategis.ic.gc.ca/sc_mrksv/corpdir/corpFiling/engdoc/) where you can submit certain documents online that are required under the *Canada Business Corporations Act*. To file an application for federal incorporation, a notice of change of directors, or a change of registered offices, the forms can be filled out and submitted online, without the need to print off and submit several copies manually. Payment can be made by submitting a credit card over a secure Internet connection.

The Corporations Directorate site, like most government sites, highlights another of the benefits of the Internet. In addition to information about corporate filings and data, contact numbers are provided for those wishing to obtain further information.

Not only can you get at information more readily over the web, but you can also more easily track down who to contact to get *more* information. And via email you can *initiate that contact immediately*. No flipping through phone directories or wading through recorded phone messaging systems. At most government websites, you can now simply click on the email link of a contact person for information you are seeking, compose a short note describing what you are looking for, and click the send button. Your web browser handles all the addressing niceties, allowing you to focus on the substance of the communication.

Searchable email and phone directories are also available at most government websites, and can also dramatically speed up the process of communicating with government employees. At the federal government's main website, for example, the Government Electronic Directory Services (http://canada.gc.ca/search/direct500/geds_e.html) allows you to search for contact information by the name of a public servant or by government department. The search results include the address and phone number for each employee listed, as well as links to the department in which that person works. Other government directories show the results of your search as a list of email links, so that you can send an email directly from the screen to the person for whom you are looking.

BUSINESS & FINANCE

The volume of business news, company information, and market data on the Internet is simply staggering. For the uninitiated, the amount of information about stocks on the web can be downright frightening. Since lawyers so often deal in business information, though, this increased access is mostly a very good thing.

BUSINESS & COMPANIES

You do not have to go very far online to find business news. The CNNfn (http://www.cnnfn.com/) website, for example, features up-to-the minute market and financial news and resources from CNN's financial network. The financier's bible, Bloomberg.com (http://www.bloomberg.com/), is another site chock full of all the business and financial news you could ever want.

Such important sources of Canadian business news as the *Financial Post* (http://www.nationalpost.com/) and the *Report on Business* magazine (http://www.robmagazine.com/) have their entire editions online, often before you can secure a print copy.

Do be aware, however, that some of the best sources of business news are charging for their content on the Internet. *The Wall Street Journal Interactive Edition* (http://interactive.wsj.com/) and *The Economist* (http://www.economist.com/) both charge roughly 30 per cent of their print subscription rates to access their Internet editions. Print subscribers are offered additional discounts.

Other sources of business information on the Internet are the many websites that allow you to search for information about specific companies. For example, Carlson Online (http://www.fin-info.com/) provides one-stop shopping for Canadian company information, with links to company home pages, stock quotes, news releases and more. It also automatically searches

and links to SEDAR for company filings. Yahoo! Finance (http://finance.yahoo.com/) provides a similarly deep archive of information about United States-based companies, including articles in the news, company profile information, and links to the company's home pages, stock quotes, and SEC filings.

MARKETS

In addition to business news, the Internet is home to an unprecedented volume of stock market data. At sites such as the Globe Investor website (http://www.globeinvestor.com/), from the folks at *The Globe and Mail*, you can get stock quotes (to within the previous 15 minutes) on any company listed on an American or Canadian exchange, financial reports and analysis, charting and reporting tools, and customized "portfolio trackers" that allow you to create your own personal list of stocks that you want to follow. Some sites, such as the investor community site Raging Bull (http://www.ragingbull.com/), allow access to free real-time stock quotes.

A driving force behind this increased access to information that has historically been reserved for investing professionals is the explosion in online trading. One out of three stock transactions are now placed through an "e-broker." Discount brokers such as E*Trade (http://www.etrade.com/) are luring investors away from traditional brokers with low transaction fees, after-hours trading, and access to market data. The result for the user is more choice, and much more information.

FACTUAL RESOURCES

The web offers new ways to access people, experts, and reference material.

PEOPLE

This may come as a surprise, but you can find people on the Internet. In fact, you may be able to find yourself. There are dozens of websites that serve as giant Internet phone books, listing names, numbers, and addresses for millions of people.

Some of these sites have been created, quite literally, from phone books. Canada 411 (http://canada411.sympatico.ca/), for example, is the Internet version of Canada's telephone companies' residential white pages and business yellow pages. It includes over 10 million listings supplied by participating telephone companies from across the country. Other sites such as the Lycos Network's WhoWhere Directory (http://www.whowhere.lycos.com/) gather their data from activity on the Internet — for example, by having users submit their email

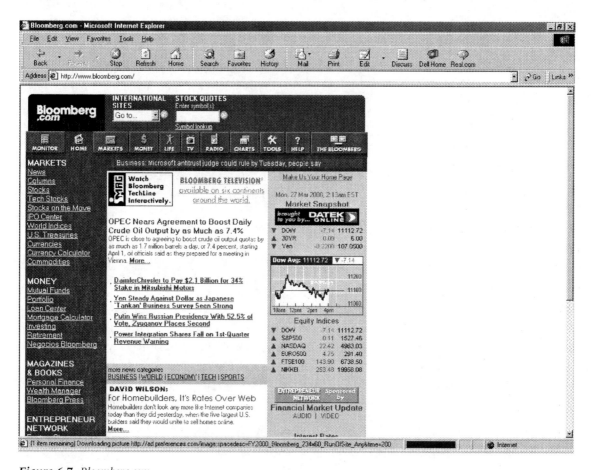

Figure 6.7. Bloomberg.com

addresses and other contact information to the directory itself, or by mining email addresses from other sites that users visit on the web.

The end result for a user is that there are dozens of people directories on the Internet that you can search over when looking for contact information for a person. You will typically be presented with a search form into which you can type a first or last name, and (optionally) a city or province or even an email address.

Some people directories provide, somewhat more sinisterly, a reverse lookup feature. InfoSpace (http://www.infospace.com/canada/) allows you to type in a phone number, address, or area code to turn up listings that match. Once you have a listing in front of you, another click can bring up a map displaying the location of the subject's address, as well as all surrounding streets and businesses, and even the names of neighbours. Very eerie. Especially if you happen upon your own listing in one of these directories.

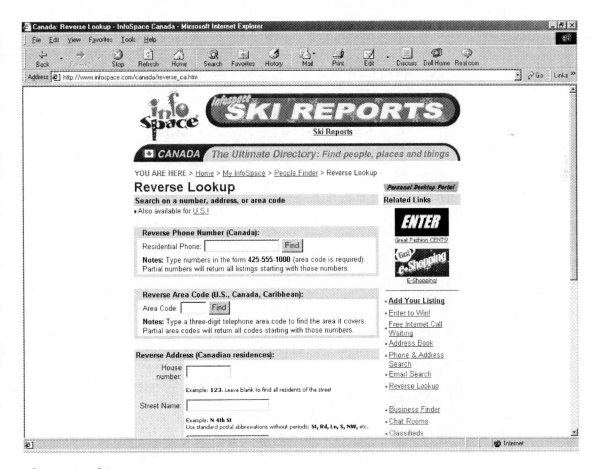

Figure 6.8. InfoSpace

EXPERTS

The web is providing increased access to expert witnesses. There are many United States-based expert witness directories online, such as the National Directory of Expert Witnesses (http://www.claims.com/index.html), published by Claims Providers of America. This searchable directory includes over 1,200 experts and consultants in several hundred categories of technical, scientific, and medical expertise. For Canadian-based experts, the websites of the Trial Lawyers Associations in both Ontario (http://www.otla.com/) and British Columbia (http://www.tlabc.org/) feature (for members only) searchable databases of expert witnesses. Such databases can be kept up-to-date more efficiently than can print directories, and the ability to search over the listings makes finding relevant entries much easier.

There are also directories that specialize in helping you locate lawyers in a particular field, which can be useful when trying to track down specialists. The Canadian Legal LEXPERT Directory (http://www.lexpert.ca/) identifies leading Canadian law firms and lawyers in over 50 practice areas across Canada. The Martindale-Hubbell Lawyer Locator (http://www.martindale.com/locator/) provides searchable access to the worldwide Martindale-Hubbell Law Directory. And the Canadian Law List (http://www.canadianlawlist.com/) is a searchable listing of Canadian law firms, lawyers, and judges. The latter two directories both provide excellent search forms that allow you to locate a lawyer by name, firm, location, practice area, and more. Listings include contact information, including email addresses, and practice profiles.

REFERENCE

One of the areas where the Internet excels is in providing access to reference material, from encyclopedias to dictionaries to specialized information collections.

For example, it is now possible to access medical information that historically was available only to medical professionals. The US National Library of Medicine offers access to MEDLINE (http://www.nlm.nih.gov/nlmhome.html) a huge database of over 11 million article references published in biomedical journals and magazines. Healthfinder (http://www.healthfinder.org/), a site developed by the US Department of Health and Human Services, assists researchers in finding reliable health-related information online. MedicineNet (http://www.medicinenet.com/), a network of American physicians and health professionals, provides medical news and articles, detailed information about medications (including much of what researchers can find in Physicians Desk Reference), and an extensive medical dictionary.

Encyclopedias are also increasingly available online. In 1999, the publisher of the traditional multi-volume Encyclopedia Britannica went with the prevailing trend and launched Britannica.com (http://www.britannica.com/), a free website offering the complete Encyclopedia Britannica as well as enhanced coverage. Encarta (http://encarta.msn.com/) is an abridged online version of Microsoft's CD-ROM encyclopedia, and includes over 16,000 reference articles as well as photos, maps, charts, and tables.

Also of value are the many dictionaries now online. Searching for a definition is now as easy as typing a word into a search form and clicking a button. Merriam-Webster Online (http://www.m-w.com/home.htm) provides searchable access to Merriam-Webster's well-known dictionary.

For each definition that you find, you can also link to the same word in the site's extensive thesaurus. Specialized dictionaries are prevalent on the web. Medscape (http://www.medscape.com/), a rich source of medical news and information, includes an extensive dictionary of medical terms. Webopedia (http://www.webopedia.com/) is one of many online dictionaries of technology and Internet terminology. Oran's Dictionary of the Law (http://www.wld.com/conbus/orans/) from the West Group provides concise definitions

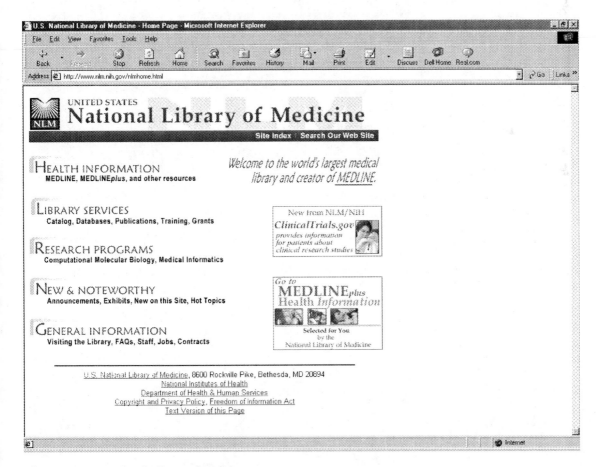

Figure 6.9. US National Library of Medicine

Libraries on the Web

It should come as no surprise that libraries have created some very useful sites on the web. Librarians, after all, are specialists in information, the currency of the Internet.

The website for the National Library of Canada (http://www.nlc-bnc.ca/ehome.htm), for example, features Canadiana Quick Reference (answers to reference questions most asked of the National Library librarians), and extensive links to Internet resources organized by subject.

Law libraries in particular offer extensive resources for lawyers and other legal professionals. The British Columbia Courthouse Library Society website (http://www.bccls.bc.ca/) features updates on legislative developments both at the federal and provincial level, and a searchable library catalogue of resources available in all court house libraries in British Colum-

bia. From the convenience of your desk you can type keywords into an easy-to-use search form and find out whether your local library has copies of any relevant texts.

The website of the Bora Laskin Law Library (http://www.law-lib.utoronto.ca/) at the University of Toronto Faculty of Law features research guides, links to law-related Internet resources (organized by source and by topic), and a listing of electronic law journals. This latter resource is an excellent way to start a search for a law journal article. It provides a list of full text law journals available on either Lexis-Nexis, Westlaw, QuickLaw, or the Internet. The list includes links to law journals available on the Internet and the database codes of law journals available on Lexis-Nexis, Westlaw, or QuickLaw.

---

of legal terms. Even Nolo's Law Dictionary (http://www.nolo.com/dictionary/wordindex.cfm), although aimed at lay persons, offers easy-to-read definitions of legal terms that can be useful for the legal professional.

UNITED STATES & INTERNATIONAL LAW RESOURCES

The Internet, of course, is not limited to Canadian resources. The Internet is a truly

global medium, and one of its greatest strengths is the ease with which you can access resources from distant places. If your firm works even occasionally on matters that have an international spin, even if no more exotic than the United States, then you will very quickly discover that the web can make your life much easier. From countries as diverse as Australia and Zimbabwe you will find government documents, court decisions, legislative proceedings, statutes and constitutions. And the Internet is now the most efficient way to track down the text of an international treaty, from the 1648 *Treaty of Westphalia* to the 1994 *World Trade Agreement*.

Part of the credit for this is due to the country that designed the network's infrastructure: the United States. They are some two years ahead of everyone else in putting legal material on the Internet, be it domestic or international law. Among the best sources of international laws and treaties on the Internet are some American law schools and institutes. The Fletcher School of Law and Diplomacy at Tufts University, for example, offers the full text of hundreds of international treaties at its excellent "Multilaterals Project" website (http://fletcher.tufts.edu/multilaterals.html). Searches can be run over the text of the treaties, which can also be browsed chronologically and by subject (Atmosphere and Space, Cultural Protection, Human Rights, and so on). A resource like this one is simply not available in any other medium.

As for domestic American law, there is a tremendous volume of outstanding material online. The website of Cornell Law School's Legal Information Institute (http://www.law.cornell.edu/), for example, includes a database of United States Supreme Court decisions that is a resource a commercial service would be proud to offer. The subject topic and case name indices seamlessly link you to the text of relevant cases as well as to case summaries. Searches can be run over the database, and can be limited to case summaries, party names, or the judge rendering the decision. Cases are available the same day as they are released by the Court, and are archived from 1990 onwards.

Other critical sources of United States law on the Internet include:

- THOMAS (http://thomas.loc.gov/), an indispensable service from the Library of Congress to current (and historical) United States legislation;

- the consolidated and searchable United States Code (http://uscode.house.gov/) from the Office of the Law Revision Counsel; and

- EDGAR (http://edgar.sec.gov/index.html), a searchable database of company filings, reports, and background information filed with the US Securities and Exchange Commission (SEC).

These kinds of sophisticated resources are not unique to the United States. One of the most impressive legal websites anywhere is the Australasian Legal Information Institute (http://www.austlii.edu.au/), which provides free access over the web to a huge collection of (mostly Australian) legislation, treaties, and decisions of courts and tribunals. The United Kingdom Parliament (http://www.hmso.gov.uk/acts.htm) is one of hundreds of law-making bodies across the globe that publishes all new Acts on the Internet, and like many courts, the United Kingdom House of Lords (http://www.parliament.the-stationery-office.co.uk/) now posts all recent judgments on the web within hours of their release.

With all of the outstanding American and international legal resources available online, we would love to provide extensive

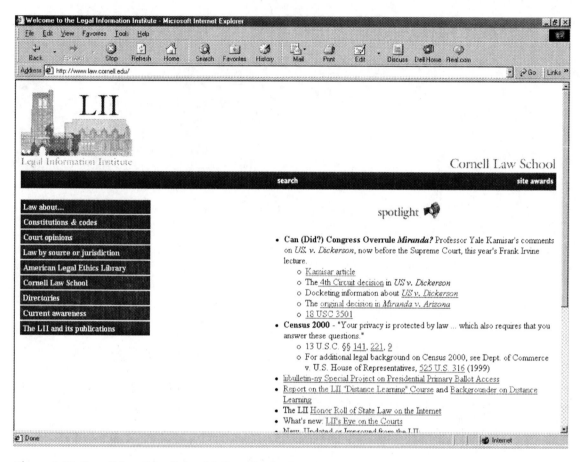

Figure 6.10. Cornell Law School's Legal Information Institute

listings of each, but to do so would easily consume an entire book. In the sidebar, Some Leading US and International Resources, we settle for listing some key starting points.

NEWS & MEDIA

It is now easier and faster to get updated on the news on the Internet than by any other medium. Media powerhouses like MSNBC (http://msnbc.com/news/) and CNN (http://cnn.com/) carry superb up-to-the-minute coverage of major world events and breaking news. The Bill Clinton-Monica Lewinsky story was initially broken on the Internet, in the Drudge Report (http://drudgereport.com/), a legendary Internet political tabloid. Local media outlets are everywhere on the web, from your local newspaper to local entertainment listings.

Some Leading US and International Resources

For US legal resources on the Internet, some good places to start include:

Cornell's Legal Information Institute. A rich collection of legal material (including US Supreme Court judgments, the US Code, and other key documents) and links (organized by jurisdiction and source). http://www.law.cornell.edu/

FindLaw. The Yahoo! for law resources online, featuring a huge directory to websites of interest to lawyers. http://www.findlaw.com/

LAWlink. From the American Bar Association, a directory to US legal research and information resources on the Internet. http://www.abanet.org/lawlink/home.html

For international legal resources, you could start your explorations at any of these sites:

Australasian Legal Information Institute. This ambitious site includes an extensive collection of links to legal materials around the globe. http://www.austlii.edu.au/

Hieros Gamos. Another ambitious site that aims to chart much of the world's laws online. http://www.hg.org/

Lex Mercatoria. Extensive materials and links dealing with international trade and commercial law. http://lexmercatoria.net/

United Nations. Links to UN sites with international treaties and laws. http://www.un.org/

In fact, most print media is now fully on the web, and much of it remains free. *The New York Times, The Financial Post, The Globe and Mail*: all of these excellent publications and thousands of others have the entire editions of their print offerings and more available at their websites, free of charge. Some publications, such as *The Wall Street Journal* and *The Economist*, have opted to charge for access to their online editions, although the cost is typically considerably less than for print subscribers. See the sidebar, Media Sites Worth Tuning In To for some suggestions of the better news and media sites on the web.

As discussed above in the Business & Finance section, the business and market news available online is downright overwhelming. Sites like Bloomberg.com (http://www.bloomberg.com/) and Globe Investor (http://www.globeinvestor.com/) are chock full of financial news, stock quotes, financial reports and analysis, even charting and reporting tools that allow visitors to customize their own analysis of market trends.

As you start working with the media sites on the web, you will notice that many offer information in formats that require special programs to use. For example, many media sites provide audio files that you can listen to only if you have audio software installed on your computer (and a computer with speakers). Such special programs are called "plug-ins," and many come pre-installed in recent versions of the major web browsers, or can be downloaded for free off the Internet. See the sidebar, Working With Browser Plug-ins for a list of some of the key plug-ins you may want on your computer, and how and where to get them.

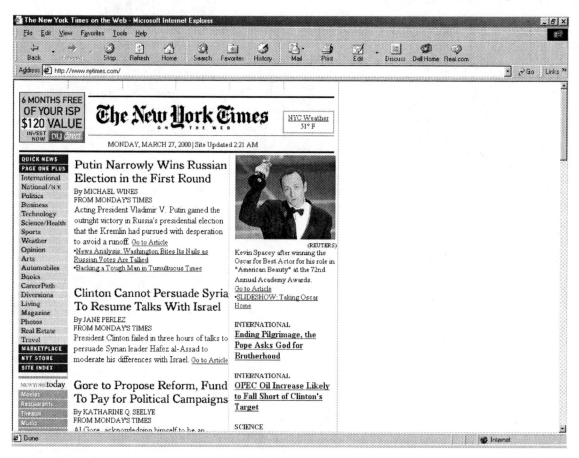

Figure 6.11. *The New York Times*

Media Sites Worth Tuning In To

Media outlets abound on the web. Magazines, newspapers, TV broadcasters, and new media players compete to keep you up-to-date on breaking news and information. Here are some of the better sources of news online.

CBC News. Still staffed sufficiently to have a snazzy website. If your system is set up for it, you can listen to streaming real time audio and video.
http://cbc.ca/news/

The Globe and Mail. Online news stories, investor tools, discussion groups, and more.
http://www.globeandmail.com/

The National Post. A stylish site featuring stories from today's Post, supplemented by breaking news through the day.
http://www.nationalpost.com/

The New York Times. All the news that's fit to post. Must register to use.
http://www.nytimes.com/

Slate. Lively online magazine focusing on politics and culture; part of the Microsoft Network.
http://www.slate.com/

Plus a few sites that may not enhance your billable hours, but can be fun to check in on from time to time.

ESPN.com. Perhaps the best sports site on the web, chock full of news, stats, and commentary from the folks at ESPN. Close your office door and we'll see you in three hours.
http://espn.go.com/

Salon Magazine. One of the most stylish online magazines, featuring literature, culture, and criticism.
http://www.salon.com/

Internet Movie Database. An astonishing collection of news, reviews, facts, and figures about movies and the film industry. Good for resolving those film trivia disputes that are otherwise so disruptive in the workplace. Also, good for informing the complex decision: What shall I rent this weekend?
http://www.imdb.com

Dilbert Zone. For a daily hit of the workplace comic strip.
http://www.unitedmedia.com/comics/dilbert/

Working with Browser Plug-ins

From time to time you'll happen upon a website that offers information in a format that requires a special program to use. For example, many media sites provide audio files that you can listen to only if you have audio software installed on your computer (and a computer with speakers). Such special programs are called "plug-ins," as they install on top of, or "plug-in" to, your web browser. Think of them as web accessories. For example, the Shockwave plug-in adds multimedia capabilities to your web browser, so that you can view animated and interactive pages on a website.

Here are some of the key plug-ins that you may want to have installed on your system (note that the current version of Netscape Communicator and Microsoft Internet Explorer come with some of these plug-ins already installed). Some of these sites offer commercial versions with more capabilities, but you should be just fine with the free versions.

Adobe Acrobat Reader to view Portable Document Format, or PDF, files.
http://www.adobe.com/products/acrobat/main.html

Apple QuickTime to view video offerings.
http://www.apple.com/quicktime/

RealPlayer to listen to audio files.
http://www.real.com/player/index.html

Shockwave to view interactive web content like games, business presentations, and entertainment offerings.
http://www.macromedia.com/shockwave/

To install a plug-in, first download it from the site in question. Be sure to check any installation notes you find to ensure that your browser will be able to operate it. Note, too, that many plug-ins, such as Apple's QuickTime, offer a variety of installation files for download. Read the descriptions carefully — choosing the most appropriate file may save you some download time. After downloading the plug-in to your computer, exit your web browser and then double-click on the file you just downloaded. Each plug-in runs through its own installation procedure, but the process is usually similar to other software installations.

Once installed, your plug-in will open automatically the next time you click on a web page that requires the plug-in.

7 THE WEB: FINDING TOOLS

The Internet's greatest asset—the ease with which information can be delivered to a vast audience—is also its greatest liability. In a few short years, the Internet (led by the explosion of material on the web) has become the world's largest library. So large that it defies cataloguing. And there's no librarian to help you find your way around. The question arises: how do you go about finding anything?

Fortunately there are hundreds of tools available to help you find what you're looking for. Some are better than others. Some are suited to certain tasks. This chapter is designed to help you work with the finding tools that exist on the web, and to help you decide what finding tool you should use in what circumstance.

As well, the latter part of this chapter focuses in on using the web to find specific types of material: to find company information, people, legal information generally, case law, and statute law.

AN INTRODUCTION TO FINDING TOOLS

Even if you've only occasionally tried to find information on the Internet, you'll be familiar with these thoughts:

- While there's an enormous amount of material on the Internet, it's hard to find what you want in the great sea of data out there.

- The quality of information on the Internet is highly variable.

- Information on the Internet is often lacking in depth. Case law collections, for example, tend to go back only a few years.

- There is no uniformity in site organization and presentation, or in search syntax and commands.

Still, there are several reasons why the Internet has quickly become a key tool for anyone looking for information:

- For certain types of information, such as international legal materials or product information (directly from a company), the Internet is already the best place to look.

- Almost all of the information on the Internet is free.

- The information on the Internet is growing at a dizzying pace, and it's also quickly improving in quality and functionality.

WHEN TO LOOK ON THE INTERNET

The first step in trying to use the Internet to find information is to consider whether you should be on the Internet at all. There are tasks that quite simply are better suited to books, CD-ROMs, or commercial online services such as QuickLaw or *e*Carwsell, either because the information is of higher quality or you can find it faster.

You should not be looking on the Internet if:

- you need to search over predictable, stable, and deep archives of information—for example, a case law collection going back several decades (a law report collection or online service will be better sources);

- you want to access secondary materials, such as textbooks, encyclopedias, or journal articles (print books and online services will be better sources); or

- you need to note up a case (an online service will be a better source).

On the other hand, the Internet is often a good starting point if:

- you need to find legislation, particularly if you're looking for recent amending legislation;

- you are looking for information about hot factual topics. The web is stocked full of information on matters of popular interest, from tobacco litigation to post traumatic stress disorder;

- you are looking for information about a company. If a client is considering investing in or acquiring a company, a search on the web can turn up that company's website as well as other resources that include information about the company;

- you want to access information about technology issues;

- you are researching an Internet legal issue. There is a tremendous amount of material online on legal issues relating to the Internet, from the legal aspects of registering an Internet domain name to privacy concerns arising out of email use; or

- you want to ask someone a question—see Chapter Eight (Discussion Groups) for an overview of using web-based discussion groups and email mailing lists to ask questions of others.

SEARCH ENGINES AND DIRECTORIES DEFINED

The finding tools available on the web come in two principal varieties: search engines and directories. Many people use the term "search engine" to describe both types of finding tools. In fact, there are key differences between search engines and directories, both in terms of how they are compiled and how you use them.

Search engines allow you to search through a database of information for certain terms. The database can be (in theory at least) as large as the entire web, as in the case of such major search engines as HotBot (http://hotbot.lycos.com/) and AltaVista (http://www.altavista.com). (As we'll see below, however, no single search tool covers the entire web, as it is simply growing too quickly for any one tool to map comprehensively.) Or the database that the search engine allows you to search over can be limited to the resources at a specific website, such as the collection of cases at the

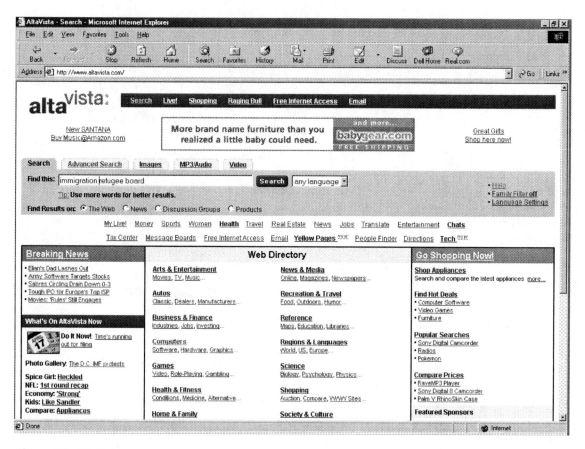

Figure 7.1. AltaVista

Supreme Court of Canada website (http://www.scc-csc.gc.ca/). Search engines create their listings automatically, by sending out programs that collect pages to store in its database of information. The way you actually use a search engine is to type the terms you're looking for into a search form, and then tell the search engine (typically by clicking a button that says "search" or "submit") to find material in its database that includes those terms.

Directories, on the other hand, allow you to find material based on how it fits into a classification structure. This structure, which is created not by machines but instead by people, might be based on subject matter or geographic location or some other logical way of organizing material. Similar to search engines, the scope of a directory might be (in theory) as wide as the entire web, as in the case of the best-known directory, Yahoo! (http://www.yahoo.com/). Or a directory might be restricted to a specific topical area, such as Canadian law, or lawyers. The way directories work on the web is that you can browse through a listing of categories, clicking categories of interest to link to more specific topics and ultimately to relevant sites.

Search engines and directories have their respective strengths and weaknesses. Search engines generally have a broader reach, but they can be blunt instruments if not used properly, turning up hundreds of only vaguely relevant materials. Directories rely more on human intervention, which can be good in that someone else will have given thought to what materials are relevant to a particular topic. But human intervention can be bad in that classifiers naturally have their own classifying biases: is scientology a religion or a cult?

This is why the best kind of finding tool is a site that includes both a search engine *and* a directory. Such "hybrid" search services allow you to track down information both by searching via keywords and by browsing a listing of categories.

Thankfully, most of the major search engines have evolved into hybrid finding

Figure 7.2. Google web directory

tools, having recently added directories to complement their search engines. HotBot, AltaVista, Excite, Go, Google, and many other popular search engines now also offer topical directories that allow you to find material by drilling down listings based on subject.

USER'S GUIDE TO FINDING TOOLS

DECIDING WHAT KIND OF TOOL TO USE

Even if you are using a hybrid finding tool, as described above, you will still want to have some appreciation for when to use the search engine and when to use the directory offered by that site. Deciding whether to search via keywords or browse directory listings to find what you're looking for is part personal preference, part experience, and part the nature of your task. In very general terms, here are some broad guidelines to consider in making the decision.

Search engines are generally most effective when you are:

1. **Able to identify unique keywords.** Can what you're looking for be readily captured in a few unique keywords? For example, if you have the name of a specific organization or a combination of words that is relatively unique, a search engine will often be the best place to start. The more specific the terms, the better. "Human rights age

discrimination" will generate more fruitful results with a search engine than will the more broad "human rights."

2. **Looking for new information.** Search engines tend to turn up more recent information than do directories. As search engines index automatically, using spiders that crawl the web, they tend to capture recent material more quickly than do directories, which are compiled by human beings.

3. **Field searching and limiting.** When your search lends itself to specifying a field to search over, such as the titles of documents, then a search engine will be the more productive place to start your explorations.

4. **Looking for the needle in the haystack.** When what you're looking for is very specific, and quite likely to be on a page buried deep within a website, a search engine will be a better place to start than a directory.

Directories, on the other hand, tend to be good places to start when:

1. **Getting the lay of the land.** Directories tend to be good places to start when you want to access a broad range of materials on a particular topic, rather than track down something very specific.

2. **Looking for a specific website.** If you're trying to find a website for a specific organization, a directory such as Yahoo! can often be your fastest route, as directories index sites rather than specific pages.

Search Strategy #1: URL Guessing and Cutting

When you are searching for a specific organization's website, you may not even need to go to the trouble of using a directory or search engine. Instead, consider first trying to guess the URL for the organization, and typing that directly into the address or location window of your web browser. The following steps may help:

1. With Netscape and Internet Explorer, leave off **http://**

2. Try the common **www.** to start the address.

3. Use the name, acronym, or shortened name of the organization (globeandmail, cba, findlaw) in the middle.

4. Add the appropriate top-level domain, most often .com or .ca See page 76 for a fuller list of top-level domains or try one of the following common endings:

   .com for commercial
   .ca for Canada
   .org for nonprofit organizations
   .on.ca for Ontario, Canada
   .bc.ca for British Columbia, Canada
   .gc.ca for Canadian government

URL guessing can also help in finding pages for URLs that no longer work and links that lead to dead ends. Try chopping off parts of the URL starting on the right-hand side and stopping at every /.

USING A SEARCH ENGINE

Search engines have three major elements. The first is something called the spider, also known as the crawler. The spider visits a web page, reads it, and then follows links to other pages within the site. The spider returns to the site on a regular basis, such as every month or two, to look for changes.

Everything the spider finds goes into the second part of a search engine, the index. The index, sometimes called the catalogue, is like a giant book containing a copy of every web page that the spider finds. If a web page changes, then this book is updated with new information.

Sometimes it can take a while for new pages or changes that the spider finds to be added to the index. Thus, a web page may have been "spidered" but not yet "indexed." Until a page is indexed—added to the index—it is not available to those searching with the search engine.

Search engine software is the third part of a search engine. This is the program that sifts through the millions of pages recorded in the index to find matches to a search and rank them in order of what it believes is most relevant.

From the user's perspective, a search engine works by allowing you to type a word or a string of words into a form. The engine will then grind away searching and return to you with the results. The results are presented in the form of a list, where each item on the list is a hypertext link itself, usually accompanied by a description of what lies at the far end of the link. In other

Search Engine Terminology

Boolean search: A search allowing the inclusion or exclusion of documents containing certain words through the use of operators such as AND, OR, and NOT.

Concept search: A search for documents related conceptually to a word, rather than specifically containing the word itself.

Fuzzy search: A search that will find matches even when words are only partially spelled or misspelled.

Hit: A single site returned by a search request.

Index: The searchable catalogue of documents created by search engine software. Also called a "catalogue."

Keyword search: A search for documents containing one or more words specified by the user.

Phrase search: A search for documents containing an exact sentence or phrase.

Relevancy: How well a document provides the information a user is looking for, as measured by the user.

Search engine: The software that searches an index and returns matches. Search engine is often used synonymously with spider and index, although these are separate components that work with the engine.

Spider: Software that visits websites and builds a search engine's index.

Stop words: Common words such as AND, TO and A that are not indexed by search engines.

words, once you've got your search results, you can begin exploring directly from the results page to evaluate the success of your search.

Let's have a look at an example to see how this works.

Problem: You are looking for information about recent changes to environmental protection laws.

With this type of matter, where you can identify specific words or phrases that will probably be included in the documents you want – such as environment, protection—it is better to use a search engine than a directory.

For this example, we'll use the popular HotBot search engine. You type the URL (http://hotbot.lycos.com/) into the address window of your browser, or select the site from your Favourites list (see Chapter Five (The Web: An Overview) for discussion of how to work with favourites, also known as bookmarks). The screen in Figure 7.3 appears.

Figure 7.3. *HotBot*

You enter the search terms "environment protection laws canada" and press the search button. The results are brought back to you in the form of a listing of linked pages with short descriptions that are automatically generated from the pages themselves, as in Figure 7.4.

As with many searches on the web, there are thousands of documents that match your search terms. Fortunately, the search engine uses a sophisticated algorithm or formula to rank the results in order of their relevance to your search terms. The most relevant documents appear first. A relevancy ranking or confidence score is sometimes expressed as a percentage (for example, 72 per cent relevancy). Each search engine has a unique relevancy ranking algorithm, but generally the rankings are a result of several factors:

1. **Location.** Pages with keywords appearing in the title are assumed to be more relevant than others to the topic. Search engines will also check to see if the keywords appear near the top of a web page, such as in the headline or in

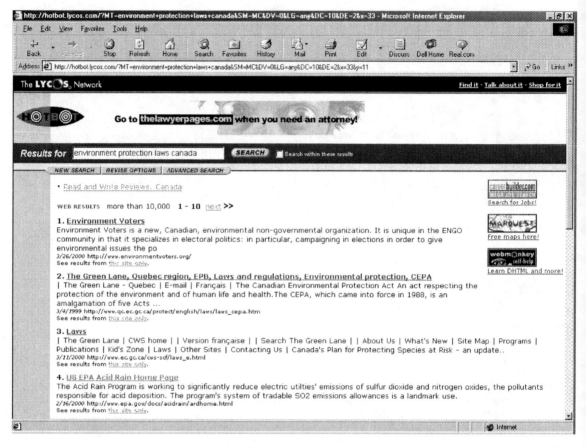

Figure 7.4. HotBot search results

the first few paragraphs of text. They assume that any page relevant to the topic will mention those words towards the beginning.

2. **Frequency.** Frequency is the other major factor in how search engines determine relevancy. A search engine will analyze how often keywords appear in relation to other words in a web page. Those with a higher frequency are often deemed more relevant than other web pages.

3. **Link popularity.** Some engines give a relevancy boost to pages that many other sites link to. The idea is that users across the web have in essence voted for good sites by linking to them, and that these more "user's choice" sites should appear higher in a search results list.

4. **Meta tags.** Some search engines give a slight relevancy boost to pages with keywords in their meta tags. (A meta tag is applied by the document creator

to facilitate searching, and is invisible to the user.)

The search results are shown in sequences of ten results at a time at the HotBot site. To visit any result, you click on the highlighted title to link to the site where the document in question is posted. Exploring some of the top results reveals several highly relevant pages, including:

1. The CEPA Environmental Registry, a large collection of orders, guidelines, and regulatory material under the *Canadian Environmental Protection Act*, located at the Environment Canada website (http://www.ec.gc.ca/).

2. The full text of the *Canadian Environmental Protection Act* and corresponding regulations at the Department of Justice website (http://canada.justice.gc.ca/).

3. Environmental assessment legislation and guidelines at the Canadian Environmental Assessment Agency website (http://www.ceaa.gc.ca/).

4. News of developments relating to environmental legislation at the website of West Coast Environmental Law, an environmental public interest group (http://www.wcel.org/).

And these materials are just a selection of thousands of sites found by your search. (As we discuss below in the section "Search Engine Tips," this tendency for web searches to turn up thousands of documents can seem overwhelming; in that section, we suggest ways to make your

searches more precise and by extension more productive.) This kind of quick access to a broad range of material is part of the wonder of the Internet. Of course, the success of your explorations will depend on what kind of material you're looking for and how well you use the available search tools.

LIMITATIONS OF SEARCH ENGINES

Search engines are by no means without flaws. One thing you will notice very quickly is that search engines do not produce results with anything like the level of certainty you can expect on commercial online services like *e*Carswell or QuickLaw. In fact, different search engines can produce vastly different results.

Just for fun, run exactly the same search on three or four of the major search engines and compare the results. You will see entirely different sites turning up, different ordering of results, and different numbers of sites returned. There are several reasons for this:

1. **No one search engine covers more than a relatively small percentage of the web.** Studies in early 2000 estimated that of the roughly 1 billion indexable pages on the web, no one search engine indexed more than 40 per cent. Large popular search engines such as AltaVista, Excite, and Northern Light index only 25 to 35 per cent of the web. This low coverage is partly a result of the incredibly swift growth of the Internet—no search engine can

keep up—and partly due to the fact that search engines don't index all web pages. For example, engines don't pick up the content of Adobe PDF files, the content of sites requiring a log in, or CGI output such as data requested by a form.

2. **Some search engines are more current than others.** Some engines index web pages more often than others, meaning that the engines will differ in their ability to serve up more recent information.

3. **Search engines don't really search the web.** Search engines search only the databases they have created to replicate the web, not the web itself. Many search engines take only top level pages from websites, or partial pages, so in many cases you are searching over partial websites rather than entire sites.

4. **No two search engines have identical relevancy ranking algorithms.** As described above in the section "Using a Search Engine," the algorithms that search engines use to rank the relevance of results vary from engine to engine.

For these reasons, if you need to conduct a thorough search on the web, it is essential that you use more than one search engine because the results will differ. As well, you will want to be sure to use the better search engines, and to use them to maximum effect. The following sections are designed to help in these areas.

THE BEST SEARCH ENGINES

There are hundreds of search engines available, and you will no doubt develop your own preferences over time. You may choose your favourites based on the speed with which results are returned to you, the breadth of the search engine's coverage, the look of the search form, or the range of power features the search engine makes available to you. To help identify some of the leading contenders, here are descriptions of six popular major search engines:

AltaVista (http://www.altavista.com). This engine consistently ranks as one of the largest search engines on the web, in terms of pages indexed. Researchers like its comprehensive coverage and wide range of power searching commands (found under "Advanced Search"). It also includes a topical directory. AltaVista was initially created by Digital in 1995, and has since been spun off into a separate company that is now controlled by CMGI. A subsite (http://www.altavista.ca/) focuses on Canada-only material.

Excite (http://www.excite.com). One of the most popular search services on the web, Excite also offers personalization features and free email. It boasts a large index of web pages and also integrates non-web material such as company information and sports scores into its results, when appropriate. It features easy-to-use advanced search forms for power searching, and a topical directory for browsing. Excite was launched in 1995, quickly grew in prominence, and consumed two of its competitors, Magellan and WebCrawler, in 1996.

Keeping Up with the Search Engines

The major search engines are constantly adding new features and services. To help you keep up with recent developments, and to extend your knowledge of search engines generally, these two resources are well worth a visit:

- **Search Engine Watch.** Created by Danny Sullivan, an internet consultant and journalist who continues to maintain the site for Internet.com, this site is an exceptional resource for web searchers. It's loaded with search engine reviews, comparisons, tutorials, tips, and news about recent developments.
  http://searchenginewatch.com/

- **Search Engine Showdown.** Produced by Montana State University Reference Librarian Greg Notess, this excellent site features search engine comparison charts, reviews, strategies to searching, and more. Of special interest are the long-range surveys on search engine sizes and dead links, as well as the coverage of search "inconsistencies" – when search engines don't operate the way they are supposed to.
  http://www.searchengineshowdown. com/

Similar to AltaVista, a subsite (http://www.excite.ca/) focuses on Canada-only material.

Go (http://infoseek.go.com/). Formerly Infoseek and now part of the expanding "Go Network" (a portal site produced by Infoseek and Disney), Go offers portal features such as personalization and free email, plus a search engine and directory. It consistently returns quality results in response to many general and broad searches, thanks to an effective search algorithm. Go also has an impressive human-compiled directory. Go was launched in January 1999; the former Infoseek service launched in 1995.

Google (http://www.google.com/). A more recent entry into the search engine wars, Google makes heavy use of link popularity as a primary way to rank websites. For this reason, Google can often return good sites in response to general searches such as "medical" or "mutual funds," because users across the web have in essence voted for good sites by linking to them. It also includes a directory based on the Open Directory project, which uses volunteer editors to catalogue the web.

HotBot (http://hotbot.lycos.com/). This is a favourite among researchers due to the quality of the results it generates and its many power searching features. Its search forms are easy to use and flexible, and HotBot also features an extensive directory based on the Open Directory project. HotBot's first page of results comes from Direct Hit, a company that works with other search engines to refine their results. Secondary results on HotBot come from the Inktomi search engine, which is also used by other services. It was originally launched by Wired Digital, the folks behind Wired Magazine. The portal site Lycos purchased Wired Digital in 1998 and continues to run HotBot as a separate search service.

Northern Light (http://www. northernlight.com/). Another favourite among researchers, Northern Light features one of the largest indexes of the web, along with the ability to cluster documents by topic. It also has a set of "special collection" documents from thousands of sources, including newswires, magazines, and databases. Searching these documents is free, but there is a charge of up to $4 to view them. There is no charge to view documents on the public web. Northern Light was launched in 1997.

SEARCH ENGINE TIPS

Search engines offer a variety of ways for you to refine and control your searches, for you to be more precise in your searching. Precision is good, as you will quickly find searching over the great body of data on the web. The notion of wading through 250,000 web pages that match your search terms is not one that most users welcome.

This section describes some key ways to make your searches more precise. These tips work for nearly all of the major search engines. Note that some search engines offer drop-down menus from which you can select options. Others require you to use special commands as part of your search. Some key commands are listed in the Search Engine Comparison Chart on page 137. As well, all the major search engines feature detailed and easy to use help material on how to use the engine.

1. Be specific.

Before starting any search, keep in mind that the more specific your search is, the

more likely you will find what you want. Don't be afraid to tell a search engine exactly what you are looking for. For example, if you want information about mutual fund RRSPs, search for "mutual fund RRSPs," not "mutual funds." Or even better, search for exactly what you're looking for: "mutual funds that qualify as RRSPs" for example. You'll be surprised at how often this works.

2. Note whether the search engine defaults to *alternative* or *inclusive* searching.

Some search engines automatically add "and" between any words you type into the search form, so that only those pages that include all of your search terms are returned. These engines are defaulting to *inclusive* searching. Examples of search engines that do this are Google, HotBot, and Northern Light.

Other search engines automatically add "or" between any words you enter, so that your results will include pages that include either search term. Examples of engines that default to *alternative* searching are AltaVista, Excite, and Go.

As you type search terms into a search engine, you will want to be aware of whether it will default to inclusive or alternative searching. For engines that default to alternative searching, an effective technique can be to list several synonyms for the concepts you are searching for. Such engines will first list pages that have all your terms, followed by pages with some of your terms. As the top results will be pages that include all of your terms, these sites will likely be more relevant. The danger of using this technique with engines that default to inclusive searching is that with these engines, you will *only* get results that include all of your terms, and you may unwittingly eliminate relevant material.

3. Use the + symbol to specify that a term must be included in a result.

Sometimes, you want to make sure that a search engine finds pages that have all the words you enter, not just some of them. As described above, some search engines will do this type of search by default. At other engines, using the + symbol lets you do this type of "inclusive search." (Note that using the + symbol will work the same way on virtually all the major search engines, regardless of whether the engine defaults to inclusive searching or not. For this reason, it is a good idea to get in the habit of using the + symbol when you want to do an inclusive search. That way, you don't have to worry about what type of searching a particular engine defaults to.)

For example, imagine you want to find pages that have references to both music and copyright on the same page. You could search this way:

+music +copyright

Only pages that contain both words would appear in your results. Here is another example:

+recovered +memory +syndrome

That would find pages that have all three of the words on them, helpful if you wanted to narrow down a search to the pages that deal with recovered memory syndrome.

The + symbol is especially helpful when you do a search and then find yourself overwhelmed with information. Imagine that you wanted to find pages describing hotels in downtown Chicago. You might start out simply searching like this:

hotel chicago

If so, chances are, you'll probably get too many off-target results. Instead, try searching for all the words you know must appear on the type of page you're looking for:

+hotel +chicago +downtown

4. Expand your search by selecting the "match any" option.

Sometimes you want pages that contain *any* of your search terms. For example, you may want to find pages that say either England or London. As described above, some search engines will do this type of search by default, without you needing to specify any commands.

At other search engines, you can do a "match any" search by using a menu next to the search box or on the advanced search page. At Northern Light, you'll have to rely on the OR Boolean command (see the coverage of Boolean search operators below) to perform a "match any" search, and there is no way to do a "match any" search at Google.

Keep in mind that most search engines will automatically first list pages that have all your terms, then some of your terms, when you perform a "match any" search.

Browser Tip: Finding Something Within a Web Page

Once you've found a web page that you believe includes relevant information, you may want to search *within* the page to find a specific word or words. You can do this by using the "Find in Page" option of your web browser. Select "Find in Page" from the "Edit" drop-down menu of your browser, type your word(s) into the test box, and click "OK." You will be brought to the first appearance of that word within the open web page. Note that this find command is entirely literal. If you type "funds," it will search for exactly that word, and not the singular form "fund" for example. Be sure to enter exactly the word you want in the Find text box.

---

5. Search for a phrase.

Phrase searching allows searching words as phrases and can be very effective in narrowing a search. For example, remember above when we wanted pages about recovered memory syndrome? We entered all the terms like this:

+recovered +memory +syndrome

That brings back pages that have all those words in them, but there's no guarantee that the words may necessarily be near each other. Doing a phrase search avoids this problem. This is where you tell a search engine to give you pages where the terms appear in exactly the order you specify. You do this by putting quotation marks around the phrase, like this:

"recovered memory syndrome"

Now, only pages that have all the words and in the exact order shown above will be listed. Your search is likely to be much more precise.

POWER SEARCHING TIPS

For those who want to take their searching a step further, here are some tips that may help make your searches more productive. Refer to the Search Engine Comparison Chart on page 137 to see which of these features are supported by the major search engines listed.

1. Be cautious using complex Boolean searches.

Boolean searching involves connecting search terms in logical ways to retrieve information from the search engine. Boolean search commands have been used by professionals to search through commercial online databases for years. The basic commands or "operators" are AND, OR, NOT, and NEAR. (See the sidebar, Boolean Search Logic 101 for an overview of Boolean commands.)

For many web users, Boolean commands are probably overkill. Use of the + symbol to specify that a term must be included in a document, as described above, and use of the – symbol to specify that a term must not be included, give similar functionality as Boolean commands and are supported by all the major search engines.

For professional searchers who are comfortable using Boolean commands, many (but not all) of the major search engines do support them. See the Search Engine Com-

Boolean Search Logic 101

Although it sounds like a mind-virus infecting the crew of the Starship Enterprise, "Boolean search logic" is, in fact, "the use of logical operators . . . in retrieving information from a computer database," according to the *Oxford Dictionary*. Named after the English mathematician G. Boole, Boolean search logic is based on the operators AND, OR, NOT, and NEAR, which can be inserted into a search query to give it more accuracy than a basic keyword search. These operators work as follows:

- **AND** e.g., immigration **and** refugee will find only materials including both the word immigration and the word refugee

- **OR** e.g., immigration **or** refugee will find materials containing the word immigration or the word refugee

- **NOT** e.g., immigration **not** refugee will find only materials that contain the word immigration but not the word refugee (it is best to use this operator with caution, as it can exclude relevant pages using your search term in a different context)

- **Near** e.g., immigration **near** refugee will find materials that contain the words immigration and refugee within a certain number of words of one another. For example, at AltaVista, NEAR means within ten words of one another.

parison Chart on page 137 to see which of the engines listed support Boolean commands. However, be aware that some experts suggest that Boolean commands do not perform well in web search engines, particularly when nested Boolean queries are submitted. (Nested Boolean queries involve the use of parentheses to combine Boolean commands in sophisticated ways— for example, "(joint or co-author) AND music AND copyright.") Web search engines are statistical search engines, and the use of Boolean commands can unwittingly skew results. Unlike exact match Boolean systems, statistical search engines return a subject territory, which is to say almost-exact matches as well as exact matches. The almost-matches can find you terminology that you can use to refine your search. However, if you use Boolean expressions, this important feature of a statistical search engine is turned off, making the search less effective. Even worse, none of the major web search engines process a nested Boolean query well, and all process it differently. (For example, Excite ignores parentheses, whereas AltaVista processes parentheses correctly—providing you use the Advanced Search form – but drops the relevancy ranking of results.) For further discussion of this topic, see the intriguing article "The Internet Search-Off" in *Searcher*, February 1998 (http://www.infotoday.com/searcher/feb98/story1.htm).

2. Use "More like this."

Many of the major search engines offer "more like this" as a feature. "More like

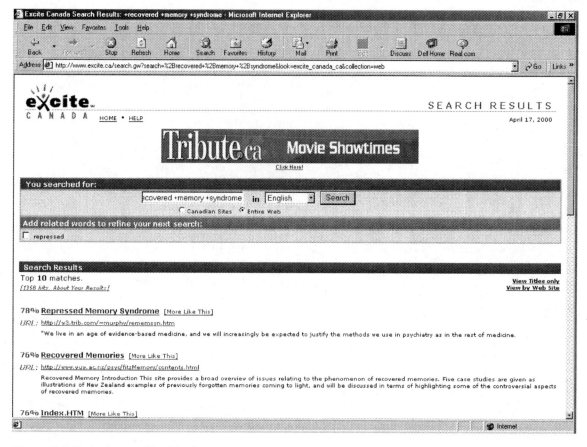

Figure 7.5. Excite's "More like this" feature

this," or "Find Similar," is actually a variation on using a lot of words in the search. It tells the search engine to seek out other pages that seem similar to those you like. Rather than your having to select all the possible terms, you let the document terminology act as your search. It is usually very effective.

3. Search within results.

After doing a search, if you feel like you have too many results, some of the major search engines allow you to search again over the results you've already generated. Go and HotBot make this easy through a "Search Within" feature that appears next to the search box. Refining your search in this way lets you define a large set of results initially and then add more parameters to it in order to narrow the initial search. This can be a more effective approach than using Boolean operators.

4. Title searching.

A web page can be considered as being made up of several fields, such as title, URL, headings, text, and so on. Many of the major search engines allow you to search within just the titles of web pages. (The title is the text that appears within the title tag of a document, and is displayed across the very top bar of your web browser when viewing the page.) Title searching can be a very effective way to narrow your search to only the most relevant material.

Those search engines that support title searching typically use the "title" command, which looks like this:

title:terms

where "terms" are the words you wish to search for in the title. Here are some examples:

title:environmental
title:environmental protection
title:"environmental protection act"

In the first example, we're looking for the word "environmental" in page titles. In the second example, we're looking for both "environmental" and "protection" in titles. In the last example, we're looking for the exact phrase "environmental protection act" in titles.

The *title:* command doesn't work at Excite or Google. It does work in the other major search engines listed in the Search Engine Comparison Chart on page 137. Several of the search engines that support the *title:* command also allow you to specify a title search using their advanced search pages.

5. Site searching.

One of the most powerful features available in web search engines is the ability to control what sites are included or excluded from a search.

For example, imagine you wanted to see all the pages from the federal Ministry of Finance. At AltaVista, you could use this command:

host:fin.gc.ca

In response, AltaVista would display all the pages it has indexed from the *fin.gc.ca* domain.

Now imagine you wanted to find all the pages from the Ministry of Finance that also mention the word "budget." You could do that this way:

host:fin.gc.ca budget

That tells AltaVista to list pages with the word "budget" that are within the Ministry of Finance site.

You can even combine other commands, such as those described above. For instance, look at this example:

host:fin.gc.ca + "budget 2000"

Here, we are telling AltaVista to list all pages within the Ministry of Finance site that also include the phrase "budget 2000."

Not all search engines provide the ability to search by site, and the command is different for those that do. The Search Engine Comparison Chart on page 137 shows which search engines have this capability and the exact command to use. Several of the search engines that support a site search command also allow you to specify a site search using their advanced search pages.

Figure 7.6. *AltaVista: site searching*

6. Using wildcards.

You can search for plurals or variations of words using a wildcard character. It is also a great way to search if you don't know the spelling of a word. The * symbol is used as the wildcard symbol at all major search engines that support wildcard searching, as listed in the Search Engine Comparison Chart on page 137.

The format looks like this:

*child** finds child, childish, children
*theat** finds theater and theatre

Some of the major search engines (for example, HotBot and Go) support what is called "stemming." This means they will find terms like "children" even if you only enter "child." This also means you may not need to use a wildcard symbol.

7. Sort by date.

Sort by date sounds like a great idea, but there are big problems with dates on the web. Some web servers report incorrect dates or no dates at all. Go estimated in 1998 that only 70 per cent of web servers

Search Engine Comparison Chart

Command	AltaVista	Excite	Go	Google	HotBot	Northern Light
Default Searching	Alternative (match any term)	Alternative (match any term)	Alternative (match any term)	Inclusive (match all terms)	Inclusive (match all terms)	Inclusive (match all terms)
Must include term	+	+	+	+	+	+
Must exclude term	–	–	–	–	–	–
Phrase searching	" " (semi-automatic)	" "	" " (semi-automatic)	" "	" "	" "
Boolean AND	AND or & (only in advanced search)	AND (must be in upper case)	N/A	automatic	AND (set menu to Boolean phrase)	AND
Boolean OR	OR (only in advanced search)	OR (must be in upper case)	N/A	N/A	OR (set menu to Boolean phrase)	OR
Boolean NOT	AND NOT (only in advanced search)	NOT (must be in upper case)	N/A	N/A	NOT (set menu to Boolean phrase)	NOT
Proximity searching	NEAR or ~ (within ten words)	N/A	N/A	N/A	N/A	N/A
Title search	title:	N/A	title:	N/A	title:	title:
Site search	host:	N/A	site:	N/A	domain:	N/A
Wildcard (*)	Yes	No	No	No	Yes	Yes
Date range	Yes	No	No	No	Yes	Yes

returned the correct date, while 20 per cent reported the current date, regardless of when the page was created or changed. The remaining 10 per cent of the time, the web servers reported no date at all.

Still date sorting is a nice feature to have, and one that many professionals want. Go and Northern Light offer it. When you choose the option, they list pages with newer dates first.

USING A DIRECTORY

Instead of relying on computers to sort data like search engines do, directories depend on human beings. People sort material into some kind of directory or classification structure. This structure might be based on subject matter or geographic location or on some other logical way of organizing material.

The way directories work for the user is that you can browse through a listing of categories, clicking categories of interest to link to more specific topics, and ultimately link to specific websites. In this way you "drill down" a directory to find the material you want. If a search engine is like a book's index, then a directory is like its table of contents.

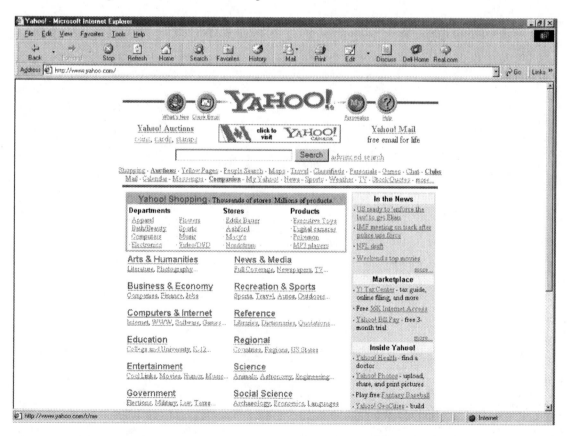

Figure 7.7. Yahoo!

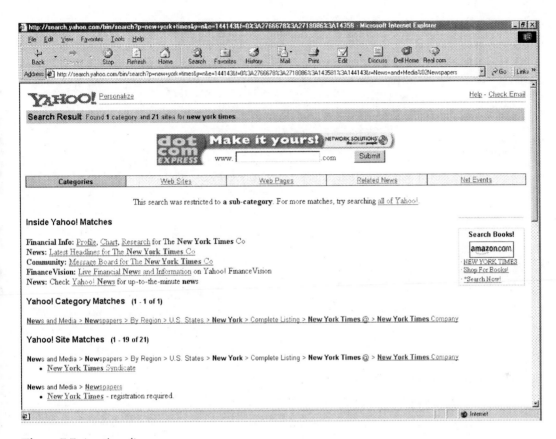

Figure 7.7. (*continued*).

Let's have a look at an example to see how a directory works.

Problem: You are looking for the website for the *New York Times*.

With this type of matter, you could type "new york times" into a search engine. However, you may be overwhelmed with pages that refer to the *Times*. Here, where you want to quickly locate the website for the *Times*, using a directory like Yahoo! can often be your fastest route. Directories typically index only the top-level page at a website, and not the vast numbers of web pages nested within sites, so can be much

more efficient in taking you to the "front door" of a particular site.

You type www.yahoo.com into the address window of your web browser, or select Yahoo! from your Favourites list. The screen in Figure 7.7 comes up. Under the category "News & Media" you select "Newspapers." One of the newspapers listed on this page is the *New York Times*, and when you click on this listing you are brought directly to the *Times'* greeting page.

An alternate way to use the directory to find the *Times'* website would be to type the words "new york times" into the search form at Yahoo!. This would bring up all site listings with those terms, as well as all categories that include those terms. This can be a very useful technique to quickly locate a site you're looking for, as well as related sites.

THE BEST DIRECTORIES

Directories are only as good as their designers. Directories work by sorting the material available out there into some kind of logical structure. The three elements of a useful directory are the quality of its directory structure, whether you can search over the directory, and whether directory listings are annotated.

1. **Directory structure.** A good logical structure is key to a good directory. If the directory has confusing or repetitive categories, it will obviously be hard to find what you're looking for.

2. **Search capability.** As mentioned in the Yahoo! example above, an extremely helpful feature of a directory is being able to search over the listings and category headings. For example, typing "web copyright" into the search form turns up all site listings as well as all category headings that include those terms, such as Internet: World Wide Web: Legal Issues: Copyright. This allows you to quickly find relevant categories, without having to browse through category branches that don't turn up information you're seeking.

3. **Annotations.** The best directories have annotations describing the contents of indexed sites. The more site annotations

the better, as it suggests someone has analyzed the site long enough to summarize its contents.

With the above features in mind, here are descriptions of three of the best directories on the web:

Yahoo! (http://www.yahoo.com)—The oldest (having been launched in 1994) and most popular directory on the web, Yahoo! has a well-deserved reputation for helping people find information easily. It's the best place to go when you're looking for just one site, particularly on a general topic. Key is the ability to search over Yahoo! categories and listings—this allows you to quickly home in on both relevant topics and sites. If a search fails to find a match within Yahoo!'s one million plus listings, then matches from the Inktomi search service are displayed. Yahoo! is the largest human-compiled guide to the web, employing about 150 editors in an effort to categorize the web.

Looksmart (http://www.looksmart. com/)—In addition to being a stand-alone directory service, LookSmart provides directory results to MSN Search, Excite, and many other partners. AltaVista provides LookSmart with search results when a search fails to find a match from among LookSmart's directory listings. LookSmart launched independently in 1996, was backed by Reader's Digest for a year, and then went independent once again.

Snap (http://www.snap.com/)—Like LookSmart, Snap aims to challenge Yahoo! as the champion of categorizing the web. The directory listings on Snap are supplemented by search results from Inktomi. Snap was launched in 1997 and is backed by Cnet and NBC.

FINDING SPECIFIC TYPES OF INFORMATION

This part of the chapter focuses in on using the web to find specific types of material: to find company information, people, legal information generally, case law, and statute law.

FINDING COMPANY INFORMATION

The web is a rich source of business and company information. Here are four steps to finding company information on the web, with some key examples of the tools available under each step.

Step #1: Find address and contact information for the company

- **Canada 411 (http://canada411. sympatico.ca/)**—A Canada-wide phone directory with over ten million listings, for both businesses and individuals.

- **InfoSpace (http://www.infospace. com/)**—A search tool to find people, email addresses, and business information. It also features reverse look-up by phone number, address, or area code.

Step #2: Locate information about the company

- **Carlson Online (http://www.fin-info.com/)**—One-stop shopping for Canadian company information, with links to company home pages, stock quotes, news releases and more. Automatically searches and links to SEDAR for company filings.

- **Dow Jones Interactive (http://djinteractive.com)**—Company and industry information from this leading information provider. Charges apply to view Dun & Bradstreet reports, historical market data from Tradeline, and other premium information.

- **Hoovers Online (http://www. hoovers.com/)**—Features corporate and business profiles for more than 10,000 North American companies. IPO Central includes latest filings, pricings, and news on companies going public.

- **Thomas Register (http://www. thomasregister.com/)**—A searchable database of over 150,000 American and Canadian companies. Allows searching by company name, product or service, or brand name, and results include business name and address and, for several companies, an online catalog and link to the company's website.

Step #3: Search public databases

- **Canadian Federal Corporations Data On-line (http://strategis.ic.gc.ca/ sc_coinf/engdoc/homepage.html)**—A searchable database of federally incorporated companies, at Industry Canada's Strategis website.

- **EDGAR Online (http://www.edgar-online.com/)**—US Securities and Exchange Commission's searchable database of public company filings. Includes up-to-the-minute SEC filings.

- **IPO Express (http://www.edgar-online.com/ipoexpress/)**—IPO headlines, filings, pricings, and much more from EDGAR Online.

- **SEDAR (http://www.sedar.com/)**—Searchable archive of all documents filed in the SEDAR system by Canadian public companies and mutual funds, as well as profiles of all SEDAR filers. Current to the most recently completed business day.

Step 4: Find news stories

- **Bloomberg.com (http://www.bloomberg.com)**—From the venerable supplier of financial information, breaking business and financial news.

- **CNNfn: The Financial Network (http://www.cnnfn.com/)**—From the folks at CNN, a rich source of financial news.

- **Globeinvestor.com (http://www.globeinvestor.com/)**—Stock market and financial news from one of the Globe and Mail's web offerings.

- **Yahoo! Finance (http://finance.yahoo.com/)**—Compiles real-time financial news from major newswire services and maintains the links for seven days.

FINDING PEOPLE

Locating an individual's address or telephone number used to be an expensive, potentially time-consuming experience. Online, it typically involved knowing a rough geographic region and spending approximately $50 per search. Offline, it meant finding a library that housed telephone directories for the locations you were interested in, and thumbing through directories one by one.

On the web, there are now hundreds of directories that can help you locate people quickly and inexpensively. Here are several of the best such resources, organized into three categories: general listings, lawyers, and government listings.

General Listings

- **Canada 411 (http://canada411.sympatico.ca/)**—Canada-wide phone directory with over ten million listings, for both businesses and individuals.

- **InfoSpace (http://www.infospace.com/)**—Search tool to find people, email addresses, and business information. Includes a reverse look-up feature by phone number, address, or area code.

- **WhoWhere People Finder (http://www.whowhere.lycos.com/)** — From Lycos, a search tool to find people and email addresses.

Lawyers

- **The Canadian Law List (http://www.canadianlawlist.com/)** — From

Canada Law Book, a comprehensive listing of Canadian law firms, lawyers, judges and government departments. Searches can be done over specific fields (such as name, organization, city, etc.) using a FolioViews search form.

- **Canadian Legal LEXPERT Directory (http://www.lexpert.ca/)** — Identifies the leading Canadian law firms and lawyers in over 50 practice areas across Canada.

- **Carswell's Directory of Canadian Lawyers and Law Firms (http://www.carswell.com/LawDir/)**—Email and website addresses of lawyers across Canada, organized by province. Searchable by lawyer's name, firm, city, and province.

- **Martindale-Hubbell Lawyer Locator (http://www.martindale.com/locator/)**—Searchable access to the worldwide Martindale-Hubbell Law Directory. Locate a lawyer by name, firm, location, practice area, and more.

- **West's Legal Directory (lawoffice.com) (http://www.lawoffice.com/)**—Profiles of over one million North American lawyers and firms; searchable by name, city, province, firm size, and practice area.

Government Listings

- **Government Electronic Directory Services (GEDS) (http://canada.gc.ca/search/direct500/geds_e.html)**—An integrated, searchable directory of all federal public servants. Includes phone numbers, addresses, and email addresses.

- **INFO-GO Telephone Directory (http://www.infogo.gov.on.ca/)**—Online Ontario government telephone directory of names, phone numbers, addresses, and email addresses.

- **BC Government Directory (http://www.dir.gov.bc.ca/)**—A searchable directory of telephone, title, address, and other public information related to British Columbia government employees.

Starting Points for Finding Legal Information Generally

There are several sites that specialize in mapping the web for legal resources. They have been created by law schools, law institutes, continuing legal education societies, and businesses with an interest in law. These sites can be good starting points when trying to find a law-related website, or when trying to track down international legal material. Here are some examples of such sites, broken into two categories: Canadian law and International law.

Canadian Law

- **Virtual Canadian Law Library (http://www.lexum.umontreal.ca/index_en.html)**—This outstanding directory to Canadian law includes pointers to legislation, case law, tribunal rulings, libraries, publishers, lawyers, and much more. The work of the CRDP (Centre for Public Law Research) at the University of Montreal Law School.

Browser Tips for Web Searchers

Finding what you're looking for on the web is made much easier by effectively using the key tool: your web browser. Here are handful of tips.

1. **Organize your bookmarks/favourites.** Using the bookmarks or favourites feature of your web browser allows you to mark the good stuff for return visits. Since bookmarking is so easy to do, your favourites list can get out of control very quickly. It helps to create folders within your favourites, such as "Government sites" or "Intellectual Property Resources," and turn your favourties list into your own personal web directory.

2. **Use the "Find in Page" option of your web browser to search within a web page.** You can search within a web page for a specific word or words by using the "Find in Page" option of your web browser. Select "Find in Page" from the "Edit" drop-down menu, type your word(s) into the test box, and click "OK." You will be brought to the first appearance of that word in the open web page.

3. **Save good pages.** Saving interesting pages to your computer can be an efficient way to manage documents you find on the web. Rather than printing

out a copy, you can "file" the electronic copy on your computer's hard drive. Note that if you save a page in HTML or web format, you can successfully open the page up again in your web browser. However, if you try to open the page in your word processor, the formatting may go awry (indeed, if you are using an older word processor the page will be so cluttered with code as to be unreadable). You can always save a web page as text format, which will strip out all formatting and retain a stripped down version of the document.

4. **Use multiple browser windows.** When you want to jump back and forth between two or more web pages or sites, an effective technique can be to open multiple windows in your web browser. You can do this by clicking the "File" drop-down menu and selecting "New Window." To jump between windows, simply click the button at the bottom of your screen for the relevant window, or press Alt-Tab to toggle between windows. This can be a particularly useful technique when you are waiting for a document to paint across your screen – simply jump to a new window and explore something else until the document fully downloads to your browser.

• **University of Calgary Law Library Links (http://www.ucalgary.ca/library/law/)**—A comprehensive and up-to-date directory to Canadian legal resources on the Internet, from the University of Calgary Law Library. Sites are organized into categories based on type of resource (legislation, judicial decisions etc.) and source of resource.

- **Continuing Legal Education Society of BC's Legal Links (http://www.cle.bc.ca/resources/)**—One of the most comprehensive directories to Canadian legal resources, with an accent on British Columbia material. Categories are based on a Yahoo-like structure that includes listings of cases, legislation, government, lawyers, practice areas, and more. Extensive annotations. You can search over the resources listed here.

International Law

- **FindLaw (http://www.findlaw.com)**—Features a Yahoo-like directory to Internet legal resources. Sites are arranged into categories based on law subject topics, legal entities, professional development, news and reference material, legal practice information, and so on. Short annotations give some hint of what lies at the other end of each link. There is also a search engine that can search over the web for law sites, or over specific sites (such as United States government sites) or resources (such as United States Supreme Court cases).

- **Australasian Legal Information Institute (http://www.austlii.edu.au/)**—This ambitious site includes an extensive collection of links to legal materials around the globe.

- **Hieros Gamos (http://www.hg.org)**—A massive global directory to legal resources, on the Internet and off. Main-

tained by Lex Mundi, a global association of over one hundred law firms.

FINDING CASE LAW

As described in Chapter Six (The Web: Its Resources), the coverage of case law on the web is very thin, and the ability to search over case collections is very limited. That said, if you are looking for a specific recent decision, the web can now be the fastest way to get a copy in some jurisdictions. As well, the case collections at some court websites can be used for rudimentary research.

For example, at the Supreme Court of Canada decisions site (http://www.droit.umontreal.ca/doc/csc-scc/en/) developed by the University of Montreal's Centre for Public Law Research (CRDP), a fielded search form offers the ability to focus a search on a specific type of information in an SCC judgment. You can restrict a search to such fields as case name, abstract, judge's name, cases cited, or statutes cited. You could, for example, search for employment law decisions on which Sopinka J. rendered a decision. In offering an increasingly comprehensive collection (the site includes decisions from 1989 forward) and adding a powerful search facility, the Supreme Court site offers a hint of what may be in store for court websites in the years ahead.

The Canadian courts that have websites featuring case collections include:

Alberta Courts (http://www.albertacourts.ab.ca/)—Full text cases from the Alberta Court of Appeal and Pro-

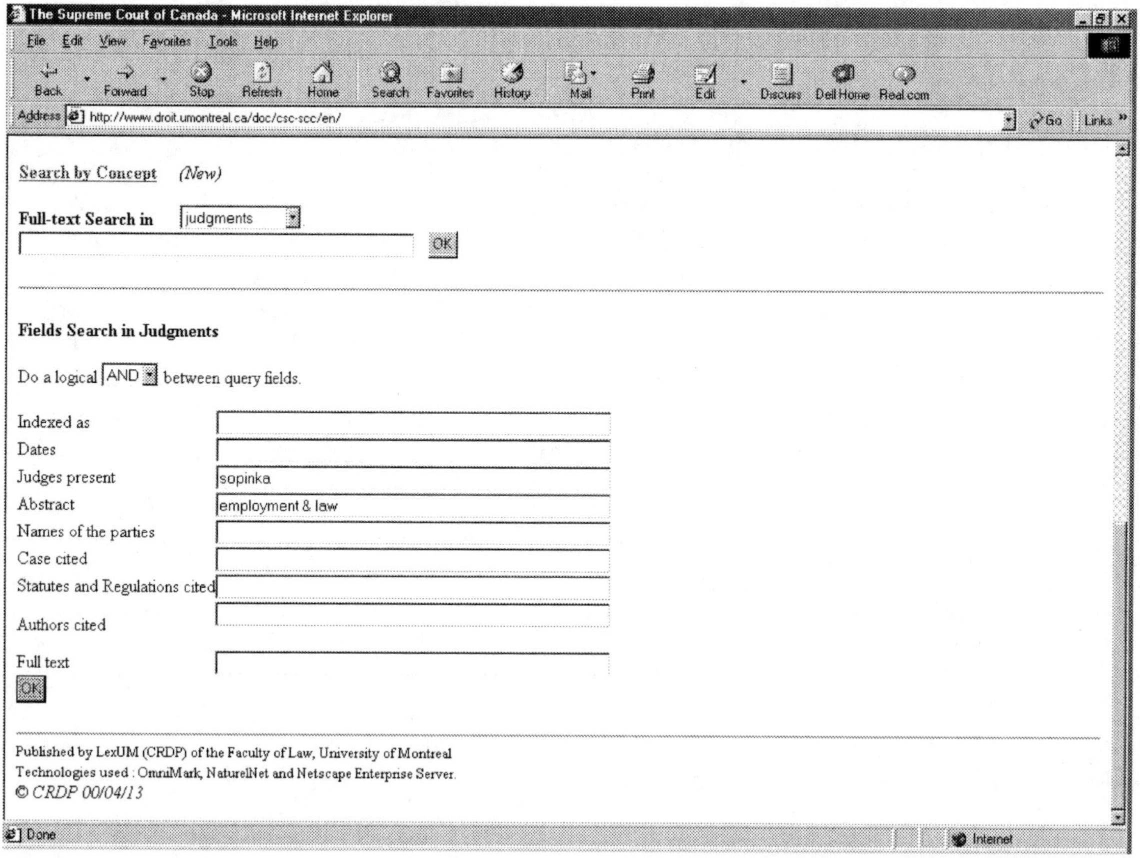

Figure 7.8. Supreme Court of Canada fielded search form

vincial Court since 1998 are featured here. Cases can be browsed by date, or searched by keyword. The search tool supports Boolean and proximity searching.

British Columbia Superior Courts (http://www.courts.gov.bc.ca)—Cases from the BC Supreme Court and Court of Appeal are available in full text, archived since January 1996. The search engine is quite basic, allowing limited date searching and Boolean searching. A topical listing divides cases into several broad subject areas

ranging from Civil Procedure to Trusts and Estates.

Federal Court of Canada (http:// www.fja.gc.ca/en/cf/index.html)—The Federal Court site includes a database of Federal Court decisions from 1993 forward. The decisions can be browsed by Federal Court Report volume, searched by keyword, or browsed using a topical directory.

Ontario Courts (http://www. ontariocourts.on.ca/)—The full text of

Ontario Court of Appeal cases, dating from 1998, are featured here. Cases can be browsed by date, but (at least for now) cannot be searched by keyword.

Prince Edward Island Supreme Court (http://www.gov.pe.ca/courts/supreme/)—Features the full text of PEI Supreme Court decisions since January 1997 (in Acrobat PDF format). Decisions can be searched by keyword, date, and area of law.

Supreme Court of Canada cases (http://www.droit.umontreal.ca/doc/csc-scc/en)—The Supreme Court of Canada website includes a database of SCC judgments from 1989 forward. Decisions can be browsed by Supreme Court Report volume number, or you can search the database using keywords. An advanced search feature allows you to search by such fields as case name, judge's name, cases cited, or statutes cited. A topical directory allows browsing by subject matter.

In using such case collections on the web, keep the following considerations in mind:

1. **How comprehensive is the collection?** Does the site post every decision rendered by the court? Not all do: for example, the Ontario Courts' website posts only decisions of the Ontario Court of Appeal; the Alberta Courts site does not include judgments of the Court of Queen's Bench. Also, how many years of judgments does the site offer? The depth of the collections on the web is not great. Most courts provide judgments from only the last few years; the Supreme Court of Canada's collection is the deepest, going back to 1989. If you need to search over a comprehensive collection that goes back several decades, you should be looking in print law reports or on commercial online services like *e*Carswell and QuickLaw.

2. **What kind of currency does the collection have?** That is, how quickly are new judgments posted to the court's website? At many court sites, judgments are posted very quickly, within hours or a day of their release.

3. **How do you use the search tool at the site?** Most court websites now provide a search tool to allow you to find judgments in the site's collection. There is a wide range of search tools in use on court sites, so be sure to check the site's help material to see what search syntax and approach you should use when searching the collection. The sidebar, Case Collection Searching Chart lists some of the key search features for the court websites listed.

FINDING STATUTE LAW

As described in Chapter Six (The Web: Its Resources), providing access to legislation is an area where the Internet excels. The Department of Justice website (http://canada.justice.gc.ca/) provides the full text of every federal statute (except, the *Income Tax Act*) and regulation, consolidated to a date within the previous six to nine months. Most provinces' statutes are also available on the Internet (see the Legal Resources Directory for a complete listing and URLs). For a lucky few provinces (Alberta, Ontario, New Brunswick, Nova Scotia, and all three territories), complete sets of regulations are also online.

One thing you will notice very quickly as you explore the legislation on the web, however, is that there is no consistent approach to the material. From site to site, you will find that the presentation differs, as do the search tools and syntax, the currency dates, and even whether the material

Case Collection Searching Chart

	Alberta Courts	BC Superior Courts	Federal Court of Canada	Ontario Courts	PEI Supreme Court	Supreme Court of Canada
Coverage	Alta. C.A. and Prov. Ct. decisions since 1998	B.C. S.C. and B.C. C.A. decisions since 1996	Federal Court decisions since 1993	Ont. C.A. decisions since 1998	P.E.I. S.C. decisions since 1997	S.C.C. decisions since 1989
Default searching	phrase search	phrase search	Alternative (match any term)	N/A	phrase search	Alternative (match any term)
Phrase searching	automatic (no quotations required)	automatic (no quotations required)	insert ADJ between terms	N/A	automatic (no quotations required)	insert ADJ between terms
Boolean AND	AND	AND	&	N/A	N/A	&
Boolean OR	OR	OR	space	N/A	N/A	space
Boolean NOT	NOT	AND NOT	–	N/A	N/A	–
Proximity searching	Can select "Within 10 words", "Within a paragraph of", "In same paragraph as" from menu	NEAR finds words within 50 words of each other	#w finds words within the number specified by the #	N/A	N/A	#w finds words within the number specified by the #
Field searching	Can search by court; civil or criminal	Can search by court, year	N/A	N/A	Can search by month	Can search by indexed name of case, abstract, name of parties, cases cited, and legislation cited
Wildcard (for truncating)	* or !	*	*	N/A	N/A	*

is free or not. (One province, Saskatche-wan, has an Internet collection of statutes and regulations that is accessible only for a subscription fee. The more common approach is for a free collection to be available over the web with relatively basic search capabilities, and an enhanced version to be available for a fee either over the web or on CD-ROM.)

Many statute sites use specialized search software called FolioViews, a powerful search program favoured by legal publishers. Unfortunately, FolioViews is not the most intuitive search program for a user (see the Federal Statutes pictured in Figure 7.9). Note that if you know what statute or regulation you're looking for and want to access it quickly, you can opt for the text format of the document at the Justice site. However, if you want to search over the statutes or regulations, you'll need to learn how to use the Folio commands.

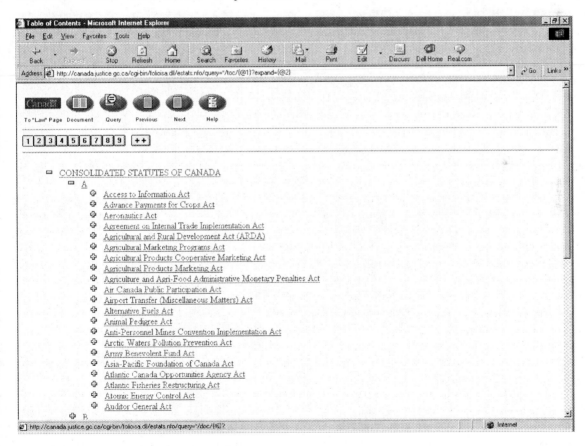

Figure 7.9. *Department of Justice: Federal Statutes*

With Folio, there are a couple of ways to find what you're looking for. One is to browse a listing of statutes. When you first link to the Statutes, you will be presented with a screen with some buttons on the top (these are tools to navigate through the database), as well as a row of numbers from 1 to 9, and a listing of statutes beginning with A. What you are looking at is called the "Contents" view, which offers a table of contents-like view of the database. The row of numbers represents levels in the statutes, such as Act, Part, Division, and Section. Note that number "3" is depressed when you first link to the Statutes. This tells you that you are looking at the third level headings, which are the names of the Acts. Clicking on "2" will give you the letters of the alphabet, the second level headings. Clicking on the plus sign beside any entry will expand that branch to the level below.

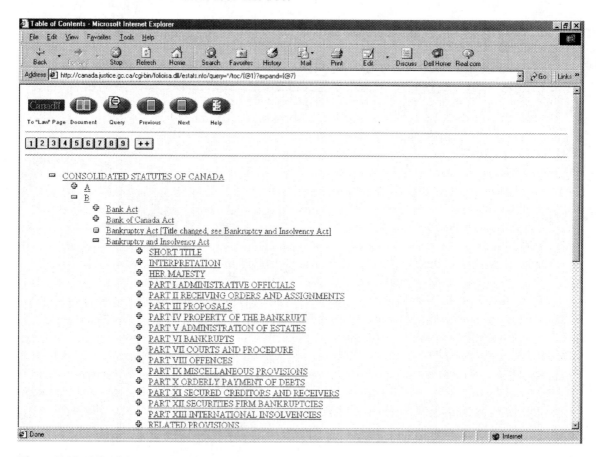

Figure 7.10. Federal Statutes: Browsing

So if you wanted to find the *Bankruptcy and Insolvency Act*, you would click on the number "2" in the row of buttons, then click on the plus sign beside "B," and then the plus sign beside the *Bankruptcy and Insolvency Act*.

Browsing the statute listing, however, can get a little cumbersome, particularly if you don't have a fast connection to the Internet. A faster way to get at material you're looking for is to use the search feature. To do so, click on the "Query" button near the top of the page.

A search form will come up. In the form, you type the terms that you want to find. You can use Boolean operators (AND, OR, NOT) and the truncation wildcard (employ* for employee, employer, employed, employment). You can also search for phrases (put your terms inside quotation marks). (Note that if you don't use any connectors between multiple terms, AND is by default inserted between them.)

Once you've typed in your search terms, wait a moment before starting your search. Note the Display Options (see below). A check mark in the box beside an option means the option is turned on. It is easiest to navigate through your search results when you have "Records w/Hits Only" turned to OFF, "Headings w/Hits" turned ON, and "Words Around Hits" turned OFF. Click on the check boxes to get the appropriate settings. Now, start your search by clicking the "Search" button. In a moment, you'll get a nifty display of the number of records that match your search terms (called the "Results Map").

Here things get a little tricky. Note the "Document" and "Contents" buttons above the Results Map. Clicking the "Document" button brings you into the full text of the statute featuring your first search hit. You can now use the "Previous Hit" and "Next Hit" buttons near the top of the page to navigate between your search results.

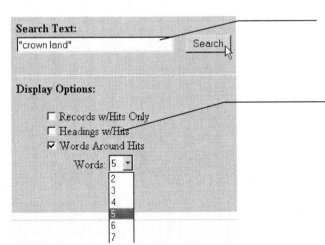

Type search terms — using quotes will search for a phrase

Check box to left of Headings with Hits to see Contents view displaying only those sections with search results (**recommended**)

Figure 7.11. Federal Statutes: Searching

Results Displayed with the "Headings with Hits" option selected:

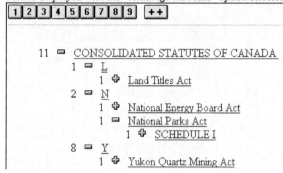

Figure 7.12. *Federal Statutes: Navigating Search Results*

Clicking the "Contents" button brings you to the table of contents view of the statutes. Clicking on the number "3" in the row of numbers along the top will give you the titles of statutes that include your search terms (recall that you set Display Options to "Headings w/Hits"). Note that the number of hits under each statute title is shown on the left. This can be a very useful feature. Click on the plus sign beside the title of a statute you want to explore, and you will narrow in on the section of the Act that includes your search terms.

8 DISCUSSION GROUPS

Often, the best way to find an answer to a problem is to phone a knowledgeable peer and exchange thoughts. One of the more powerful features of the Internet is that it takes this concept to a completely new level. Internet discussion groups, which come in several forms, offer ways to interact with others online. You can ask a question, and it is very likely you'll get several replies in a short time. Then there will be replies to those replies, and typically you'll find what you are looking for—and often a whole lot more. Internet discussion groups have in fact been so successful in linking people with like interests and concerns that an entire industry now serves emerging "online communities." Particularly for lawyers in solo or small firm settings, who don't have ready access to others to bounce ideas off of or seek advice from, such online communities can be excellent places to turn to solve a problem, to find a resource, or to simply share experiences.

This chapter describes four types of Internet discussion groups or online communities:

1. **Mailing lists**, which are the most popular and useful type of discussion group, allow Internet users to interact through email.

2. **Web-based discussion forums**, which are accessed using a web browser, and work like online bulletin boards.

3. **Newsgroups**, which have been eclipsed somewhat by the rapid growth in web-based discussion forums, also work like electronic bulletin boards, supporting online exchanges on thousands of discrete topics.

4. **Internet chat**, long perceived to be a time waster, but recently discovered by the business world and renamed "instant messaging," or the ability to join people from various geographic locations and allow them to interact online, in real-time.

MAILING LISTS

Mailing lists were actually the original type of online community, dating from the mid-1970s. They allow Internet users to interact through email. Participants send a message via email to a remailing program that duplicates the message and remails it to every participant on the list. Mailing lists are often referred to as "listservs," the name of a popular mailing list management software program. Users of the list open up their email inbox to a stack of the most recent messages sent by list participants. Everyone sees every message, and can contribute with new messages and replies as they desire. There are thousands of mailing lists in existence, on every conceivable topic, which can link you with people and resources you would otherwise not be able to communicate with easily.

Law librarians, law firm administrators, and technology lawyers have been using mailing lists for years. For example, the Canadian Association of Law Libraries List, CALL-L (http://www.callacbd.ca/), began operation in 1991, and has been an extremely effective way for those interested in law librarianship in Canada to exchange information. Topics discussed on the CALL-L mailing list, now with over 700 subscribers, include reference questions, online databases, legal websites, and law library administration. NET-LAWYERS (http://www.net-lawyers.org/), a list dealing with Internet developments and sites related to law, has been very active since its inception in 1994, with some 2000 subscribers. The US-based list includes many Canadian subscribers, with such cross-border discussion threads as law firm websites, Internet legal issues, and new software. Similarly, the Canadian Society for the Advancement of Legal Technology (http://www.csalt.on.ca/) has operated a mailing list, CSALT-TALK, since the mid-1990s, which focuses on law and technology matters.

More recently, mailing lists have emerged that are aimed at the typical practicing lawyer. For example, the Trial Lawyers Associations in both Ontario (http://www.otla.com/) and British Columbia (http://www.tlabc.org/) operate mailing lists for their members, providing a new venue for association members to research problems and network.

Even law firms are hosting their own mailing lists. Pushor Mitchell (http://www.pushormitchell.com/), a mid-size British Columbia firm, is one of many firms using an announcement, or one-way, mailing list to send legal update newsletters to clients. Such one-way mailing lists, where mail is sent only from the list owner to subscribers, are increasingly popular marketing tools, used by bar associations, vendors,

and law firms to get information quickly to their members/customers/clients.

Note that discussion-style mailing lists can be moderated or unmoderated, public or private. A moderated list has a person in control. Moderation styles naturally vary, with some vetting every message for relevance and appropriateness before it is posted to the list, and others merely trying to guide the discussion. Generally, moderated lists tend to be of higher quality, as a good moderator will help reduce the number of irrelevant (or offensive) postings. Some lists are open to anyone who wants to subscribe, whereas others require a moderator's approval or (as in the case of lists like the Ontario and British Columbia Trial Lawyers Associations lists) membership in a particular organization.

USING MAILING LISTS

To participate in a mailing list, you will first have to subscribe to the list (see the sidebar on How to Subscribe to a Mailing List). Note that there are two email addresses you will need to keep track of: the address of the mailing list management software that handles subscription matters, and the address of the list itself, where you send messages to have them distributed to list participants.

Once subscribed, keep the first email you receive from the list. This message will contain the instructions and the two addresses you need to manage your subscription and post messages to the list. In due course, you will receive postings to the list by other list participants in your email inbox. To send a message to the list is simply a matter of composing an email message and sending it to the mailing list email address.

The more popular (and hence useful) mailing lists can generate a large number of postings each day. To avoid being overwhelmed by a constant flow of messages from the list, you may want to consider having list messages delivered to you in digest form, if the list supports that option. With a digest, individual messages are combined into one large message before sending, typically daily. You still get all the messages, but they are often easier to handle in a digest form. Check the mailing list's help to see if a digest option is available, and how to set yourself up for it. For example, if the list is managed using LISTSERV, a popular mailing list management software program, then to change your delivery method to digest form, you would send the following message to the list's subscription address:

set *listname* digest

Filters can also be a good way of handling mailing list messages. Filters, which are a feature of most email software programs, set rules on how to handle incoming messages. With filters, you can direct mailing list messages to their own individual folder or mailbox as they arrive. This keeps your inbox smaller, and keeps all the mailing list messages together so they are easier to read.

Finally, note that you can post a message to many mailing lists without being a subscriber. Make sure to ask subscribers to send any responses to your email address and not to the list, as you won't get the responses otherwise.

FINDING MAILING LISTS

There are thousands of different mailing lists. To locate lists on topics you are interested in, you can try searching by keyword at one of the many sites that indexes mailing lists. Two of the better ones are:

- **The Liszt (http://www.liszt.com/).** Provides a searchable index and topical directory of over 90,000 mailing lists. Mailing list entries include subscription information and (for some lists) searchable archives of past postings.

- **CataList (http://www.lsoft.com/).** The official catalog of LISTSERV lists, hosted by L-Soft, the vendor of the LISTSERV software. Some 40,000 public mailing lists can be searched, and entries include subscription information and (for some lists) searchable message archives.

To focus in on law-related lists, one of the better sources is the Law Lists site (http://www.lib.uchicago.edu/~llou/lawlists/info.html), maintained by Lyonette Louis-Jacques at the University of Chicago Law Library. The site includes a brief description and subscription information for hundreds of law-related mailing lists around the globe.

MAILING LIST NETIQUETTE

When sending an email to an individual, you generally know your correspondent, and can tailor your message accordingly.

How to Subscribe to a Mailing List

Mailing lists work by email, so you won't have to learn a new piece of software to participate in discussions taking place on lists of interest to you. Posting a message to a mailing list is simply a matter of composing an email message and sending it to the appropriate address. Here, though, things can get a little tricky.

That is because there are two email addresses you need to keep track of when dealing with a mailing list. For the Canadian Association of Law Libraries List, for example, call-l@listserv.unb.ca is the email address of the list itself, and where you send messages to participate in discussions. listserv@listserv.unb.ca is the address of the mailing list management software, otherwise known as the subscription address. This latter address is where you send messages to subscribe or unsubscribe to the list, or to send other commands to the list, such as to change your delivery method to digest form.

So, to subscribe to a mailing list, send an email message to the subscription address — to listserv@listserv.unb.ca in our example — in this form (note that the form varies slightly depending on which mailing list management software program the list uses — LISTSERV, ListProc, and Majordomo are three of the most popular programs):

For LISTSERV or ListProc lists:
subscribe *listname* firstname lastname

For Majordomo lists:
subscribe *listname* email address

Replace the word "listname" with the name of the mailing list you're subscribing to, and the words "firstname" and "lastname," or "email address," as the case may be, with your real first name and last name or email address. Leave the subject line blank and include nothing else in the body of the email.

Messages you post to a mailing list are read by anyone and everyone (most, complete strangers). As a result, mailing lists have developed their own rules of conduct, which are best observed if you want to get the most out of your list experience:

1. **Be a little bit informed.** Don't ask painfully obvious questions or questions that are inappropriate for the group. If in doubt about something, try first to find a Frequently Asked Questions (FAQ) list, which may be posted at a website that the list uses to archive previous list messages.

2. **Lurk.** This is what Internet users call it when you follow a mailing list, reading the messages but not actually posting anything yourself. You get the flavour for the conversation. You learn some of the basic stuff without asking. You get up to speed.

3. **Use the right address.** Messages go to the list address; unsubscribe, help, and configuration settings (for example, di-

gest requests) go to the subscription (aka administrative) address.

4. **Don't post ads.** Most mailing lists explicitly or implicitly prohibit advertising messages. Posting an ad can make you very unpopular very quickly.

5. **Send personal messages to the author, not to the list.** If you want to send a personal message to the author of a message, send the reply directly to that person, not back to the list address. Take out the list address in the To field, and put in the author's address (which can often be found at the end of the message text, in the signature lines). Even if the message isn't "personal" personal, some things simply don't need to be seen by everyone on the list.

6. **Watch what you send.** Remember that what you say is being seen by many people, including possibly colleagues at your firm, lawyers on the other side of a file, and existing and prospective clients. Mailing list messages can be archived and accessed for a very long time. What you say could come back to haunt you, even several years later.

7. **Avoid confrontation.** It is wise to employ high diplomacy in criticizing another posting or engaging in friendly argument. The lack of physical context cues (which we take for granted in personal conversation) can quickly escalate a misunderstanding into a "flame war." This is the colloquialism used on the Internet to describe volatile exchanges between online discussion participants.

8. **Don't send long messages if the information is easily available elsewhere.** For example, if a court judgment is posted on the web, don't paste the text into a message and send it to the list. Instead, send the URL of the web page for the judgment. Most email programs recognize an URL and display it as a hypertext link within the message text. The recipient can simply click on the link, launch their web browser, and be looking at the page in moments.

WEB-BASED DISCUSSION FORUMS

Web-based discussion forums are perhaps the most visible form of online community on the Internet. Virtually every major website seems to host their own set of discussion forums, from the large Internet portals such as America Online, Yahoo!, and the Microsoft Network, to niche sites about sports (ESPN.com at http://espn.go.com/), seniors (SeniorNet at http://www.seniornet.org/), or movies (Internet Movie Database at http://www.imdb.com/). All the media sites have their own forums, also called message boards, from the National Post (http://www.nationalpost.com/) to CBC (http://cbc.ca/). Discussion forums focused on professional users are more common every month, ranging from stock sites like Raging Bull (http://www.ragingbull.com/) to magazine sites like the Harvard Business Review (http://www.hbsp.harvard.edu/).

Web-based discussion forums work like electronic bulletin boards. When you drop into a forum, you select a topic from a list of discussion topics, and you begin to browse through the messages already posted there. They will be listed in chronological order, generally with a Subject line, author, and date, very much like email. You read some. You skip some others. You may reply to one or two, by emailing the authors directly, or by posting your response to the forum itself for everyone to read.

Interestingly, despite the explosion of web-based discussion forums generally, there still are not that many forums focused on legal matters. Findlaw (http://www.findlaw.com/), a large US-based legal site, has hundreds of ongoing discussions on law-related topics, and some forums are hosted by other American legal sites such as the American Bar Association (http://www.abanet.org/), some state bar associations, and even some enterprising law firms (see, for example, Siskind, Susser, Haas & Devine's immigration law website at http://www.visalaw.com/). But in Canada, relevant (that is, useful) discussion forums on

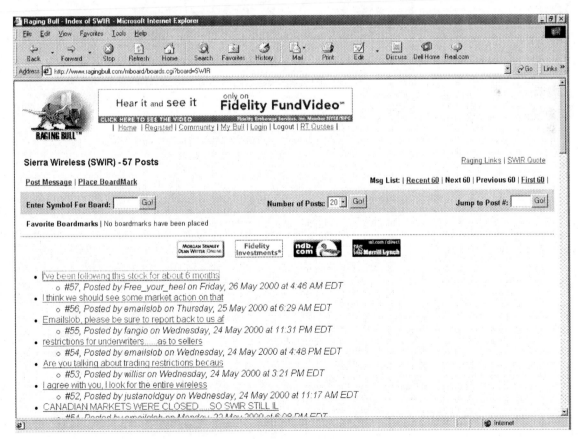

Figure 8.1. Raging Bull's stock discussions

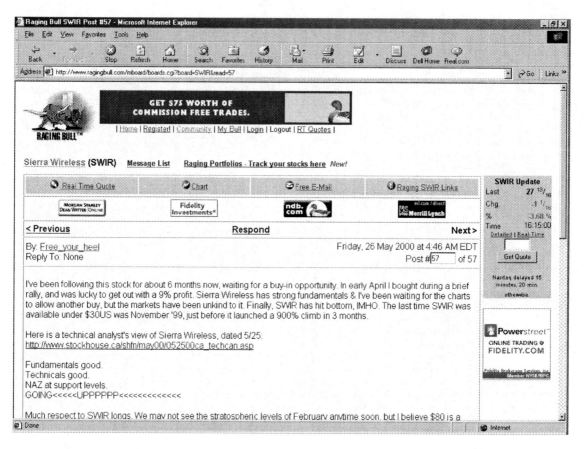

law-related topics have not yet really emerged on the web. By contrast, mailing lists on law-related topics are almost as prevalent in Canada as in the United States (although the US is somewhat ahead of us here as well, as it tends to be with anything Internet-related).

There are two theories that might explain the different growth patterns of mailing lists and web-based discussion forums. Theory one is that the exchanges that take place via mailing lists, including mailing lists relating to legal matters, tend to be a distinct step up in quality from the exchanges in discussion forums. Some discus-

sion forums are riddled with off-topic, rude, or just plain useless postings (Internet users describe such forums as "noisy" or having a "poor signal to noise ratio"—not much signal; an awful lot of noise). Perhaps the notion of an email ending up in someone's personal email inbox gives the writer pause more so than does the idea of posting a message to a public place on the web. Or the greater ease with which someone can find and subscribe to a web-based discussion forum may open up forums to more off-the-wall users. Whatever the reason, the fact is that discussion forums more than mailing lists are places to exercise a little caution before dropping in on.

Theory two is that for busy professionals like lawyers, the "pull" of a mailing list is key in getting users to participate. With a mailing list, an email comes in to your email inbox, serving as a reminder that a discussion is going on that may be of interest, and making it very easy to jump in to the exchange. With a web-based discussion forum, you need to remember to go onto a website to check in on the discussion, and often you need to enter a username and password (which are very easy to misplace) to participate in the discussion.

USING DISCUSSION FORUMS

To participate in a web-based discussion forum, you may need to register at the website hosting the forum. This typically involves typing several bits of personal information into a form at the site, such as your name, email address, and street address. Be aware of the privacy policy on the site before you register—any self-respecting website (that is, any site worth registering at) will post a policy explaining what they will and will not do with the information they gather from you.

Once registered, you will be given a username and password (which you can sometimes select yourself—be sure not to use the same password you use on your own computer system, for security reasons), often in the form of an email sent to you immediately after you register. Be sure to save this email. You'll be amazed at how quickly you can amass (and forget) passwords to access various websites.

Discussion forums are typically very intuitive to use—the popularity of forums has meant fast strides in improved ease of use. At the *New York Times* website (http://www.nytimes.com/), for example, once in the forums area of the site, you can drill down through a listing of categories to select a forum of interest. Clicking on "Business" will bring up a series of discussions on business issues, one of which is "Interest Rates, Inflation and the Federal Reserve." Once in the discussion, you can scroll through recent postings, and then post a reply to any one of them by clicking on the "Post Message" button. This brings you to a form where you type in your comments, and then click "Post my Message."

Also available in most discussion forums will be links to areas where you can change your preferences (to display messages in a certain format), search over message postings, or access help on how to use the forum.

MORE NETIQUETTE

The rules of conduct, or netiquette, described in the section on mailing lists above apply equally to participating in web-based discussion forums. As well, here are a couple of additional suggestions that you may want to consider as you foray into discussions taking place on the web:

1. **Exercise a bias for moderated discussion forums.** This is optional, but you may find it useful to stay away from forums that are not moderated or hosted by someone, or at least conscientiously monitored by the organization hosting the forum. A moderator can help by either deleting the rude and

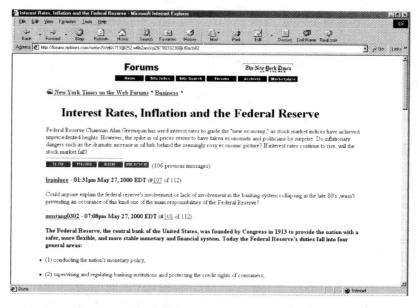

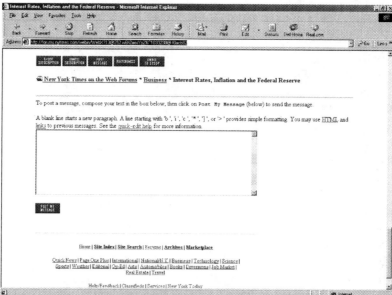

Figure 8.2. New York Times *Forums*

off-topic posts that can plague some forums, or guiding the discussion in more
valuable directions.

2. **Resist the temptation to give legal
   advice.** Even more so than mailing
   lists, discussion forums that are law-

related tend to feature questions from non-lawyers on legal topics. Lawyers are often posting answers, and it is true that this can be a good way to present yourself to the Internet community as a knowledgeable, approachable professional. But if you do post answers, you will of course want to include a clear disclaimer that your post is not to be taken as legal advice. A disclaimer is doubly important in the context of the Internet's global reach: many questions may very well come from users located in a jurisdiction where you aren't licensed to practice.

NEWSGROUPS

Newsgroups have been eclipsed somewhat by the rapid growth in web-based discussion forums. Like discussion forums taking place on websites, newsgroups work like electronic bulletin boards, supporting online exchanges on thousands of discrete topics. Newsgroups are actually a cluster of different newsgroup networks or bulletin board systems, the largest of which is called Usenet, which can be accessed through the Internet or through such online services as America Online and the Microsoft Network. Usenet alone contains more than 14,000 newsgroups, covering every imaginable interest group.

One feature of newsgroups to be aware of at the outset is that if you find the ex-

changes on web-based discussion forums to be freewheeling, you'll be even more alarmed by the gloves-off discussions that take place on some newsgroups. Usenet, for example, has some individual newsgroups that are moderated, but no person or group has authority over Usenet as a whole. The end result is that more than any other corner of the Internet, newsgroups tend to be for the more adventurous souls.

That said, there are very useful discussions taking place on newsgroups. Not on law-related matters, alas. The vast majority of newsgroups that touch on law are overwhelmed with postings from people looking for free legal advice, commenting on the latest sensational legal case, complaining about the lawyer they recently fired, and so on. But newsgroups can offer value in other areas. Technology is one example. There are countless newsgroups on computer-related topics, and these discussions are among the more valuable resources on the Internet. There are entire newsgroups dedicated to virus fixes, firewall installation issues, Windows 2000 configuration problems, and so on. Other areas where newsgroups offer excellent value include fact finding (determining the location of an Australian nuclear power plant, for example), hunting for resources (locating a textbook on environmental disasters), and hobbies and recreation (discovering a great restaurant in New York).

The bottom line with newsgroups is that there are thousands of discussions going on. Some will be of utterly no interest to you, but some will be, depending on what kind of information you're seeking.

ACCESSING NEWSGROUPS

You can access newsgroups using any recent version of the popular web browsers, which include built-in news reader programs. To use the news reader, you will need to configure it, which means typing in your display name (the name that will be shown with any newsgroup postings you make), email address, and the address of a news server (which you can get from your Internet Service Provider). Alternately, you can simply go to a website such as Deja.com (http://www.deja.com/) or HotBot (http://hotbot.lycos.com/), and access newsgroups in your regular web browser exactly the same way you would access web-based discussion forums. If you are a light newsgroup user, this approach will be easier and likely sufficient.

Another approach for more regular users of newsgroups is to obtain a stand-alone news reader software program, which will have more features than the built-in reader in your web browser. The Gravity news client from MicroPlanet (http://www.microplanet.com/) is one of the more popular news reader programs, and makes it easy to work through a large volume of messages, subscribe and unsubscribe to groups, and make rules for organizing and prioritizing groups and messages.

USING NEWSGROUPS

Newsgroups are arranged in a hierarchical fashion. The name of each newsgroup has three or four parts, which increase in specificity as you read from left to right.

Example: **rec.photo.equipment.35mm**

. . . from the **recreation** hierarchy (>1000 groups)
  . . . the **photo** subset (20 groups)
    . . . **equipment** subset (4 groups)
      . . . **35 mm** issues (1 group)

The first part of the name is the so-called senior hierarchy, and as you can see from the example, it describes the most general class into which the discussion falls. The most common senior hierarchies include:

alt   alternative newsgroups, unmoderated, many topics
biz   business and advertisement
comp computers, high technology issues
misc miscellaneous
news about the newsgroup system itself
rec   recreational, hobbies
sci   science
soc   social issues

Given this organization, one can browse for interesting newsgroups in the master list. For example you might try computer groups (comp), look for security discussions, and look for one focusing on firewalls. And there you have it—comp.security.firewalls, which is a real group in fact.

Of course browsing can be time consuming given the sheer number of groups. Fortunately, there are ways to search the newsgroups using keywords. A good starting point is the Deja.com site (http://www.deja.com/), which allows you to run keyword searches over Usenet newsgroup discussions. Using such a site you could turn up all discussions relating to virus software programs, for example, by typing in the words "virus software." An added benefit of searching newsgroups is that you can discover relevant postings from a range of different discussions in progress in different newsgroups. One search on software piracy might uncover several different groups of people discussing the issue: software developers, retailers, hackers, law enforcement authorities, etc.

Several of the major search engines also allow you to search over newsgroups. At AltaVista (http://www.altavista.com/) or HotBot (http://hotbot.lycos.com/), for example, you can search newsgroup discussions by topic or by author, search within a specific newsgroup, or search the entire universe of newsgroups. If you are looking for a discussion group on a certain topic, this is also a quick way to locate the right newsgroup.

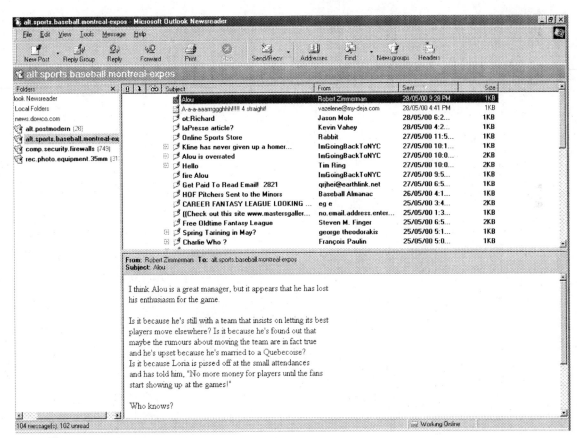

Figure 8.3. *Microsoft Outlook Newsreader*

INTERNET CHAT

Internet chat has had a reputation for being a time waster. Indeed, the traditional chat medium on the Internet, Internet Relay Chat or IRC as it is known, is not typically a forum for serious discussion. (In fact, it's a lot like the old party phone lines that you might have stumbled onto once or twice in your teens. Most of the "chat" by far is socially oriented to put it politely.) But the role of online chat is quickly evolving. The business world and professionals have discovered that the concept of being able to participate in real-time discussion with other people by typing your comments on-screen is actually quite useful.

The term "instant messaging" has emerged to describe the ability to join people from various geographic locations and allow them to interact online, in real-time. The value of instant messaging is that it allows spontaneous communication and collaborative work, in ways that are more immediate and interactive than email, vastly less expensive than video conferencing, and more flexible and cost effective than conference telephone calls.

Instant messaging is taking off both in the public Internet arena and in private business settings. ICQ (http://www.icq.com/) is a public instant messaging service that informs you who's on-line at any time and enables you to contact them instantly, to chat or send files back and forth. Internet portals, such as America Online, the Microsoft Network, and Yahoo!, offer instant messaging tools as part of their online communities. On the higher end, products like Lotus Sametime (http://www.lotus.com/) let businesses collaborate in real-time over an intranet or the Internet, with online chat, threaded discussions, shared whiteboards, and remote application sharing.

These kinds of online conferencing tools hold promise to take online interactivity to entirely new levels as they become more widespread.

9 BEING AN INFORMATION SUPPLIER

Now that we've considered the ways you can use the Internet as an information consumer, we'll switch to the other side of the information exchange. For those law firms that effectively use this new medium to *supply* information, there can be enormous advantages. A well-designed website can allow a firm to serve existing clients better and provide an edge when it comes to gaining new business or new talent. An Internet presence is not going to solve every business problem, but it can effectively reinforce and build on the firm's other client service and marketing efforts.

This chapter focuses on the three most effective ways that a law firm can participate in the Internet phenomena as an information supplier.

1. **Setting up a firm website:** the single most effective way to use the Internet to improve communication with existing clients and attract new clients.

2. **Setting up an intranet:** supplying information not to Internet users, but to your own firm lawyers and staff via web technology over an intranet.

3. **Establishing an extranet:** the latest client service trend, in which Internet technology is used to provide clients with private access to files, materials, and applications that relate to the clients' specific matters.

WHY WOULD YOU WANT TO BECOME A SUPPLIER?

GAINING A COMPETITIVE ADVANTAGE

The popular press would have us believe that if you don't have a website by now, there must be something wrong with you. Beyond the hype, there are in fact sound strategic reasons to participate as a supplier in the Internet information exchange. Even for those who already have a website, it's worth taking a moment to review the key benefits to establishing an effective presence on the Internet (with the accent on the word *effective*, which we try to address in the balance of this chapter):

1. **Enhance Communication.** Establishing an Internet presence can allow you to communicate with more people more efficiently than you can through traditional means. Your firm newsletter, for example, can be distributed at virtually no cost to hundreds of recipients in seconds using an email mailing list. Visitors to your website can click on an email link or fill in an online form and immediately communicate with you. Where the person seeking a lawyer from the yellow pages has to pick up the phone, dial your number, and often leave a message for you to call, the visitor to your website can with a click send a detailed message directly to you, requesting specific information. Also, web traffic analysis tools allow you to see exactly who has visited your web-

site, and you can target frequent visitors with specific promotional efforts.

2. **Build Your Reputation.** Having an Internet presence can impress upon potential and existing clients that you're an innovative organization, alive to using technology to gain a competitive advantage. Moreover, the content of your website, or a newsletter you distribute via an email mailing list, can persuade prospective clients that you're a knowledgeable and approachable organization worth contacting the next time they need legal help.

3. **Service Existing Clients.** One of the best uses for a website can be to keep existing clients updated on your firm and on legal developments relevant to their business. Consultants will tell you that communication is the single most important factor in maintaining clients. An Internet presence can add to your ability to communicate with existing clients and provide them with enhanced service.

4. **Recruit Talent.** Many new lawyers and law students are Internet savvy. All universities now offer Internet access for students, and you can safely assume that law students considering your firm as a place to article are going to be very familiar with the web. Having a web page can allow prospective recruits to quickly learn about your firm and convince them that yours is a forward-thinking organization that would be an interesting place to practice.

5. **Extend Your Reach.** The Internet community is a massive audience. Over 13.5 million Canadians over age 18 had Internet access at the beginning of 2000, and 71.5 per cent of North Americans are projected to be *regular* Internet users by 2005 (see page 4 for sources). Professionals and managers make up 40 per cent of the Internet community (compared to only 25 per cent of the overall population). These are the clients you are trying to reach and service.

6. **Reduce Your Marketing Costs.** Having a presence on the Internet is (comparatively) cheap. To put up a web page can be less expensive than running a handful of newspaper advertisements. Of course it's possible to spend more, but even the cost of setting up a dedicated web server is not significantly greater than the annual cost of taking out a large yellow pages ad.

7. **Set-up Easily.** Internet technology is very easy to work with. Point-and-click graphical software is the norm, and that goes for the software needed to supply information as well as the programs used by info-consumers. Preparing a web page, for example, is now possible using the most popular word processors. And due to the Internet's open standards, you can call on the whole community of users for support if things go wrong.

To illustrate a few of these points, let's look at some examples. Bennett Jones (http://www.bennettjones.ca/), with offices in Alberta and Toronto, has a section on their

Figure 9.1. *Pushor Mitchell's website*

website devoted to their client base, featuring links to websites of key clients, a detailed listing of significant recent transactions the firm has handled, and information for clients on recent legal developments and issues. The section serves both to showcase the firm's blue chip client list to prospective clients, and to provide some valuable content for existing clients.

The website of Branch MacMaster (http://www.branmac.com/), a Vancouver litigation firm that specializes in class actions, features articles, case summaries, and links

relating to past and potential class actions in British Columbia. New material is added often. The site serves as a tremendous mechanism to pull together the critical mass of applicants that a class action requires. A prospective client is left with the impression that the firm is committed to and knowledgeable in its area of practice; an existing client can keep up with the progress of other class action lawsuits.

Another British Columbia firm, Pushor Mitchell (http://www.pushormitchell.com/) in the province's Interior, uses an email newsletter to provide legal updates to clients. Clients can subscribe to the newsletter by filling out a simple form at the firm's website, and receive by email regular news about changes to the law that may affect the client's situation. This way of distributing information to clients is extremely inexpensive, allows for very timely delivery of information, and can help maintain contact with a client base that is distributed over a large area (as is Pushor Mitchell's Okanagan clientele).

There are hundreds of other examples of law firms using the Internet to great effect (including several listed on page 180). In short, if you are willing to invest the time and energy to make effective use of this new medium, it can create a competitive advantage—something that is extremely important in today's highly competitive marketplace.

AN INTERNET MARKETING PRIMER

Before you begin using the Internet to attract and service clients, you need to be aware of the unique culture of the online world, and the short but vibrant history of marketing on the Internet. Internet marketing strategies have come in three waves:

1. **First Wave: Mass marketing blitzes.** The initial rush of marketers to the Internet realized the medium's power to reach thousands of prospective clients instantly and for pennies. "MAKE MONEY FAST" is now a depressingly familiar subject line in bulk emailings and discussion group postings. The First Wave of mass marketing blitzes has re-

vealed that, in the wrong hands, Internet tools have an unprecedented capacity to inconvenience and annoy huge numbers of people—a few bad marketers have threatened to spoil the game for everybody. This First Wave of Internet marketing is characterized by lack of relevance to recipients, poor netiquette (that is, bad online manners), a high nuisance factor, and low effectiveness.

2. **Second Wave: Broadly targeted marketing to specific groups of users.** Smarter marketers appreciate the importance of marketing being relevant to the prospective client. The Second Wave of Internet marketing features sending emails to users thought to be interested in the marketer's subject area, and posting short, relevant notes to specific, targeted discussion groups.

3. **Third Wave: Highly targeted, one-to-one database marketing.** The Third Wave of Internet marketing strives to reach the right person, with the right offer, at the right time. This strategy, called "one-to-one database marketing," involves developing "intelligent lists" of potential clients, and using techniques to deepen the marketer's understanding of each targeted client on a one-to-one level.

Fortunately for law firms, the evolution of marketing on the Internet is moving steadily away from the First Wave "junk mail" phase of evolution and towards the more focused efforts of the Third Wave, aiming marketing efforts at particular people who need particular goods and services. This new kind of marketing is much better suited to the business development efforts of law firms, which is to say, to the process of selling the unique set of skills available at your firm. There are many people, as an example, who do not need to know about your firm's deep expertise in insurance litigation, but there is a group of people who might like to know about this expertise very much.

As for how you can identify these people and communicate with them directly, gathering information about your clients is central to your efforts to market "one-to-one" with them. "Database marketing" is the practice of gathering and deepening information about existing and prospective clients, and using this information in service of your firm's business development efforts. Sources of client information include past

Third Wave Internet Marketing Tips for Law Firms

There are many ways to market "one-to-one" with prospective or existing clients using the Internet. Here are a few ideas:

- **Establish individual email addresses for each member of your firm.** To allow "one-to-one" contact, make sure that clients can communicate easily with individual lawyers, rather than only with lawfirm@lawfirm.com.

- **Put your email address on your business card.** Hand out your card to prospective clients and invite them to drop you an email. If they do, email them a copy of your online brochure.

- **Provide a service for free.** A brief, regular newsletter that is on topic with your target client's interests will be appreciated and will keep your name top-of-mind. Email your firm newsletter on insurance developments to your insurance clients.

- **Set up that firm website.** A website offers a great way to make information

about your firm available to existing or prospective clients when they want to access it. Put information about your firm, practice areas, and individual lawyers on the site, and include something of value for vistors—again, the firm newsletter is an obvious start, but also consider, for example, a section answering frequently asked questions relating to bankruptcy law (or whatever areas for which you want to be known).

- **Establish a two-way dialogue with your existing and prospective clients.** Put individual lawyers' email addresses on your firm's website, so that visitors can send an email directly to a particular lawyer. Include at your firm's website a questionnaire asking what areas your visitors are interested in, what industry they work in, and so on. Such an online survey can depen your profiles of clients and prospects.

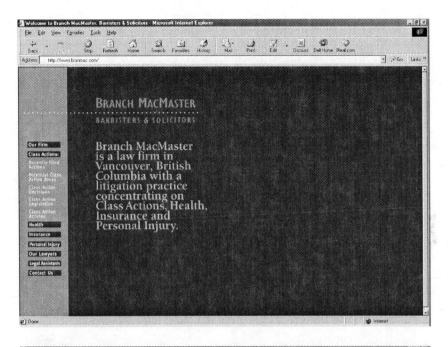

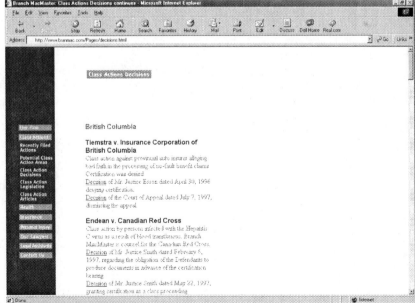

Figure 9.2. Branch MacMaster's website

dealings with the firm, the results of client surveys that you may carry out, responses to mailings of your firm's newsletter, and other client feedback as such can be gathered. The underlying motive is to give your firm an understanding of the legal needs, the interests, and other general preferences of your clients. The result of an effective marketing database is an unprecedented ability to highly target your business development efforts in order to reach the right person, with the right information, at the right time.

SETTING UP A WEBSITE

The process of setting up a website can be distilled to seven key steps:

1. **Determining the site's purpose:** You need to be clear as to why you are establishing the site. Is it to provide information or to sell new services to existing clients? Or is it to generate new clients, either directly from the site or in conjunction with other marketing efforts?

2. **Reserving a domain name:** Domain names, which are the familiar, easy to remember names for computers on the Internet, are handed out by various registries on a first-come, first-served basis.

You will want to take early steps to secure the most compelling variation of your law firm's name as a domain name.

3. **Deciding where to host the site:** You will need to decide whether to set up the site on someone else's computer, or on a web server that you buy and host yourself.

4. **Identifying content:** Easily the main concern in building a website, content is what will draw visitors back to your site.

5. **Designing the site:** Establishing the look and feel of your site and authoring the site, either by yourself or by contracting the work to a web developer.

6. **Advertising the site:** Spreading the word about your website.

7. **Maintaining the site:** Taking the time to keep your site current is key if you want visitors to return often.

DETERMINING THE SITE'S PURPOSE

As a first step in establishing a website, you need to think carefully about how you expect the site to benefit your firm. Are you setting up the site:

1. **To service existing clients?** Is the purpose of the site to provide information to existing clients? To sell new services to existing clients?

2. **To attract new clients?** Is the purpose of the site to generate new clients di-

rectly from the site? To supplement other marketing efforts?

The answers will guide the content you put up, your advertising strategies, and the way you maintain the site. If your purpose is to service existing clients, you will want to put more energy into providing a continual stream of information of value to your existing client base, rather than into advertising the site widely. If your purpose is to attract new clients, a priority will be to advertise the site extensively, both online and offline.

Be sure to set goals that are specific, well defined, and attainable. If you want to draw ten thousand visitors a day, different efforts will be required than if you are simply providing client newsletters or supplemental information to existing clients.

RESERVING A DOMAIN NAME

An early step in setting up a website is to reserve a domain name. (In fact, you really want to take this step when you open an email account, as an email address such as "you@yourfirm.com" is much more compelling than "you@yourISP.com.")

Domain names are the familiar, easy to remember names for computers on the Internet. They correspond to a series of numbers (called Internet Protocol numbers) that serve as routing addresses on the Internet. In the case of your firm, the domain name represents the location on the Internet of the firm's website or email address, as the case may be. Domain names always have two or more parts, separated by dots. Law firm domain names typically include an ab-

breviation of the firm name, although some strive to be more creative. So, for example:

osler.com in the case of Osler, Hoskin & Harcourt LLP
mccarthy.ca in the case of McCarthy Tetrault
envirolaw.com in the case of Dianne Saxe's environmental boutique firm
patentable.com in the case of Oyen Wiggs Green & Mutala, an intellectual property firm

Note the two different suffixes: .com and .ca. These represent the two registration options available to Canadian law firms: registering a .com domain with one of many registrars who have been accredited by the Internet Corporation for Assigned Names and Numbers (ICANN); or registering a .ca domain, which is the top level domain code for Canada, with one of the registrars accredited by the Canadian Internet Registration Authority (CIRA).

A .com domain typically takes the form **yourorg.com**, where **yourorg** is a string derived from the name of your organization or your registered trademark, and **.com** represents a commercial organization.

A .ca domain typically takes the form **yourorg.province.ca**, where **yourorg** is a string derived from the name of your organization or your registered trademark, **.province** is a two letter abbreviation such as .bc if you have a provincial (as compared to a national) presence; and **.ca** represents Canada. Note that until 2000, a .ca domain was given out only if there was some link between your organization's name and the sought after domain name. This requirement was removed in 2000, which means that now anyone can register virtually any untaken .ca domain name (similar to the situation with .com domain names).

The critical thing to keep in mind as far as domain names are concerned is that the registries hand out domain names on a first-come, first-served basis. If you want to ensure that you can use your preferred firm domain name, you must register it. To find out whether your preferred name is still available, you can search one of the many domain name databases maintained by registrars and others. For example, for .com domains, you can search the database of a registrar such as Network Solutions (http://www.networksolutions.com/) or Register.com (http://www.register.com/), or a site that monitors domain issues such as Domain Watch (http://www.domainwatch.com/); for .ca domains, you can search the CIRA database (http://www.cira.ca/).

As for registering a domain name, the process differs for the two types of domains:

To register a .com domain. File an application with one of the dozens of ICANN accredited registrars for .com names. See http://www.icann.org/ for a current list of accredited registrars, including links to their websites. Once at a website for a registrar, you can quickly work through an online application form. The leading registrars were charging a US $35 fee for a one-year registration at the time of publication. It may take up to three days after you submit

the application for the domain name to be accessible.

To register a .ca domain. In late 2000, the .ca Registry function was transferred from CDNet to a newly created body called the Canadian Internet Registration Authority (CIRA). Applications for a .ca domain name can be filed with one of the CIRA accredited registrars for .ca names. See the CIRA website (http://www.cira.ca) for details. At the time of publication, a $50 fee for a one-year registration was expected to be implemented as part of the transfer of the .ca Registry function to CIRA.

DECIDING WHERE TO HOST THE SITE

A website can be set up on someone else's computer, or on a web server that you buy and host yourself. In deciding which approach to take, the key considerations are cost, ease of set-up, and control over access.

From a cost standpoint, $200 to $5,000 per year will cover you if you intend to mount your site elsewhere (depending on the amount of data you want to publish and the scope of services you are provided). To set up your own web server will be more like a $10,000 to $30,000 proposition once all the hardware, connection, software, and other expenses are considered.

As for set-up, to mount your website on someone else's machine involves remarkably little technical effort on your part. At most, you'll want to consider the design options available using HyperText Markup Language (HTML), the language in which web documents are written (although you

A One-Page Guide to Finding a Home for Your Website

A Home Away From Home

To minimize the costs of establishing a website, you may decide to mount it on someone else's machine—for example, that of your Internet Service Provider. These are the kinds of questions to ask in choosing a home for your web page:

1. Will your material be on a shared or dedicated server?

2. How much bandwidth does the ISP support from visitors? 56 Kbps access? ADSL access? A T1 link?

3. How much bandwidth does the ISP itself have? An ISDN (128 Kbps) line, a T1 link, a T3 link or higher?

4. How many visitors can browse your web page simultaneously?

5. What kind of third party support does the ISP have? Do they have 24-hour support in the event of a system failure?

6. Can the ISP assist you in reserving a domain name? What is the cost for this service?

7. What does it cost for the ISP to host your website? Do extra charges apply if visitors exceed a certain maximum? If data stored exceeds a certain maximum?

Setting up Your Own Web Server

Should you decide to set up your own web server, these are the basic building blocks you need:

Hardware: You need to dedicate a computer to the undertaking. Some opt for a UNIX machine (a Sun workstation, for example) for their greater stability and performance. Others prefer the lower cost and easier set-up offered by a PC or a MacIntosh. A Pentium III, for example, with 512MB of RAM, should come in around $10,000 and handle moderate Internet traffic.

Network access. You need a dedicated connection to the Internet. To support moderate traffic, you'll likely want at least an ISDN line (64 or 128 Kbps), or preferably an ADSL line (384 Kbps and up) or a T1 line (1.5 Mbps). See page 35 for a comparison of the speed and cost of various Internet connection options.

Software. You need to be running the communication package that lets your computer talk to the Internet in its own language, which is TCP/IP. You'll also need web server software for your platform. There are many programs available, for all platforms. Among the best and most popular are web servers from Microsoft, Sun Microsystems, and Novell.

Security. A firewall is mandatory to keep visitors away from the data on your office network. Refer to the discussion of trespassers and firewalls in Chapter Three.

won't have to learn the language itself if you don't want to; there are scores of web page designers eager to help you prepare your web page, as discussed below). To set up your own server, on the other hand, is by no means a quantum leap into techno-hell (learning UNIX is no longer a requirement), but it does involve a number of substantial considerations, from securing a beefy enough computer to adequately serve the anticipated traffic, to establishing a dedicated connection to the Internet, to configuring web server software and setting up a firewall.

Finally, with respect to control, if you mount your site elsewhere, visitors can access it only on the terms established by your website landlord (although many website hosts are very flexible in negotiating terms). This means that the bandwidth of your web host's connection to the Internet determines the speed at which visitors can view and download data from your site. The number of visitors accommodated overall by your web host can also impact the way users see your page: if visitors to other web pages hosted by your landlord are sharing the lines with your page's visitors, this will slow data transfer. And if your web host's machine goes down, people can't see your page. Plus, some web hosts don't support certain types of web technology, such as customized database programming, which is becoming a very popular way to serve up content on more dynamic websites. If you set up your own web server on the other hand, you have complete control over all of these matters: the bandwidth offered to visitors, the number of visitors sharing the same lines, the stability of your server machine, and the type of underlying technology used. But you also have the resulting responsibility for these issues as well.

IDENTIFYING CONTENT

Content is easily your main concern in building a website. The whole point of this exercise, after all, is to persuade clients and potential clients to visit your website and learn more about your law firm and its services. If you don't provide them with content of interest to them, you can't count on them making return visits. You may be satisfied with this: mounting a firm brochure on the web can still put your firm name before a large audience. But it's not exploiting the web's enormous potential to do much, much more—to put your knowledge before the world and to enhance communication with current and prospective clients, as well as with your peers.

So, what information can you mount on your web page? Try your internal firm newsletter for starters. Remember that content isn't just for new clients. One of best uses for a website can be to keep existing clients (or even lawyers and staff within the firm) updated on your firm.

Many firms now offer as part of their web page a section on firm activities—an online hypertext bulletin, if you will, keeping clients and others informed about the firm. Heenan Blaikie (http://www.heenanblaikie.com/), for example, features news of firm lawyers appointed as partners, presentations or publications by firm lawyers, and news of major client developments in a What's New section. Other firms feature media articles highlighting the firm, individual lawyers, or cases the firm has handled.

If you also currently prepare a newsletter for clients, put it on your web page. The cost is minimal compared to mailing or faxing copies of the newsletter to clients. A web newsletter is also easier and cheaper to update. Best of all, it can be archived at your website permanently, creating a kind of online library of newsletters for clients and others to browse when they're seeking specific information.

Some firms are going further and putting on their websites collections of materials in their areas of specialization. Articles on significant legal issues, Frequently Asked Questions (FAQ) lists on legal topics, summaries of key cases or statutes, and links to related information elsewhere on the Internet are featured on many Canadian law firm websites. For example, Clark, Wilson (http://www.cwilson.com/) has distinct areas of their website for each of 20 industries, where firm publications, representative transactions, and relevant industry links are combined with photos and biographies of the firm lawyers whose practice

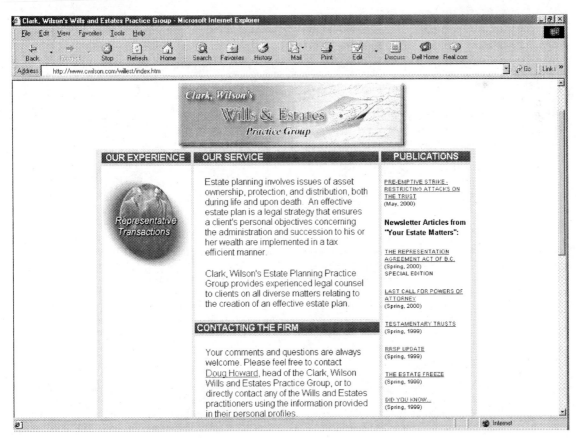

Figure 9.3. Clark Wilson's website

Top 10 Law Firm Websites

Of the hundreds of law firms that are now on the Internet, many have created attractive and valuable sites. Here is a (by no means exhaustive) selection of ten of the better firm websites:

Bennet Jones. Lots of fresh content, and a good dose of personality in the form of community and individual pursuits.
http://www.bennettjones.ca/

Bereskin & Parr. Extensive commentary, updates, and links on intellectual property law.
http://www.bereskinparr.com/

Blake, Cassels & Graydon. Extensive collection of newsletters and publications.
http://www.blakes.ca/

Branch MacMaster. Articles, case summaries, and links relating to past and potential class actions in British Columbia, from this Vancouver litigation firm that specializes in class actions.
http://www.branmac.com/

Clark, Wilson. "Industry focus" areas of their site combine firm publications and relevant industry links with descriptions of the firm lawyers whose practice relates to that industry.
http://www.cwilson.com/

McCarthy Tetrault. Extensive publications section, and lots of updated content.
http://www.mccarthy.ca/

Joel Miller's Family Law Centre. A remarkably extensive collection of family law resources from this Toronto practitioner.
http://www.familylawcentre.com/

Osler, Hoskin & Harcourt LLP. Well-designed site features deep and often updated collection of newsletters and publications.
http://www.osler.com/

Pushor Mitchell. This mid-size BC firm uses an email newsletter to provide legal updates to clients.
http://www.pushormitchell.com/

Dianne Saxe's envirolaw.com. Updates and resources in environmental law from this environmental boutique firm.
http://www.envirolaw.com/

relates to that industry. Visitors can immediately see who the lawyers are that service that area, and the quality of the work and information produced by those lawyers.

There are countless other law firms using their websites effectively, but the sidebar, Top 10 Law Firm Websites, lists ten of the better ones.

DESIGNING THE SITE

Once you've established what content to include in your firm's website, the next step is designing and authoring it.

The language used to create documents for the web is HyperText Markup Language (HTML). HTML is a simple implementation of Standard Generalized Markup Language (SGML), an international standard for the description of marked-up electronic text. You don't have to know anything about HTML. The most popular word processors already have added the capability to automatically generate a web document. There are also easy-to-use web page editing programs available such as Microsoft Front-Page (http://www.microsoft.com/) and Allaire HomeSite (http://www.allaire.com/). Moreover, there are scores of web developers eager to help you prepare your web page—consult your local business and computer papers, or the web, for listings.

If you do retain a web developer, be aware that there are several things to pay special attention to as you negotiate an agreement with the developer:

1. **Who owns copyright to the site?** You and your developer may be considered "joint authors" of the site under copyright law, with the result that both of you will have complete rights to exploit the material, subject to a duty to account to the other for profits. Be sure to specify in the contract with the developer that the firm owns copyright to the site.

2. **Who owns the domain name?** Many developers will automatically register the domain name for sites they design. Be sure to specify that the firm owns the domain name, and (particularly important where the developer is your Internet Service Provider) that the firm can move the domain name to a new host at any time.

3. **Who owns the underlying code?** Be clear on what is included in the contract price: does the price include ownership over the underlying programming behind the web pages?

4. **Who has artistic control?** Deciding what constitutes an attractive website design is a highly subjective matter. Be clear on how the decision will be made as to the final design, and how many different iterations of the design are included in the contract price.

5. **Will the developer receive credit for its work?** Many developers will want to see a credit line on your site, with a link back to their website. Consider specifying whether to allow such a credit, and if so, where and how prominent the credit will be.

For those (even those who are using a web developer to design your site) who want a taste of the nuts and bolts of HTML, we have provided a one-page primer (see below). Whether or not you author your own page, you will want to consider the key design goals of any web page: **good layout**, **easy navigation**, and **minimizing bandwidth**.

1. **Layout.** The best web pages are aesthetically pleasing, balanced, and un-

Learning HTML in a Page

HTML, or HyperText Markup Language, is the language used to create documents for the web. As a markup language, HTML is not so much concerned about the appearance of a document as its structure. An HTML document contains tags, or code, defining its elements: headings, paragraphs, lists, emphasized text. It doesn't worry so much about indicating the exact font size, typeface, or style of the text – that can be left up to the web client software to determine. The client software sees a chunk of text defined as a heading and shows it as 16-point Helvetica, or 24-point Times New Roman. The web author doesn't have to specify this (although in fact many web authors do).

Web page editing software programs are fully graphical, so you never have to see raw HTML code if you don't want to. Still, it is useful to understand the underlying structure of a web page, to appreciate the possibilities of web page design. In general, HTML tags begin with a "<" and end with a ">." Most tags have a beginning tag and an end tag. A document's title, for example, would appear between the beginning title tag <TITLE> and end title tag </TITLE>.

Basic HTML Tags Include:

<TITLE> document title

<H1>–<H6> heading 1–6

<UL> unnumbered list

<ADDRESS> email address

<IMG SRC . . . > inline GIF image

 line break

<I> italic

<B> bold

<A HREF . . .> hypertext link

Linking to Other Documents:

The chief power of HTML comes from its ability to link text to another document. HTML's single hypertext tag is <A>, which stands for anchor. The use of the anchor tag takes this form:

<A HREF="**destination URL**"> The text that will be highlighted as the hypertext link</A>

So the example

<A HREF="http://cba.org">Canadian Bar Association</A>

makes the words "Canadian Bar Association" the highlighted hypertext link to the website for the CBA. By clicking on the highlighted text, the user would be transported to the CBA's web page.

If you want to explore HTML and web authoring issues further, there are many outstanding resources on the web, including CNET.com (http://www.cnet.com/), WebDeveloper.com (http://www.webdeveloper.com/), and webmonkey (http://hotwired.lycos.com/webmonkey/).

cluttered. Strive for readability. You want the first page of material to appear clearly on a standard 15 inch monitor. Try to avoid the cutesy options offered by so many authoring tools: avoid background colours that obscure text, for example. And don't even think about using the <BLINK> tag (which causes text to blink on and off). Everyone but its creator agrees that it's irritating.

2. **Navigation.** The best web pages are intuitive to navigate. They flow well from page to page, and provide links to drill down to more detailed information. Be careful not to create culs-de-sac and dead ends: always give users a way to get back to the opening page of your material.

3. **Bandwidth.** A good web page takes up a minimum of bandwidth, to ensure quick response times. Your page should be lean enough to download within thirty seconds on a 33.6 Kbps modem. Few things are more frustrating for users with modest desktop set-ups than waiting for two minutes while a massive image of a firm nameplate loads. Consider using thumbnail anchors for any graphic over 60 Kb: this allows the user to decide whether to take the time to view the larger graphic.

ADVERTISING THE SITE

Once your website is complete, you'll want to spread the word. A stunningly designed website is only useful if people come and look at it.

Search engines such as AltaVista, HotBot, and Excite are one way visitors can find your site. Although some search engines will "find" your site with software that spiders the web for new sites, it is worth spending a few hours submitting your site to the major search engines (see Chapter Seven for a discussion of, and addresses for, the major sites). You can typically submit your site to a search engine by clicking an "Add URL" button on the engine's website and submitting the requested information. Or you can use one of the many search engine submission services, but you lose the opportunity to customize your information for each search engine.

There are also several ways to enhance your findability with search engines. You can use programming techniques such as metatags—hidden codes in the pages on your website that help you specify certain keywords by which a search engine will index your site. You can buy banner advertising that will appear when anyone searches for certain keywords using a search engine. Or you can use word placement strategically on your site to give it a higher priority in response to certain keyword searches. All these techniques require a good understanding of how search engines work, a topic that is discussed beginning on page 123.

Also important in advertising your site will be getting your page listed in the major directories and search engines that specialize in law. See page 142 for a listing of some key directories to law and to Canadian law.

As well, don't forget offline advertising. Include news of your new website anywhere you normally advertise: in your firm brochure, in your print ads, in your client newsletter. Be sure to include your website address in your letterhead and business cards. Have firm lawyers mention the website in any presentation or seminar they give. Tell your clients, employees, colleagues, and friends about the site. Even on the Internet, nothing works better than word of mouth.

Maintaining the Site

If you want users to return often to your web page, you should be sure to set aside time to keep it current. A list of inoperative links to other sites that have since changed their URLs can be thoroughly frustrating for the user, greeted at every click with a "Destination Not Found" message. A discussion of "the hottest legal cases" that is approaching a year old betrays a waning interest in being an information supplier. Establishing a website, in fact, is not really worth the effort unless you are willing to keep the information up-to-date and useful.

As well, consider that ideally, putting information on the web will not be a one-time affair. The whole point is to facilitate communication and information exchange, so be prepared to respond to email and other enquiries flowing from your website. Visitors to your site that are moved to send a message will be hoping for a timely response.

Using Internet Tools Within the Firm

Whether or not you're interested in providing information over the Internet, the technology involved offers a powerful and modestly priced way to supply information internally, to your own lawyers and staff. In other words, you don't need to be on the Internet in order to make use of Internet software. In fact, the use of web-based technology on an internal network to distribute information within an organization is so popular that a term has evolved to describe the practice: the *intranet*.

Why Create an Intranet?

Indeed, the term intranet has become something of a technology buzzword. Market research studies of intranet use (by O'Reilly & Associates and Forrester Research, for example) are glowing, reporting that approximately 50 per cent of surveyed companies have created or are actively working on intranets. Many very successful companies (like Federal Express and 3M) are using their intranets on an every-day basis for selected corporate applications. VISA says that its intranet has allowed them to eliminate two million paper documents every day.

Why would a law firm want to join the intranet revolution? Consider one example. Precedent materials and research memorandums are at the core of every law firm's practice. Many firms have spent thousands of person-hours and dollars collecting these documents into paper-based archive systems, only to see the system underutilized and documents rewritten from scratch over and over. A paper-based archive is hard to keep up-to-date, can be hard for individual lawyers to find, is accessible by only one lawyer at a time, and is prone to having pages go missing.

The resources to convert the paper archive into electronic form, on the other hand, have been (prior to intranet technology) enormous: the software is typically expensive, a programmer needs to set it up, training costs are high, and at the end of the day, the programs often aren't easy for users to learn.

An intranet effectively solves these problems. With web technology, a firm's intellectual property can be organized and distributed at a low cost, with modest set-up effort, in an easy-to-use medium. Precedent and research materials that are in electronic form can be converted with relative ease into web format. Firm staff and lawyers can access the documents from any kind of computer, using their preferred web browser, and using easy-to-learn point and click commands. No special training is required; if an employee has browsed the web, they will know how to get around the intranet. And best of all, the intranet can deliver other kinds of information to internal users. The firm newsletter, policy manuals, the phone directory, training materials, a schedule of firm events, employee manuals—all of these materials can be delivered to every desktop in the firm from an internal web server.

Indeed, the benefits of an intranet are many:

1. **Rich format.** The web's vaunted multimedia capabilities allow information of all types to be delivered over the network: not just news of the firm retreat, but a photo of the hotel where everyone will be staying, and a map of how to get there.

2. **Platform independence.** There are web client programs for virtually every hardware platform and operating system on the planet. If your office has a mix of machines, delivering information with an internal web server means that everyone can access it, using their preferred platform and browser software.

3. **Ease-of-use.** The web's point-and-click graphical interface is intuitive and easy to learn. Moreover, the web's hypertext linking makes navigation a breeze, allowing users to painlessly drill down to information they want.

4. **Ease of set-up.** Unlike most proprietary solutions, the web is simple technology not only for users but for those administering the system. Web server software uses a graphical interface for point-and-click server installation, configuration and maintenance. As well, the web supports multiple data types, so that much current firm data can be easily converted to web format. Text files, word processed documents, databases, even spreadsheets can be programmed to dump information seamlessly into web format.

5. **Open standards.** Web technology is based on open standards. It's not a proprietary solution, so it doesn't lock you in to a particular vendor. In the event things go sour for the company that helps you set up your intranet, you can switch to another supplier without losing any of your legacy data or incurring conversion costs.

6. **Third party support.** In the event things go awry with your intranet, you can call on the expertise of thousands of system administrators and consultants participating in discussion groups on the Internet. The web, in fact, is supported by an enormous global community capable of producing products and services that no single vendor could possibly hope to match.

WHAT CAN YOU PUT ON YOUR INTRANET?

The web, as discussed, supports a broad range of data types and media. What you put on your firm intranet is limited only by your imagination and resources. Start by considering what you already have in electronic form that people in your office need to access. Consider as well whether the current process for reaching that data is cumbersome or ineffective. Here are a few suggestions for what could form part of your law firm intranet:

• links to frequently used external websites;

• client matter lists;

• conflicts checking;

• office Rolodex;

• tickler calendar;

• outstanding bills;

• client billing histories;

• client payment histories;

• office-wide announcements;

• office policies;

• frequently asked questions;

• firm research memorandums;

• firm precedents;

• recommended CLE materials; and

• practice area web pages.

HOW DO YOU BUILD AN INTRANET?

You will need five pieces to build a basic intranet:

1. TCP/IP running on your Local Area Network;

2. a web server;

3. web browsers for every machine that will be using the intranet;

4. something to publish (content—the reason you're doing this); and

5. some way to convert your content into web format.

TCP/IP. TCP/IP is a network protocol, or more specifically the set of protocols that governs Internet operations. Even though TCP/IP is different from Novell Netware or Appletalk/Ethertalk, it doesn't conflict with those other network architectures, and you can run them all over the same network wiring (using the same network adapters)—all at the same time. You do have to install a TCP/IP "communications stack" (a set of drivers) on each machine in your network. Fortunately, Windows 95/98 now comes with a TCP/IP stack built-in, as do Windows NT, OS/2 and UNIX.

Web server. Functionally, the web server is simply where your web-based documents are stored. Technically, the web server is the software that runs HTTP (HyperText Transfer Protocol), making web pages available to users. There's server software for almost every type of hardware platform, and every price range. Among the best and most popular are programs from Microsoft, Sun Microsystems, and Novell. For best performance, a server should be installed on a dedicated machine. Remember that web technology doesn't require that you match your server and your user workstations—even if all your user machines are running Windows, you can use a UNIX machine as your server. Finally, if you're setting up your network for office-wide access to the Internet, then you'll need a good firewall as well (see Chapter Three for a discussion of security and firewalls).

Web browsers. The web browser is the software that runs on the users' workstations, allowing them to look at web pages and files stored on the server. Most people in your office will already be familiar with

web browsers and have their favourite program, be it Microsoft's Internet Explorer, Netscape's Navigator, or another browser. Fortunately, if some people in your office prefer one browser and others want to use another, they will all work fine.

Content. The content, of course, is the reason you're doing this. Look for content that's already in electronic form, possibly starting with the suggestion list included above. An attractive feature of intranet technology is that the technical pieces are relatively easy, which means you can concentrate on choosing and organizing content.

Converting content to web format. Converting your content into web format, or HyperText Markup Language (HTML), is a lot easier than you might think. You can automatically generate an HTML document using any of the most popular word processing programs. Alternatively, there are separate programs that can be used to create web documents, or convert documents in other formats into HTML code. Some of the leading web editors are Microsoft FrontPage, Allaire HomeSite, and Macromedia Dreamweaver.

That's it. You're set to launch your intranet. For further details on implementing these building blocks, the Internet is, not surprisingly, chock full of resources to help you out. The Intranet Journal website (http://intranetjournal.earthweb.com/) features white papers and demonstration sites, as well as links to various providers of intranet tools. Many of the technology publications online also have extensive resources relating to intranets—PC Magazine Online is among the better ones for non-technical users (http://www.zdnet.com/pcmag/).

EXTRANETS: THE NEXT WAVE OF ACTIVITY

Yet another trendy web technology term has emerged in recent years: the *extranet*. Like an intranet, an extranet lets you distribute information in a way that's (comparatively) easy to maintain and allows users to access the information through an easy-to-use web browser. The difference between an intranet and an extranet is the audience. Instead of (in the case of an intranet) providing information only to staff and colleagues inside your office, an extranet opens the electronic door to Internet-connected clients as well—providing access to files, materials, and applications related to the clients' specific matters.

Building an extranet is a more complicated undertaking than building an intranet, since you've got to deal with additional levels of security and carefully segregate each client's information into a private area. But the effect can be significant; fundamentally changing the mechanism by which you deliver legal services to your clients. When done right, this improves not only the timeliness of your services, but the overall value of those services to your client as well.

Examples of information that might be included on a law firm's extranet include:

- working drafts of documents for review or comment;

- status reports on files;

- timelines and due dates;

- settlement papers and instructions;

- transcripts of evidence;

- lists of documents and full text documents;

- client-oriented FAQ lists; and

- billing information.

For example, in a larger litigation matter, an extranet could be used to provide client representatives with access to transcripts of evidence given on discovery and witness statements. On a grander scale, all relevant documents could be scanned and indexed for an extranet, which could then serve as a kind of document repository for the case. Searching the repository would be similar to searching a website, a task with which non-technical users are increasingly comfortable.

Litigation support and case management activities are in fact especially well suited to extranet technology. A recent trend has seen Application Service Providers (ASPs) offer extranet-like features over their websites that firms and clients can make use of for litigation management. Instead of setting up your own extranet, you effectively contract with the ASP to provide you and your clients with extranet-like capabilities on the ASP's website. CaseCentral.com (http://www.casecentral.com/) is a United States-based web-hosted document management service that's targeted at large-case litigation support, but that can be used for smaller litigation just as well. And Ringtail Solutions (http://www.ringtail.com.au/) is an Australian company that's starting to offer a suite of web-hosted case management products in North America.

In building an extranet, security is absolutely key. Confidential client information must remain confidential, for the integrity of the site and for the preservation of solicitor-client privilege (see the discussion of this point at page 204). Although no security measure can be labeled foolproof, web-based solutions have developed to dramatically decrease the likelihood of breach of security. Internet Service Providers and ASPs with experience in security issues can implement layers of protection by using techniques such as IP filtering, IP tunneling, Secure Socket Layers (SSL) client/server key encryption, and server-resident username and password restrictions. Now that the technology is maturing, extranets offer tremendous promise as a way for firms to truly alter the ways in which they service clients.

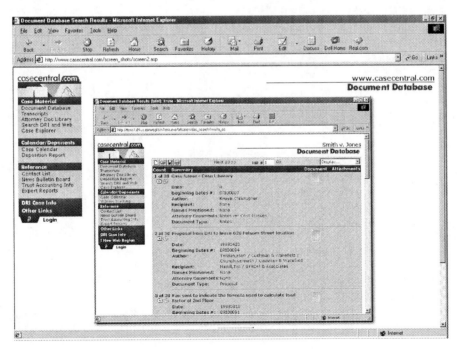

Figure 9.4. *CaseCentral.com's website*

10 INTERNET LEGAL ISSUES

THE CENSORSHIP/FREE SPEECH DEBATE
A BRAVE NEW WORLD
OBSCENITY
DEFAMATION
HATE PROPAGANDA
HARASSMENT
PUBLICATION BANS

PRIVACY

SECURE COMMUNICATIONS

INTELLECTUAL PROPERTY LAW ISSUES
COPYRIGHT
TRADEMARKS

ECOMMERCE LEGAL ISSUES
RULES GOVERNING ELECTRONIC COMMERCE
INTERNATIONAL ECOMMERCE

In her book *When Old Technologies Were New* (New York: Oxford University Press, 1988), Carolyn Marvin uncovered a 1905 editorial in the journal *Telephony* that considered the impact of the introduction of the telephone one hundred years ago:

> The invention of new machinery, devices and process is continually bringing up new questions of law, puzzling judges, lawyers, and laymen.

This chapter is where we take a look at some of the many legal issues raised by the Internet. Entire books have already been written on Internet law, and we can't possibly provide a comprehensive discussion in the few pages available here. But we will attempt to introduce the broad concepts as they are now emerging in several areas:

1. **Censorship and free speech:** the debate between those who want the Internet to be a place where all are free to speak their minds and those who want to protect other interests and potentially vulnerable parties. A tour of the main battlegrounds in the conflict: obscene material, defamatory statements, hate propaganda, harassment, and publication bans.

2. **Privacy:** the threat posed by the Internet to individual privacy by making information about us more accessible to others, and by increasing the chances our exchanges will be overheard.

3. **Confidential communications:** the special case of electronic communication between lawyer and client: whether sending an unencrypted email is a waiver of privilege.

4. **Intellectual property:** the threat posed by the inexpensive copying and distribution facilities of the Internet to those who create or own information. Also, the many trademark legal issues that have emerged with the Internet.

5. **Ecommerce legal issues:** among the many commercial legal issues spawned by the rush of business to the Internet are what rules should govern electronic commerce, and to what legal system should a company doing business on the Internet be subject.

THE CENSORSHIP/ FREE SPEECH DEBATE

"Freedom of the press is guaranteed only to those who own one," runs the A.J. Liebling quip. Well, you now *do* own one. The Internet has made it dead easy for almost anyone to put their thoughts before a large audience (275 million and counting). Even the most disenfranchised can load up their musings or their manifesto for that matter on any one of hundreds of online community websites, for free, so long as they have access to a computer.

This Everyman's Press quality has led many commentators to describe the Internet as the most powerful democratizing force of our time. In his article "Freedom of Speech and Privacy in the Information Age,"[1] Mr.

Justice Sopinka characterized the Internet as an invaluable and inexpensive way to communicate ideas—especially critical ones—to a wide audience: "electronic media such as Internet are the posters of the late twentieth century."

Of course, just like posters, the Internet can offend. Democracy reveals not just the good in people; it also can expose the dark side. People who are free to say and do more or less what they choose sometimes say things that aren't very nice, or do things that are just plain evil. The Internet is no exception to this reality. If you look for it on the Internet, you will find obscene material, statements that defame, violent or hateful speech, and behaviour that is harassing.

A BRAVE NEW WORLD

Marshall McLuhan wrote in *Understanding Media* (New York: McGraw-Hill, 1964), "It is one of the ironies of Western man that he has never felt any concern about invention as a threat to his way of life." Considering the recent hype—indeed hysteria—tying the Internet to pornographers, terrorists, hackers, software pirates, pedophiles, and other evils, McLuhan may have been wrong this once. With the explosive growth of the Internet has come the inevitable backlash, and a good part of the finger pointing has been at offensive material available online. As we'll see below, the Internet is viewed as a threat by many.

This is somewhat understandable. The Internet is a complicated place. There is the usual potential for material to offend others. But the Internet has added to the mix four other features, complicating the debate over whether the Internet should be censored: it has made speech cheap and therefore more plentiful, the Internet's culture and its design resist censorship, the Internet makes it easier than ever to do offensive things without getting caught, and the Internet spans a planet of varying legal systems.

1. **Cheap speech.** As mentioned, the cost of being heard on the Internet is virtually nil. To get a printed document before a wide audience would ring up substantial paper, production, and distribution costs. To put a web page, an email, or a discussion group posting before a worldwide audience can cost as little as a few cents. In an article in the *Yale Law Journal*, Eugene Volokh of UCLA described the Internet as offering "cheap speech." Never before has it been so cheap to talk, and inevitably more people are talking, which multiplies the chances someone will be offended.

2. **Internet culture and design.** "The Net interprets censorship as damage, and routes around it." This quote from John Gilmore, co-founder of the Electronic Frontier Foundation, appears often on the Internet. It reflects the feeling of many Internet users that the network, designed to resist nuclear attack, can also shrug off attempts to regulate it. The Internet's global reach and decentralized design, the sentiment goes, make it unpoliceable. Also evident in Gilmore's quote is the libertarian

ethos that some still say defines the Internet: no one owns us, we can say and do whatever we want, regulators be damned.

3. **Anonymity and encryption.** The Internet provides entirely new ways to do offensive things without getting caught. To post material anonymously, for example, is surprisingly simple. Programs called anonymous remailers can accept a message from anywhere on the Internet, automatically strip out any information that identifies the source, and then post the message to a mailing list or discussion group. Forging a posting is also trivially easy. Digital signatures provide a way to confirm the real author of a message, but the underlying encryption technology actually opens up another can of worms. Offensive material can be sent across the Internet in encrypted format using free, publicly available programs. This creates a potential law enforcement problem. Indeed, authorities in Canada and the United States complain that encryption technology is so strong that they often can't crack it.

4. **Virtual community.** The Internet spans the globe, and hundreds of different legal systems. Material available on the Internet may be legal under one system, but illegal under others. Should the law of the locale where material is mounted apply? Or does it make more sense to enforce the law of the locale where material is viewed? Or are new laws required that reflect the standards of the virtual community itself?

With all of these unique concerns to consider, it's no wonder that many are frightened by the way free speech plays out on the Internet and want to clamp down on it. As we'll see below, government, universities, online providers, even Internet users themselves have all been involved in attempts or plans to censor material available on the Internet.

The following discussion is broken down by the main battlegrounds in the Internet censorship-free speech debate: obscene material, defamatory statements, hate propaganda, harassment, and publication bans.

OBSCENITY

The fact that obscene material exists on the Internet has been well documented. Media reports on obscenity online are so plentiful that a non-user could not be blamed for thinking that pornography dominates the Internet. It doesn't of course, although there have for years been corners of the Internet that contain pornographic material.

Long-standing examples are the newsgroups in the alt.sex hierarchy. Over the years, many organizations that carry newsgroups on their servers have blocked access to these newsgroups. In 1995, for example, the online provider CompuServe temporarily blocked its estimated 4 million users from accessing all sex-related newsgroups, citing pressure from law enforcement authorities in Germany who purportedly threatened a crackdown on pornography online. Access to all but the most obscene groups was later reinstated, but with filters that parents could use to keep their children from accessing undesirable material. America Online and many other major portal sites offer similar filters for not just newsgroups but also for websites that contain material that is deemed obscene.

Newsgroup bans can be traced back as far back as 1988, when the University of Waterloo banned several newsgroups after a controversy erupted over jokes posted to the newsgroup rec.humor.funny. In 1992 when the issue of pornography on the Internet first entered the media spotlight in Canada, several universities responded by cancelling newsgroups, mostly in the alt.sex hierarchy. The University of British Columbia, one of the universities to initially impose a ban, struck a Task Force on the Appropriate Use of Information Technology at the University of British Columbia. The task force concluded that the university shouldn't ban electronic communication between willing participants that others find offensive. The task force's report noted that no such ban applied to other forms of communication, and existing laws and policies applied to data communication. That included obscenity laws, human rights legislation, and the university's sexual harassment policy. The task force recommended that it should be made clear to users of the Internet that they are responsible for what they say. UBC revoked its newsgroup ban soon after.

Most commentators agree with the UBC task force, even though other campuses are still banning newsgroups many years later. Mr. Justice Sopinka, for example, wrote in "Freedom of Speech and Privacy in the Information Age":

Difficult issues also arise in the context of universities which take action to ban certain communications found to be offensive and undesirable. First, one must ask whether it is not preferable to permit the expression and allow the criminal or civil law to deal with the individual who publishes obscene, defamatory or hateful messages rather than prevent speech before it can be expressed. Otherwise, individuals may be putting themselves in the positions of the courts to determine what is obscene and what is acceptable.[2]

Courts, in other words, should act as censors; not university administrators or online providers.

Obscenity laws, for their part, are well established in Canada, and extend to online communication. The *Criminal Code* makes it an offence to make, print, publish, distribute, or circulate "...any obscene written matter, picture, model, phonograph record or other thing whatever... ."[3] An obscene posting to a newsgroup or a web page would surely fall within this definition. The definition has been found to include obscene images stored on an adult-oriented Bulletin Board System: *R. v. Hurtubise.*[4] (A Bulletin Board System, or BBS, is based on older technology that uses the regular telephone line system instead of the Internet, but is otherwise analogous to a website.)

The courts have made clear in cases such as *R. v. Butler*[5] that obscenity laws impose a reasonable restriction on the right to free expression. That is so even though the right to speak freely is constitutionally affirmed by section 2(b) of the *Charter of Rights,*[6] and in the words of Cory J. in *Edmonton Journal v. Alberta (Attorney General)*, "it is difficult to imagine a guaranteed right more important to a democratic society than freedom of expression."[7]

In the United States, an attempt to legislate in this area failed. The *Communications Decency Act*[8] *(CDA)* was voted into law in 1996, and made it a criminal offense to send "indecent material by the Internet into others computers." The American Civil Liberties Union challenged the CDA on the ground that it banned speech protected by the First Amendment and subjected the Internet to restrictions that were out of line with regulations faced by other mediums. In *Reno v. ACLU*,[9] the United States Supreme Court agreed, unanimously holding that the act violated the First Amendment.

So why are universities and online providers getting involved and acting as censors? The answer is simple: exposure. They're worried about being pursued under obscenity laws themselves. And not without reason. Several countries have passed legislation making online providers liable for any obscene material passing through their lines.

Which raises one of the core issues in the debate over Internet censorship: who is liable for offensive material posted to the network? Clearly the party posting such material is liable. But the ability to post messages anonymously and the global reach of the Internet can make it hard to catch the original offender. Which has made many wonder whether those providing access to the material or who carry the material are also liable. Are online providers liable for offensive content users load up on web pages residing at their site? Are newsgroup servers hosted by online providers and universities liable for offensive postings to newsgroups carried by the servers?

At the root of this debate is whether online providers and newsgroup servers are to be treated as *publishers* or *common carriers*. If they are to be treated as publishers, then like newspapers and radio stations they would be liable for the content on their systems. If they are to be treated as common carriers, then similar to telephone companies, they would not be liable for the content of the information flowing over their wires.

Many argue that to treat online providers as publishers imposes an impossible burden on them to check every file on their systems, not to mention raise privacy concerns for their users. And it realizes the situation Mr. Justice Sopinka feared: individuals— online operators, university administrators, and so on - are put in the position of having to determine what is obscene and what is acceptable. Yet if such a burden is not imposed, it's unlikely online providers could be held liable for any obscene content they carry. That is because the courts have struck down as unconstitutional a section of Canada's obscenity law stating that ignorance of the nature of the material is no defence: *R. v. Metro News Ltd*.[10]

However, where an online provider *did* know the nature of the material on their system, the provider has been held criminally responsible. In *R. v. Hurtubise, supra*, a British Columbia couple operating an adult-only pornographic Bulletin Board Service was convicted of distributing obscene material contrary to section 163(1)(a) of the *Criminal Code*. It is open for debate whether a court would impose this kind of responsibility on an Internet provider, with their infinitely more varied content than that of an adult BBS. It would be hard to believe a pornographic BBS operator's claim that they weren't aware of the pornographic nature of the material on their own system. But it would much harder to disprove an Internet provider's claim to be unaware that mixed in with the array of professional and benign hobbyist material on their system was a web page with obscene pictures available for downloading.

One final point is worth noting relating to obscenity online. In a world where everyone on the planet can view the content of a website, which community's standards should be applied to judge the offensiveness or legality of the material? In *United States v. Thomas*,[11] the accused operated an adult only pornographic BBS out of Milpitas, California, but they were prosecuted in Memphis, Tennessee. Authorities actually enlisted a Tennessee postal inspector to download images from the BBS. The jury then considered the content of the computer system against the community standards of Tennessee, not the arguably more liberal community standards of California. The Thomas' were convicted of transmitting obscenity through interstate phone lines, a conviction later upheld on appeal. The borderless community issue raises its head.

For each issue raised by obscene material on the Internet, there are several proposed solutions. As mentioned, portal sites like America Online use technological filters that screen out material that has been "tagged" as adult oriented. Programs such as SurfWatch and NetNanny include databases of sites containing offensive material—"porno-troves"—and block a user's attempts to go to such sites. In Singapore, a regulatory agency maintains a list of banned sites and requires Internet providers to block users from accessing sites on the list. And then there are others who say leave things exactly as they are, and let time-honoured strategies like parental responsibility and peer review oversee Internet behaviour.

DEFAMATION

There are millions of messages sent across the Internet every day. So it's not surprising that some of them get a little testy, insulting, even defamatory. Internet users have a term for this kind of message. It's called a flame. Some users even announce FLAME ON before lashing into a rant (though you never see FLAME OFF when they're done).

The question arises: can you sue a "flamer" for defamation?

Several court cases have held that you can. An expression is defamatory if it tends to lower a person's reputation in the estimation of right-thinking members of society generally, or to expose a person to hatred, contempt, or ridicule. To be actionable, the expression must be communicated to a third person. In *Campbell v. Cartmell*,[12] the Ontario Superior Court found that the test for defamation was met when it considered several letters posted on the Toronto District School Board's website. The court awarded damages totalling $17,000 to the Board, three former school board officials, and a teacher, over defamatory letters falsely alleging criminal acts that were given "broad written publication on the [Board's] website as well as to the employees, peers and staff of the School Board and to municipal and provincial politicians." The letters were also posted to the Board's internal bulletin system. The criminal acts alleged included fraud, forgery, theft, harassing phone calls, and threatening. In *Southam Inc. v. Chelekis*,[13] the plaintiff journalist was awarded $875,000 in damages for libel for the "worldwide distribution" of a newsletter article by means of "electronic communication" to private investors and to "news distributors, particularly Star Data and Bloomberg." The award was upheld on appeal.

Thus parties can be sued for defamatory statements they make on the Internet. Less clear is the liability of online providers.

We return to the publisher/carrier debate. In the United States, section 230(c)(1) of the *Communications Decency Act* grants online providers and ISPs absolute immunity from defamation lawsuits over expression authored by other persons. Court cases decided after the *CDA* was enacted also suggest that the provider would have a defence at common law. In *Lunney v. Prodigy Services*,[14] the Court of Appeals of New York dismissed a defamation lawsuit against the online provider Prodigy Services over an email message and bulletin board postings disseminated by an imposter, who had

opened accounts under the plaintiff's name with Prodigy. The New York Court of Appeals held that Prodigy was protected by common law privilege, calling email "the day's evolutionary hybrid of traditional telephone line communications and regular postal service mail." Like the telephone company, Prodigy could not be considered a "publisher" because it did not participate in preparing the defamatory expression or exercise any discretion or control. See also *Ben Ezra, Weinstein & Co. Inc. v. America Online Inc.*[15]

By contrast, a recent United Kingdom case establishes that in Great Britian, ISPs are publishers and liable for what is posted on their systems. In *Godfrey v. Demon Internet Ltd.*,[16] a message was posted on the ISP Demon Internet's newsgroup servers by an unknown user and made to look as if it came from the plaintiff, a physicist and university lecturer. The message was obscene and defamatory. Despite receiving several written requests by the plaintiff to delete the postings from its servers, the ISP refused to do so until the posting was automatically taken off two weeks after its initial posting. The court found that the ISP could not claim "innocent dissemination" nor could it ignore requests to remove defamatory material. The parties settled on the eve of the ISP's appeal, with Demon Internet agreeing to pay the plaintiff $24,000 in damages, plus legal costs.

The scope and nature of ISP liability has not yet been determined by any Canadian court decision or legislation.

Another issue with allegations of online defamation is jurisdiction. In *Braintech, Inc.*

v. Kostiuk,[17] a Canadian defendant was sued in Texas for posting allegedly defamatory statements on an Internet discussion group. The British Columbia Court of Appeal unanimously refused to enforce a default judgment from a Texas court for US $300,000 for libel and disparagement. A key element of the court's ruling was the lack of any evidence that anyone in Texas actually viewed or downloaded the allegedly defamatory matter, which had been posted on a computer located outside Texas. Accordingly, there was no evidence of any "publication" to a third party within Texas.

HATE PROPAGANDA

In places where people are free to speak their minds, there are always some people who ignore the boundaries of civility and say hateful things. The Internet is such a place. Newsgroups like alt.skinheads and alt.revisionism are clogged with racist postings. Ernst Zundel operates one of many websites that continue to deny the existence of the Holocaust. White supremacist groups have mounted web pages with names like the "Stormfront White Nationalist Resource Page," posting frightening imagery and extremist views.

As with obscene material, current laws apply to prevent hate propaganda on the Internet. The *Criminal Code* makes it an offence to communicate statements in a public place that wilfully promote hatred against an identifiable group.[18] There can be no doubt a website or a newsgroup is a public place, and in *R. v. Keegstra*[19] the Supreme Court of Canada has held that the offence of wilfully promoting hatred imposes a reasonable restriction on the right to free expression.

As well, the *Canadian Human Rights Act* makes it a discriminatory practice to communicate "telephonically or ... by means of the facilities of a telecommunication undertaking" anything likely to expose an identifiable group to hatred.[20] A cease and desist order can be made to stop such a practice. Again, communications on the Internet would be subject to this provision, as the Internet runs on the facilities of a telecommunication undertaking: phone wiring. And the Supreme Court has ruled this provision to be a reasonable restriction on free speech: *Canada (Canadian Human Rights Commission) v. Taylor*.[21]

But as with obscene material, the problem with hateful speech on the Internet lies not in the laws but in their enforcement. Anonymous postings make it hard for authorities to track down the source of hateful statements. Even more problematic is the global reach of the Internet. Much of the hateful material available online is mounted on sites outside Canada. Even Torontonian Zundel's "Zundelsite" is loaded on a web server in Atlanta, Georgia. You can view his page anywhere in Canada, of course. More easily, in fact, than you can find one of Zundel's print publications. But can Canadian laws be enforced against material that doesn't reside in the country?

HARASSMENT

There is also the possibility that some will feel harassed by material on the Internet, for example, by getting offensive email, or by sharing a computer lab or workstation with someone who constantly views pornographic images online. There have even been documented cases of "net-stalking"; strangers using email and newsgroups to stalk victims, threatening them with physical harm.

Harassment laws, as well as criminal laws, apply to this kind of online conduct just as they do to face-to-face exchanges. The *Canadian Human Rights Act*, for example, makes it a discriminatory practice in the marketplace or workplace, to harass an individual on a prohibited ground of discrimination, including sexual harassment.[22] Sexually harassing email would be a discriminatory practice if it met the test set out by cases like *Janzen v. Platy Enterprises*:[23] unwelcome conduct of a sexual nature that detrimentally affects the work environment or adversely impacts the victim's job.

If harassment takes place at work or school, victims can often file complaints with an appointed anti-harassment officer. In a British Columbia case, a university student made such a complaint after another student posted an open letter to her to a newsgroup. The anti-harassment officer agreed with the complainant that the letter was threatening and violated the university's harassment policy. The student who posted the message was ordered to apologize, failing which his computer account would be suspended. He sued, saying his right to free speech was violated. The Court dismissed his claim, saying the *Charter of Rights* had no application to a decision made by the university in disciplining a student: *Blaber v. University of Victoria*.[24]

This possibility that the *Charter* protection of free speech doesn't always apply to on-line communication caused Mr. Justice Sopinka to write in "Freedom of Speech and Privacy in the Information Age":

> Although electronic mail can be used as a medium of expression, the *Charter* is essentially "an instrument for checking the powers of government over the individual". It only applies to government action. Given that much of the world of electronic communications is controlled privately, without any government regulation, the *Charter* may be an ineffective tool to protect this type of free speech.[25]

Consider in this context the Internet's capacity to censor *itself*. One of the most notorious cases relates to the Arizona lawyers who, in the mid-1990s, posted an advertisement for their immigration legal services to thousands of newsgroups on the Internet. This act of "spamming" outraged those who resisted the commercialization of the Internet. They were further angered when the lawyers refused to apologize for their stunt, threatened to do it again, and then wrote a book telling others how to make money by spamming.

You will recall from The Short Happy Marketing Blitz of Canter and Seigel in Chapter Two, that the response from Internet citizens included the "cancelbot" program that hunted through newsgroups and automatically deleted any postings from the Arizona lawyers. No one online was sad to see the lawyers' "green card ads" disappear, but many were spooked by the technology that the cancelbot programmer had unleashed on the Internet. To silence spamming or posts of pyramid schemes seems harmless. But with a cancelbot, an individual can try to silence whoever they choose and still not be subject to the *Charter*. Unless a law is enacted prohibiting the use of a cancelbot, there would be no legal recourse.

PUBLICATION BANS

Canadians may be familiar with one of the most infamous episodes of censorship in which the Internet played a role. It involved a publication ban imposed by a Canadian court during the high profile and horrifying murder trial of Paul Bernardo.[26]

Kovacs J. imposed the ban preventing the media from reporting details of proceedings against Bernardo's wife prior to his trial, in order to protect Bernardo's right to a fair trial. The Internet, however, simply routed around this ban. Internet users posted details of the case as reported in the American media. A newsgroup was established called alt.fan.karla-homolka. Other newsgroups, like alt.censorship, swelled with posts on the ban and the pending trial. The print media looked on exasperated, gnawing at their typewriters.

Many Canadians were shocked by the Internet's disrespect for the publication ban. McGill University was moved by the resulting controversy to delete the newsgroup alt.fan.karla-homolka from its server. Within one month, 15 Canadian universities had followed, as well as the National Capital Freenet.

No doubt the universities were acting in part out of a concern that if they didn't delete the group, *they* could be held responsible for breaching the ban. They feared that as Usenet hosts, they would be seen as publishers of any posted material, not merely common carriers. Parker Barss Donham in his lively paper "An Unshackled Internet: If Joe Howe Were Designing Cyberspace,"[27] argued that in banning the newsgroup, university administrators assumed control over the content of their Usenet servers. The kind of control that would be consistent with the interpretation that they *were* publishers and *not* common carriers.

Donham also questions whether deleting the group was even necessary. He says that only a relative few postings revealed banned information. Mostly, postings debated the ban's merits. Many of them supported the ban, and spoke out against attempts to subvert it. So when universities deleted the group, Donham argues, they were censoring more than the judge had done.

Which reveals how Internet censorship of this kind is a blunt instrument. As Donham says, plenty of socially useful material gets thrown out with the bathwater. Even in the mostly prurient alt.sex hierarchy, there is a newsgroup called alt.sex.abuse.recovery, where victims of sexual abuse can anonymously post messages sharing their experiences, assisting one another in the healing process. To delete an entire newsgroup—or worse, a whole hierarchy—because a few postings are offensive or breach a publication ban is about as sensible a response as taking away a radio station's license because they played the gangsta rap song "Cop Killer." As Mr. Justice Sopinka wrote in "Freedom of Speech and Privacy in the Information Age," if the goal is to prevent harassing phone calls, we don't completely ban the use of the telephone. That would be an excessive impairment on free speech.

Not only is the censorship of newsgroups a crude tool, many say it's not very effective. Universities may have banned the group alt.fan.karla-homolka from their servers, but any Internet user with a little flash could have found the group at a "mirror site"—a server carrying the same newsgroup—in the United States. Mr. Justice Sopinka has suggested that the free flow of information over the Internet may in fact make the courts more reluctant to impose publication bans in the first place:

> The fact that it is becoming much more difficult to meaningfully restrict the flow of information must be weighed into the balancing equation. If the efficacy of the ban is minimal due to technology, then it becomes harder to justify its existence.[28]

PRIVACY

The Internet has opened a window to an unprecedented volume of information. It has made information cheaper to gather and assimilate, easier to search, and infinitely more public. Which is to say, not private. The Internet has also presented entirely new ways for communications to be intercepted or monitored. By making information about us more accessible to others, and by increasing the chances our exchanges will be overheard, the Internet dramatically increases the potential for invasions of our private lives. Indeed, much controversy surrounded the revelation in early 2000 that Human Resources Development Canada was keeping a database containing up to 2,000 pieces of information on every Canadian citizen, and that some of that information was accessible over the Internet.

Unlike the freedom of speech, there is no explicit right to privacy guaranteed under the *Charter of Rights*. But underlying the right guaranteed by section 8 of the *Charter* to be secure against unreasonable search or seizure is the notion that in certain contexts, people have a reasonable expectation of privacy. In *R. v. Dyment*,[29] the Supreme Court of Canada said that "privacy is at the heart of liberty in a modern state and is essential for the well-being of the individual."

The courts have held the privacy right to be violated by such actions as the police secretly recording conversations electronically[30] or videotaping events in a private hotel room.[31] But in *R. v. Plant*,[32] it was held that the right to privacy was not violated by police obtaining utilities information from a city computer. Very little personal information was revealed, and there was no intrusion into a private computer system.

Which leads us to ask: Is there a reasonable expectation of privacy in an email message? Likely yes, just as there is a reasonable expectation that private phone messages won't be surreptitiously recorded. But the reality of email is that a message is vulnerable to interception as it travels from node to node across the Internet. Or a message sent by an employee while at work might be inspected by his or her employer when it passes through the company's server. In fact, many employers assert that not only do they have the right to inspect an employee's email, they own it. They own the computers the emails are composed on, after all.

Then there's the question of the banks of data out there that contain information about you, often highly personal—and private—information. Companies maintain databases of information about individuals for various purposes—marketing, credit checks, research. The Internet has made these data banks easier to assemble, accessible to more people, and therefore more dangerous. Indeed, some warn of an emerging practice called "dataveillance." This is how it works. Data from a wide range of sources and databases is linked together to form your "electronic dossier" or "data shadow." Every time you use a credit card, make a phone call, fill out a questionnaire, subscribe to a magazine, send in a product warranty card, use airline mileage points, and so on, the information is captured electronically. Those with access to your data shadow can track your movements, your activities, your likes and dislikes, even your habits and pet peeves. Several Privacy Commissioners have warned that with the expansion of the Internet, "the ability to engage in dataveillance will grow exponentially—as will the threats to privacy."[33]

Many commentators, including Federal Privacy Commissioner Bruce Phillips, feel that existing privacy laws simply aren't adequate to deal with the threat posed to privacy rights by the Internet. The federal *Privacy Act*,[34] for its part, is referred to as a code of fair information practices: it regulates the collection, disposal, use and disclosure by the government of information about you, and it provides you with a right of access to your information. But the Act, like most provincial privacy statutes, doesn't extend enforcement of data protection rights to the private as well as the public sector. (The Province of Quebec is the only jurisdiction in Canada, and indeed in North America, to have enacted legislation applying to data protection in the private sector. Quebec's *Act Respecting the Protection of Personal Information in the Private Sector*[35] came into force in 1994.) In other words, the statutes regulate the state's collection and use of information about you, but they do nothing to regulate the collection and use of information about you by private parties. Banks, retailers, periodical subscription departments, marketing companies, even your neighbour are all free to gather and disclose whatever details of your life they can.

This will change on January 1, 2001. That is when Part 1 of the *Personal Information Protection and Electronic Documents Act*,[36] (Bill C-6) will come into force. The Act establishes rules governing the collection, use, and disclosure of, as well as access to, personal information in the private sector.

"Personal information" is defined to mean "information about an identifiable individual, but does not include the name, title or business address or telephone number of an employee of an organization." The purpose of Part 1 is stated in section 3 of the Act to be "to establish, in an era in which technology increasingly facilitates the circulation and exchange of information, rules to govern the collection, use and disclosure of personal information in a manner that recognizes the right of privacy of individuals with respect to their personal information and the need of organizations to collect, use and disclose personal information for purposes that a reasonable person would consider appropriate in the circumstances." This section appears to require that the rights of individuals to the privacy and security of their information be balanced against the reasonable needs of organizations for information in today's high technology and information-based economy.

The new law applies to organizations in relation to personal information that they collect, use, or disclose in the course of commercial activities; it does not apply to information collected by an individual for personal purposes, or to information collected by an organization for artistic purposes. Organizations are required by section 5 to comply with ten overarching principles spelled out in detail in Schedule 1 to the Act: accountability; identifying purposes; consent; limiting collection; limiting use, disclosure and retention; accuracy; safeguards; openness; individual access; and challenging compliance.

SECURE COMMUNICATIONS

Lawyers have a special concern when it comes to the confidentiality of electronic communications. It is of course a concern that any correspondence could be intercepted and read. But communication between a lawyer and client falls into a special category. Such communication is protected from disclosure to others under the principle of solicitor-client privilege, a principle that is one of the hallmarks of the common law. But some have argued that if you send an email to a client without using an encryption program, it is likely that you waive any solicitor-client privilege over the message.

This is because of the possibility that a snooper can intercept your unencrypted message as it travels from node to node across the Internet. This isn't likely or even common. The sheer design of the Internet with its variable routing ensures this much. But it can happen. For this reason, many liken sending an unencrypted email to sending a postcard.

Paul Dodd and Daniel Bennett in their article "Waiver of Privilege and the Internet,"[37] argue that because of this possibility that an email could be read by an eavesdropper, solicitor-client privilege is lost. They point to a line of cases holding that communications between solicitor and client lose their privilege when involuntarily disclosed, even through theft or eavesdropping. *Pfeil v. Zink*[38] quotes approvingly from Sopinka and Lederman, *The Law of Evidence in Civil Cases* (Markham: Butterworths, 1974):

> ... if a third party overhears the communication, with or without the client's consent, no privilege can be claimed and that person may be forced to reveal the conversation. Similarly, if a third party openly or covertly, secures a document or makes a copy thereof, he may produce it, notwithstanding that it would have otherwise been privileged in the solicitor's possession.

Dodd & Bennett concede that the state of the law is not clear on this issue. They cite a 1989 Federal Court decision[39] holding that a communication inadvertently disclosed to the other side can still retain its privilege. They themselves prefer the more principled approach put forward by Manes & Silver in their book *Solicitor-Client Privilege in Canadian Law* (Markham: Butterworths, 1993): solicitor-client communications should remain privileged if the parties intended the communication to be confidential and they took reasonable steps to ensure that it be kept confidential.

Under this approach, an unencrypted email sent to a client over the Internet could still retain its privilege. Dodd & Bennett suggest that particularly if the message has a covering note declaring it to be privileged, a court might see the necessary intent and precaution, once it also weighed in the illegality of eavesdropping,[40] the efficacy of email as a mode of communication, and the low probability of interception.

Many lawyers are accordingly adding to their email signature blocks language that is similar to what they have been using on fax cover sheets:

A Recap on Encryption (See Chapter Three)

Encryption programs can be used to encode a message such that only a single designated recipient can unscramble it. Encryption technology is gradually being incorporated right into the most common Internet software programs, including recent releases of the major web browser programs and some email software programs. For those email programs that don't have built-in encryption, there are encryption plug-in programs such as Network Associates' PGP Personal Privacy or InvisiMail Deluxe. These programs work on something called the public-key system. Everyone with an encryption program has their own unique set of two keys, a public key and a private key. The public key you make available to all, by giving it out or by posting it at a public key server. The private key you keep absolutely private. When you send a message, you encrypt it with your private key and your recipient's public key. They then decode it using your public key and their private key. Each message encrypted in this way can only have one sender and one recipient. No one else will have the correct combination of keys.

Encryption programs can also act as a **digital signature**, allowing a reader of your email to be sure the message is from you. To do this, you simply attach a small block of encrypted text at the bottom of the message. The text is encrypted with your private key, but without any specific public key (no recipient is specified). Anyone with your public key can unencrypt this block of text to confirm that the message is yours.

This email is confidential and may be privileged; it is for the use of the named recipient(s) only. If you have received it in error, please notify us immediately; please do not copy or disclose its contents to any person or body, and delete it from your computer systems.

Others are more cautious. They argue that given that encryption technology is cheap, accessible, and really quite easy to use, it seems unwise to send an unencrypted email to a client that includes any communication over which the client may want to assert privilege (see the sidebar, A Recap on Encryption).

INTELLECTUAL PROPERTY LAW ISSUES

As we've seen, the Internet has been a boon for those who want to be heard. As "the posters of the late twentieth century," the Internet offers an opportunity for virtually everyone to speak to a massive audience at minimal expense. But the Internet hasn't been so good to those who create or own information. In a world where the cost is virtually nil to replicate material and distribute it worldwide, right away, the creator of information is highly vulnerable. Everyone from poets to publishers to programmers are complaining about the

loose and carefree way copyrighted information and trademarks are treated on the Internet.

COPYRIGHT

When an original work is created, it is automatically copyrighted. Given that the *Copyright Act*[41] protects an original work "whatever may be the mode or form of its expression," it is clear that digital works are protected by copyright just as is the book in your hands right now.

By section 3(1)(f) of the *Copyright Act*, a copyright owner has the exclusive right "to communicate the work to the public by telecommunication." This is where things begin to get murky. Recall the client-server model of web technology. The act of "reading" a web page involves a user, working with client software (their web browser), making a request of a server holding web pages. Does posting web pages, which is only half of the information exchange, amount to "communicating" a work? Is the communication "to the public" even though the content is accessed by only one user at a time?

In its 1999 decision on Tariff 22,[42] dealing with royalties to be collected on music played over the Internet, the Copyright Board of Canada helped to clarify some of these issues. First, the Copyright Board held (at 36-37) that the person who posts a work on the web does "communicate" it:

> The person who posts a work (usually the content provider) does so for the sole purpose that it be accessed by others. Since In-

ternet transmissions are communications, one should look at the source of the transmission to find out who is responsible for it. Any communication of a work occurs because a person has taken all the required steps to make the work available for communication. The fact that this is achieved at the request of the recipient or through an agent neither adds to, nor detracts from the fact that the content provider effects the communication.

The Copyright Board went on to find that a person who posts a work communicates it regardless of whether the transmission originates from a source, cache, or mirror server. Moreover, the communication is to the "public," even though the content may only be accessed by one end user at a time.

The Copyright Board also held that by making a work available to the public on a server, a person "authorizes" its communication. The Board explained (at 44) that a copyrighted work is not communicated when it is made available, but only when it is transmitted. However, its communication is authorized as soon as the work is made available:

> "Authorization" constitutes a separate protected use under the [Copyright Act]. To authorize is to sanction, approve and countenance. The person who makes a musical work available on an Internet-accessible site authorizes its communication. The work is posted for the sole purpose of being communicated and with full knowledge and intention that such a communication would occur. The person who makes the work available does more that merely provide the means to communicate the work; he/she ei-

ther controls or purports to control the right to communicate it.

Accordingly, the moment content is posted on the Internet, its communication is authorized. If the person posting the content is not the copyright owner then there is infringement under section 3(1)(f) of the *Copyright Act*.

A more elusive problem is the question of jurisdiction. The Internet is a global medium; copyright laws are national. Given that a web page may be created by an American, hosted on a Canadian server, and viewed by a British user, how can we answer the question: where does the act of authorization or communication take place? This is particularly important in the context that copyright is seen to be a national right; section 5 of the *Copyright Act* speaks of "copyright shall subsist *in Canada* in every original literary, dramatic, musical and artistic work" [emphasis added]. On this issue, the Copyright Board held (at 48) in the Tariff 22 decision:

> To occur in Canada, a communication must originate from a server located in Canada on which content has been posted. [*Canadian Association of Broadcasters v. Socan* (1994), 58 C.P.R. (3d) 190 (F.C.A.)] makes it clear that communications occur where the transmission originates. The place of origin of the request, the location of the person posting the content and the location of the original Web site are irrelevant. As a result, the right to authorize must be obtained from the person administering the right in Canada only when the information is posted on a Canadian server, and the right to communicate must be

obtained from that same person only when the transmission originates from a server located in Canada.

The Copyright Board went on to note that posting includes "not only posting to the original site, but also posting to any mirror site." Consequently, when a work is transmitted from a server operating as a mirror located in Canada, the communication occurs in Canada.

Applying this same reasoning, the Board concluded that communications triggered by an embedded link occur at the site to which the link leads. Thus, a person who creates an embedded link from a Canadian site to a foreign site does not authorize a communication occurring in Canada. Conversely, the person who creates a link to a site on a server located in Canada authorizes its communication in Canada, regardless of where the person or the link may be.

An American case on linking, *Ticketmaster Corp. v. Tickets.com, Inc.*,[43] held that linking does not itself involve a violation of the United States *Copyright Act*, since no copying is involved. The court concluded that the user is automatically transferred to the particular genuine web page of the original author. The court reasoned that this is analogous to using a library's card index to gain access to specific items, albeit a faster and more efficient process.

Framing, on the other hand, may be a violation of copyright. Framing is a technique that divides a web page into multiple "frames," each of which can display content from the same or different websites. The use of frames can obscure the source of content, making it appear as if content within a frame comes from the site of the party using frames. In *Hard Rock Café International Inc. v. Morton*,[44] a United States court found that the framing of a CD retailer's website by the defendant's site resulted in an integration of the two sites into a single visual presentation to users, and as a result the defendant's mark was used to advertise the CDs. The court ordered the defendant to cease framing the CD retailer's website. In *Futuredontics Inc. v. Applied Anagramic Inc.*,[45] another American case, the court refused an interlocutory application to dismiss the plaintiff's claim for copyright infringement, holding that it was still an open issue whether framing constitutes the creation of a derivative work.

The Tariff 22 decision has clarified some aspects of how copyright laws apply to digital information. The larger problem with copyright on the Internet, however, again lies in the area of enforcement. John Perry Barlow, Internet pioneer and co-founder of the Electronic Frontier Foundation, has gone so far as to predict the end of copyright as we know it in his provocative article "The Economy of Ideas: A Framework for Rethinking Patents and Copyrights (Everything You Know About Intellectual Property Is Wrong)."[46] Barlow and others suggest that because it costs virtually nothing to make and instantly distribute copies of copyrighted works all over the globe, copyright protection is impracticable.

If our property can be infinitely reproduced and instantaneously distributed all over the planet without cost, without our knowledge, without its even leaving our possession, how can we protect it? How are we going to get paid for the work we do with our minds?

There are actually three components to this view: the ease with which information can be copied on the Internet, the hostility of many Internet users to the concept of intellectual property, and the difficulty in tracking down those who infringe copyright.

1. **Ease of copying.** Digital information has a unique property: the ability to make an infinite number of perfect copies, essentially for free. Copy an article, mail it to a mailing list, and with a couple of keystrokes you've robbed a writer or publisher of hundreds of sales. For publishers who felt threatened by the photocopier, the Internet seems like the end of the world. Copying and distributing information is so easy it hardly seems wrong.

2. **Internet culture.** "Information wants to be free." You'll encounter this sentiment often as you explore the Internet, and it reveals the hostility some users feel toward the concept of intellectual property. Early users, mostly scientists and academics, viewed the Internet as a public domain research archive, a place where people collaborated to develop programs and share information. The next wave of users, the younger, free-wheeling counterculture of the Internet, openly mocked the notion of ownership, period. Although the Internet is now more sociologically diverse, there

remain strong pockets of hostility to commercial efforts.

3. **Difficulty of law enforcement.** It's hard to enforce laws when you don't know who the offenders are. To publish material on the Internet anonymously is possible using anonymous remailer servers, and it's also a simple procedure to forge a posting to a newsgroup. Even if the source of a copyright infringement is traceable, the sheer volume of traffic on the Internet makes it difficult to keep track of infringement.

The difficulty of enforcing copyright has led some copyright owners to pursue online providers and site operators directly. This gives rise to the now familiar carrier-publisher debate. Online providers say they are merely conduits for the flow of information, no more responsible for activities conducted on the Internet than telephone companies are for obscene phone calls. Copyright owners disagree, arguing that typically online providers know much more about what is being done on their networks than they let on.

In fact, BBS operators and online providers have been successfully sued for copyright infringement. *In Playboy Enterprises Inc. v. Frena*,[47] subscribers of a BBS uploaded, displayed, and downloaded photographs that originally appeared in Playboy magazine. The Court held the BBS liable for infringing the magazine's copyright even though the operator claimed he did not know of the infringements. In *Sega Enterprises Ltd. v. Maphia*,[48] customers of a BBS uploaded, sold, and downloaded copies of the plaintiff's

---

Intellectual Property Alert: Shareware and Freeware Distinguished

One of the best things about the Internet is all the stuff you can get for free, for example, software. Programs that outperform commercial software can be downloaded from across globe, for the cost of your connect time (that is, 25 to 50 cents for a typical connection). But do note the distinction between freeware and shareware. Freeware is as it sounds—a software program that its author distributes without charge. (This often isn't the same as "in the public domain"—freeware authors usually try to preserve their rights to the software so that no else can sell it.) Shareware, on the other hand, is a software program that the author distributes without charge, but for which payment is required if the user decides to keep and use it. Shareware authors are really just using the enormous distribution facilities of the Internet to let prospective users give their product a whirl before buying it. The real gold is freeware; shareware merely makes test driving convenient.

---

video game software. The Court found that the BBS was liable for contributory copyright infringement because there was "copying" each time the games were uploaded to or downloaded from the system.

In a case involving the Internet, an online provider was among those sued by the Church of Scientology. The Church alleged that a site hosted by the provider included material over which the Church had copyright, including Scientology's secret scrip-tures, sold to church members for thousands of dollars. In a pre-trial application, a United States Federal Court ruled that the provider did not itself violate the Church's copyright but may have contributed to the infringement by failing to remove the documents, once told that copyrighted documents had been posted on its system. The case settled before trial, with the provider agreeing to warn its subscribers not to "unlawfully distribute the intellectual property of others": *Religious Technology Center v. Netcom On-line Communications Services Inc.*[49]

Canadian courts have not yet considered the issue of an online provider's liability for copyrighted documents posted on their system.

TRADEMARKS

Trademark law is another area that has been posed significant challenges by the Internet. Consider the case of the Internet domain name itself.

A domain name is a user's Internet identity. Something called the Domain Name System was developed in the early 1980s to govern the pattern of names. The system set up a series of top-level domains, which can either be an institutional type (e.g., commercial (.com), educational (.edu)), or a country type (e.g., Australia (.au), Germany (.de)). Several dozen domain name registrars around the world have been accredited by the Internet Corporation for Assigned Names and Numbers (ICANN) to hand out the first kind of domain, the institutional type domain. The Canadian Internet Registration Authority (CIRA) oversees the registration of .ca names, which is the two letter country code for Canada. A Canadian organization can register with either or both registries: to wit, RoyalBank.com and TDBank.ca.

These registries operate on a first-come, first-served basis. You can register anything as long as it is not already taken. From the very early days of the Internet, this has created problems. In 1994, for example, WIRED magazine writer Josh Quittner discovered that many Fortune 500 companies appeared unaware of the concept of a domain name. He singled out companies that hadn't registered an obvious version of their name, and registered one of the names (mcdonalds.com) himself. McDonalds threatened to sue him. Ultimately Quittner gave the name to the company when they agreed to buy computer equipment for a Brooklyn school.

This practice of opportunistically registering domain names that incorporate well-known trademarks has become so common place that it has acquired a name: "cybersquatting." Often the cybersquatter offers to sell the domain name to the highest bidder (usually the party that owns the registered trademark). This tension between the domain name system and trademark law flows from several fundamental differences in the two systems:

• Trademark law is generally territorial and involves national rights. Concurrent uses of similar trademarks by different users in different jurisdictions is permissible. Trademark rights arise upon use—they need not be registered.

• By contrast, the Internet is global. There is a single Internet domain name system. Internet domain names must be unique— concurrent uses of the same Internet domain name are not permissible. Domain name rights arise upon registration.

Trademark holders are not without remedies, mind you. Courts in the United States and in England have held that the administrative policy of granting domain names on a first-come, first-served basis does not trump trademark law: *Cardservice International Inc. v. McGee;*[50] *Hard Rock Café International Inc. v. Morton.*[51] To be protected by trademark law in Canada, a trademark owner must establish that its mark is distinctive and in use, and that an offending mark is likely to cause confusion regarding the source of the wares or services with which it is associated.[52]

In the United States, legislation has also been passed to protect trademark holders. The *Anticybersquatting Consumer Protection Act*[53] is designed "to protect consumers and American businesses, to promote the growth of on-line commerce, and to provide clarity in the law for trademark owners by prohibiting the bad-faith and abusive registration of distinctive marks as Internet domain names with the intent to profit from the goodwill associated with such marks – a practice commonly referred to as 'cybersquatting' ": *Sporty's Farm v. Sportsman's Market Inc.*[54] The Act protects owners of famous or distinctive trademarks by providing a civil cause of action against any person who in bad faith registers, traffics in, or uses a domain name that is identical to or confusingly similar to a distinctive mark or name.

Disputes involving alleged bad faith registration and use of institutional type domain names (.com, .net, and .org) may also be resolved pursuant to the Uniform Domain Name Dispute Resolution Policy (see http://www.icann.org). The UDRP is intended to be an efficient and cost-effective procedure for resolving cybersquatting disputes. It is incorporated by reference into domain name registration agreements. The URDP contractually binds domain name registrants to a mandatory administrative dispute resolution process for domain name disputes involving allegations of bad faith domain name registration and use. The Canadian Internet Registration Authority (see http://www.cira.ca/) introduced a similar dispute resolution process for the .ca domain in 2000.

The UDRP requires the complainant to prove that: (a) the registrant's domain name is identical or confusingly similar to the complainant's mark; (b) the registrant has no rights or legitimate interests in the domain name; and (c) the domain name was registered and is being used in bad faith.

ECOMMERCE LEGAL ISSUES

The rush of business to embrace electronic commerce has raised a host of legal issues. Among them are the still to be written rules governing ecommerce, and the interna-tional aspects of ecommerce: which legal system(s) is a business with a website subjecting itself to?

RULES GOVERNING ELECTRONIC COMMERCE

To date, the Internet and ecommerce have been subject to rules that were not developed with cyberspace in mind. That is now changing.

In 1996, the United Nations General Assembly passed a resolution adopting a model law on electronic commerce. In September 1999, the Uniform Law Commission of Canada adopted a draft *Uniform Electronic Commerce Act*, based on the UN model. The Act is intended to be used by provincial and territorial governments as model legislation to facilitate electronic commerce. Already, the Act has been adopted in Saskatchewan with a few modifications. Other Canadian provinces and territories are actively considering the draft Act.

The *Uniform Electronic Commerce Act* is designed to ensure that electronic communications are treated on the same footing as written communications. The Act establishes rules by which electronic communications and signatures have the same force and effect as those on paper. A key principle established by the Act is that no one is required to use or accept electronic communications unless they consent to do so (although that consent may be inferred from a person's conduct). As well, the Act provides that:

• contracts may be formed by communicating one's agreement electronically, including by clicking on a designated icon on a computer screen;

- contracts may be formed by the interaction of computers, either with other computers or with individuals; and

- if an individual makes an error when entering a contract electronically, the contract will not be effective unless the person has the opportunity to prevent or correct the error. However, the person must give prompt notice of the error.

Similar initiatives are underway in other jurisdictions. In the United States, several states have implemented the *Uniform Computer Information Transactions Act* (UCITA), a uniform commercial code for software licenses and other ecommerce transactions. UCITA plays the same role for ecommerce that the *Uniform Commercial Code* plays for the sale of goods. UCITA addresses all the standard contract issues that the UCC addresses for the sale of goods, including provisions relating to offer and acceptance of contract terms, warranties, transfer of contract interests, the rights and obligations of the parties in the case of a breach of the contract, and applicable remedies. It also includes rules on new issues relating to electronic contracts.

INTERNATIONAL ECOMMERCE ISSUES

As we've seen, the Internet breaks down barriers between legal systems. Businesses can offer goods and services to customers beyond their borders. But this raises issues of which legal system applies to a company that does business over the Internet.

A key United States decision is *Zippo Manufacturing Co. v. Zippo Dot Com Inc.*[55] That case identified three categories of Internet activity:

1. situations where a defendant clearly does business over the Internet by entering into contracts with residents from other jurisdictions;

2. situations where a defendant has a website that allows a user to exchange information with a host computer; and

3. situations where a defendant has a passive website that does nothing more than advertise on the Internet.

The court in *Zippo Manufacturing* found that jurisdiction asserted by an American court over a foreign party is proper in the first category, is possible in the second, and is not appropriate in the third category.

In another American case, *Mink v. AAAA Development*,[56] a Texas court decided that it did not have jurisdiction over a Vermont furniture manufacturer where the manufacturer's website merely posted information about it products. Although the manufacturer's website contained a printable mail-in order form, a toll-free telephone number, and an email address, the factors were not sufficient to establish personal jurisdiction. The court found the manufacturer did not take orders over the website and did not conduct business in Texas.

In a Canadian decision, *Braintech Inc. v. Kostiuk*,[57] a Canadian defendant was sued in Texas for posting allegedly defamatory statements on an Internet discussion group.

The Canadian defendant did not appear in Texas to defend his case, and default judgment was awarded against him. When the plaintiff tried to enforce the Texas judgment in British Columbia, the BC Court of Appeal refused to recognize the judgment. The court held that the American standards of asserting personal jurisdiction were not met.

Thus where a Canadian business has a passive website that advertises its products and services, a US court will not assert jurisdiction over the business. Where the business' website allows for ecommerce, and allows a user to exchange information with the business' server, then an American court may assert jurisdiction, although even in such cases the court may find that the company was not conducting business in the United States.

END NOTES

1. J. Sopinka, "Freedom of Speech and Privacy in the Information Age" (Address at "Symposium on Free Speech and Privacy in the Information Age," University of Waterloo, 26 November 1994) gopher://insight.mcmaster.ca/00/org/efc/doc/sfsp/sopinka.txt.

2. Sopinka, *ibid*.

3. *Criminal Code*, R.S.C. 1985, c. C-46, s. 163(1)(a).

4. *R. v. Hurtubise* (January 10, 1997), Doc. New Westminster No. X045651, X045652 (B.C. S.C.).

5. *R. v. Butler*, [1992] 1 S.C.R. 452 (S.C.C.).

6. The full text of s. 2(b) of the *Charter of Rights and Freedoms* is: "Everyone has the following fundamental freedoms: freedom of thought, belief, opinion and expression, including freedom of the press and other media of communication."

7. *Edmonton Journal v. Alberta (Attorney General)*, [1989] 2 S.C.R. 1326 (S.C.C.).

8. *Communications Decency Act*, 47 U.S.C. §223.

9. *Reno v. American Civil Liberties Union* (1996), 521 U.S. 844, 138 L.Ed.2d 874, 117 S.Ct. 2329.

10. *R. v. Metro News Ltd.* (1986), 32 D.L.R. (4th) 321 (Ont. C.A.), leave to appeal refused (1986), 32 D.L.R. (4th) 321n (S.C.C.).

11. *United States v. Thomas* (1996), 74 F. 3d 701 (6th Cir.).

12. *Campbell v. Cartmell* (September 23, 1999), Doc. 97-CV-134742 (Ont. S.C.J.).

13. *Southam Inc. v. Chelekis* (April 15, 1998), Doc. Vancouver C952513 (B.C. S.C.), affirmed 2000 BCCA 112 (B.C. C.A.), leave to appeal refused [2000] S.C.C.A. No. 177 (S.C.C.).

14. *Lunney v. Prodigy Services*, 1999 N.Y. Lexis 3746.

15. *Ben Ezra, Weinstein & Co. Inc. v. America Online Inc.* (March 14, 2000), 99-2068 (U.S. C.A., 10th Cir.).

16. *Godfrey v. Demon Internet Ltd.*, [1999] 4 All E.R. 342, settlement reached March 11, 2000.

17. *Braintech Inc. v. Kostiuk* (1999), 171 D.L.R. (4th) 46 (B.C. C.A.), leave to appeal refused [1999] S.C.C.A. No. 236 (S.C.C.).

18. *Criminal Code*, s. 319.

19. *R. v. Keegstra*, [1990] 3 S.C.R. 697 (S.C.C.).

20. *Canadian Human Rights Act*, R.S.C. 1985, c. H-6, s. 13(1).

21. *Canada (Canadian Human Rights Commission) v. Taylor*, [1990] 3 S.C.R. 892 (S.C.C.).

22. *Canadian Human Rights Act*, s. 14.

23. *Janzen v. Platy Enterprises Ltd.*, [1989] 1 S.C.R. 1252 (S.C.C.).

24. *Blaber v. University of Victoria* (1995), 123 D.L.R. (4th) 255 (B.C. S.C.).

25. Sopinka, *supra* note 1.

26. *R. v. Bernardo* (July 5, 1993), Doc. St. Catharines 125/93 (Ont. Gen. Div.).

27. P.B. Donham, "An Unshackled Internet: If Joe Howe Were Designing Cyberspace" (Address at "Symposium on Free Speech and Privacy in the Information Age," University of Waterloo, 26 November 1994) http://insight.mcmaster.ca/org/efc/pages/donham2.l.

28. Sopinka, *supra* note 1.

29. *R. v. Dyment*, [1988] 2 S.C.R. 417 (S.C.C.).

30. *R. v. Duarte*, [1990] 1 S.C.R. 30 (S.C.C.).

31. *R. v. Wong*, [1990] 3 S.C.R. 36 (S.C.C.).

32. *R. v. Plant*, [1993] 3 S.C.R. 281, 84 C.C.C. (3d) 203 (S.C.C.).

33. B. Phillips, "Privacy in a Digital Age" (Notes for an Address at "Information Issues in Transition: Access & Privacy '97," 27 January 1997) http://www.privcom.gc.ca/; B. Phillips, "Protecting Privacy on the Information Highway: Response of the Privacy Commissioner of Canada to Privacy and the Information Highway" (23 December 1994) http://www.privcom.gc.ca/; A. Cavoukian, "Preserving Privacy on the Information Highway: Fact or Fiction?" (Address at "Symposium on Free Speech and Privacy in the Information Age," University of Waterloo, November 26, 1994) gopher://insight.mcmaster.ca/00/org/efc/doc/sfsp/cavoukian.txt.

34. *Privacy Act*, R.S.C. 1985, c. P-21.

35. *Act Respecting the Protection of Personal Information in the Private Sector*, R.S.Q. c. P-39.1.

36. *Personal Information Protection and Electronic Documents Act*, S.C. 2000, c. 5.

37. P. Dodd and D. Bennett, "Waiver of Privilege and the Internet" (1995) 53 *Advocate* 365.

38. *Pfeil v. Zink* (1984), 60 B.C.L.R. 32 (B.C. S.C.).

39. *Double-E Inc. v. Positive Action Tool Western Ltd.*, [1989] 1 F.C. 163 (Fed.T.D.).

40. See the *Criminal Code*, Part VI, Invasion of Privacy.

41. *Copyright Act*, R.S.C. 1985, c. C-42, ss. 2, 5.

42. Tariff 22, Decision of the Copyright Board of Canada pursuant to section 67.2 of the *Copyright Act*, R.S.C. 1985, Ch. C-42, on the statement of royalties to be collected for the performance or the communication by telecommunication in Canada of musical or dramatico-musical works (27 October 1999) http://www.cb-cda.gc.ca/.

43. *Ticketmaster Corp. v. Tickets.com, Inc.* (March 27, 2000), CV99-7654 (C.D. Cal. 2000).

44. *Hard Rock Café International Inc. v. Morton* 1999 U.S. Dist. LEXIS 8340, supplementary reasons 1999 U.S. Dist. LEXIS 13760 (S.D.N.Y. 1999).

45. *Futuredontics Inc. v. Applied Anagramic Inc.* 1999 U.S. Dist. LEXIS 9638 (C.D. Cal. 1999).

46. J. P. Barlow, "The Economy of Ideas: A Framework for Rethinking Patents and Copyrights (Everything You Know About Intellectual Property Is Wrong)" *WIRED* 2.03 (March 1994).

47. *Playboy Enterprises, Inc. v. Frena* (1993), 839 F. Supp. 1552 (Fl. Dist. Ct.).

48. *Sega Enterprises Ltd. v. Maphia* (1994), 30 U.S.P.Q. 2d 1921 (N.D. Cal.).

49. *Religious Technology Center v. Netcom Online Communications Services Inc.* (1995), 907 F. Supp. 1361 (N.D. Cal.).

50. *Cardservice International Inc. v. McGee,* 950 F. Supp. 737 (E.D. Va. 1997), affirmed 129 F. 3d 1258 (4th Cir. 1997).

51. *Hard Rock Café International Inc. v. Morton, supra* note 44.

52. *Trademarks Act,* R.S.C. 1985, c. T-13, s. 6.

53. *Anticybersquatting Consumer Protection Act,* 15 U.S.C. §1125(d).

54. *Sporty's Farm v. Sportsman's Market Inc.* 2000 U.S. App. LEXIS 1246 (2nd Cir.), quoting S. Rep. No. 106-140, at 4.

55. *Zippo Manufacturing Co. v. Zippo Dot Com, Inc.,* 952 F. Supp. 1119 (W.D. Pa. 1997).

56. *Mink v. AAAA Development LLC* (September 17, 1999), 98-20770 (U.S. C.A., 5th Cir.).

57. *Braintech, Inc. v. Kostiuk, supra* note 17.

APPENDIX: LEGAL RESOURCES DIRECTORY

BENCH & BAR
LAWYERS
COURTS

GOVERNMENT
FEDERAL GOVERNMENT
PROVINCIAL GOVERNMENT

LAWS
CASE LAW
STATUTES & REGULATIONS
LEGISLATIVE MATERIALS
TRIBUNAL DECISIONS

LEGAL EDUCATION
CONTINUING LEGAL EDUCATION
LAW REFORM
LAW SCHOOLS

LEGAL ORGANIZATIONS
BAR ASSOCIATIONS & OTHER LAW ASSOCIATIONS
LAW SOCIETIES

LEGAL-RELATED BUSINESSES
LAW PUBLISHERS
LEGAL SUPPORT SERVICES
ONLINE DATABASE PROVIDERS

This Directory represents your yellow pages to sites on the Internet that provide material of interest to the Canadian legal professional. The Directory, which is current to the date of publication, is divided into six main categories: Bench & Bar, Government, Laws, Legal Education, Legal Organizations, and Legal-related Businesses. Each category is further broken into subcategories to assist you in navigating through the listings. For example you will find the Finance Canada website in the Government – Federal Government category. Each listing includes an URL so you can pay a visit to those sites that interest you. We have also included annotations to alert you to any interesting content available at a site.

You will see a handful of entries at the beginning of each category of the Directory in a subcategory called Finding Tools. These are the sites that will assist you in keeping track of new attractions as they emerge in that category. They are also typically good places to go to link to multiple sites within a category, or to search for hard-to-find material within that category of resource.

If you are having a hard time locating a new site, also try the better directories to law-related sites:

Virtual Canadian Law Library. This outstanding directory to Canadian law includes pointers to legislation, case law, tribunal rulings, libraries, publishers, lawyers, and much more. It comprises the work of the CRDP (Centre for Public Law Research) at the University of Montreal Law School.
http://www.lexum.umontreal.ca/index_en.html

University of Calgary Law Library Links. This is a comprehensive and up-to-date directory to Canadian legal resources on the Internet, from the University of Calgary Law Library. Sites are organized into categories based on type of resource (legislation, judicial decisions etc.) and source of resource.
http://www.ucalgary.ca/library/law/

Continuing Legal Education Society of BC's Legal Links. This is one of the most comprehensive directories to Canadian legal resources, with an accent on British Columbia material. Categories are based on a Yahoo-like structure that includes listings of cases, legislation, government, lawyers, practice areas, and more, with extensive annotations. You can search over the resources listed here.
http://www.cle.bc.ca/resources/

BENCH & BAR

FINDING TOOLS

The Canadian Law List. A searchable listing of Canadian law firms, lawyers and judges. Listings include contact information, including email addresses, and practice profiles.
http://www.canadianlawlist.com/

Martindale-Hubbell Lawyer Locator. Searchable access to the worldwide Martindale-Hubbell Law Directory. Locate a law-

yer by name, firm, location, practice area, and more.
http://www.martindale.com/locator/

West's Legal Directory (lawoffice.com). Profiles of over one million North American lawyers and firms; searchable by name, city, province, firm size, and practice area.
http://www.lawoffice.com/

LAWYERS

Alexander, Holburn, Beaudin & Lang, Vancouver, BC.
http://www.ahbl.bc.ca/

Alger, Douglas, Barrister & Solicitor, Lethbridge, Alta. This sole practitioner's website provides legal information for clients and legal software products for lawyers.
http://www.algerlaw.com/

Allen & Allen, Toronto, Ont. Free summaries of Ontario law, precedents, and links to legal resources in the "Virtual Law Library."
http://www.virtual-law.com/

Amsterdam & Peroff, Toronto, Ont.
http://www.amperlaw.com/

Baker Newby, Chilliwack, BC. Client newsletters and legal links (a nice compilation) at this Fraser Valley firm's website.
http://www.bakernewby.com/

Barrigar & Moss, Vancouver, BC/Mississauga, Ont. Patent and trademark agents.
http://www.barrmoss.com/

Bassett & Company, Westbank, BC. Articles and links dealing with real estate and First Nations law from this Okanagan Valley firm.
http://www.ogopogo.com/lawyers/

Bastion Law Corporation, Victoria, BC.
http://www.firstlinelaw.com/

Beaulieu Normandeau, Québec City, Que. Updates on business and legal issues from this Quebec City firm.
http://www.beaulieunormandeau.com

Bell Spagnuolo, Port Coquitlam, BC.
http://www.bellspagnuolo.com/

Bennett Jones, Calgary and Edmonton, Alta/Toronto, Ont.
http://www.bennettjones.ca/

Bereskin & Parr, Toronto, Ont. This intellectual property firm's site includes overviews of intellectual property law, discussions of recent cases and legislative developments, and an excellent collection of links to other IP resources.
http://www.bereskinparr.com/

Bishop & McKenzie, Edmonton, Alta.
http://www.bishopmckenzie.com/

Biss, Stephen, Barrister & Solicitor, Mississauga, Ont.
http://www.lawyers.ca/sbiss/

Blake, Cassels & Graydon, Toronto, Ont/Vancouver, BC. Features a series of excellent newsletters in several practice areas, including environmental law and intellectual property.
http://www.blakes.ca/

Borden Ladner Gervais, Toronto, Ont/Ottawa, Ont/Vancouver, BC/Calgary, Alta/Montréal, Que.
http://www.blgcanada.com/

Boyne, Clarke, Dartmouth, NS.
http://www.boyneclarke.ns.ca/

Branch MacMaster, Vancouver, BC. This Vancouver litigation firm specializes in class actions, and their excellent site includes articles, case summaries, and links relating to past and potential class actions in British Columbia.
http://www.branmac.com/

Breatross, Asher, Barrister & Solicitor, Thornhill, Ont.
http://www.interlog.com/~ash/

Brownstein, Brownstein, and Associates, Montréal, Que.
http://www.brownsteinlaw.com/

Brunet Arsenault, Montréal, Que. This immigration law firm provides an online immigration assessment form.
http://www.immcan.com/

Bull, Housser & Tupper, Vancouver, BC. The site for this long-established Vancouver firm includes lawyer profiles and extensive descriptions of legal services.
http://www.bht.com

Byck & Leckie, New Liskeard, Ont.
http://www.temlaw.com/

Campbell, Cohen, Montreal, Que. This site features a newsletter on Canadian immigration law, an online Canadian immigration assessment form, and a "databank" for prospective immigrants.
http://canadavisa.com/

Campney & Murphy, Vancouver, BC. Features such newsletters as *The Financial Counsellor*, from the Campney & Murphy Financial Services Group.
http://www.campney.com/

Carr & Company, Edmonton, Alta. This ambitious site includes the firm's Insight newsletter, as well as a search engine.

http://www.carrco.com/

Cassells Brock & Blackwell, Toronto, Ont.
http://www.casselsbrock.com/index_f.html

Catalyst Corporate Finance Lawyers, Vancouver, BC. Articles relating to securities law, and links to corporate finance resources.
http://www.catalyst-law.com/

Chait Amyot, Montréal, Que.
http://www.chait-amyot.ca/

Chang & Boos, Toronto, Ont. Publications and resources for Canadians interested in immigrating to the United States.
http://americanlaw.com/

Chown, Cairns, St. Catharines, Ont.
http://www.niagara.com/northland/cc/cc.html

Claman, Peter C., Law Offices of, Halifax, NS.
http://www.claman.com/

Clark, Wilson, Vancouver, BC. Articles, links, and resources in several core industry areas.
http://www.cwilson.com/

Cleveland & Doan, White Rock, BC.
http://www.cleveland-doan.com/

Colman, Gene, Barrister & Solicitor, Toronto, Ont. The "Family Law Centre" features articles on issues relevant to family lawyers, and links to related sites.
http://www.4famlaw.com/

Cooper, Sandler and West, Toronto, Ont. Criminal law firm with extensive experience defending allegations of white-collar crime, homicide and sexual assault.

http://www.csandw.on.ca/

Cusimano & Cusimano, Toronto, Ont.
http://www.cusimano.com/lawyers/

Dale, Bryan, Barrister & Solicitor, Toronto, Ont.
http://www.bdale.com/

David Share Associates Lawyers, Toronto, Ont.
http://www.sharelawyers.com/

Davies, Gareth John, Barrister & Solicitor, British Columbia. An extensive collection of case notes and citations on child protection law.
http://www.members.home.net/gilli2/

Davis & Company, Vancouver, BC. Features the firm's newsletters in PDF format.
http://www.davis.ca/

Davis Hara Rothschild, Montreal, Que.
http://www.hara-rothschild.ca/

Desjardins Ducharme Stein Monast, Montréal, Que.
http://www.ddsm.ca/

Doak Shirreff, Kelowna, BC.
http://www.doakshirreff.com/

Drewitz, Charles, Barrister & Solicitor, Waterloo, Ont.
http://granite.sentex.net/~cdrewitz/

Dueck, Sauer, Jutzi & Noll, Waterloo, Ont.
http://www.dsjnlaw.com/

Durocher Simpson, Edmonton, Alta.
http://www.dursim.com/

Edwards, Kenny & Bray, Vancouver, BC.
http://www.ekb.com/

Fasken Martineau DuMoulin, Vancouver, BC/Toronto, Ont/Montréal, Que.
http://www.fasken.com/

Felsky, Martin, Barrister & Solicitor, Toronto, Ont. This site is home to inTeger, the Information Technology Education Group, and its excellent publication NotInPrint, which reports on Canadian legal information on the Internet.
http://www.integeractif.com/

Fraser Milner, Toronto, Ont/Vancouver, BC. The newsletter *Financial Services News* and practice area updates are featured.
http://www.frasermilner.com/

Gahtan, Alan, Barrister & Solicitor, Toronto, Ont. His site was one of the first to link to other Canadian law sites. "Canadian Legal Resources" provides an extensive (and searchable) set of links.
http://gahtan.com/alan/

Gardiner, Blumberg, Toronto, Ont.
http://www.blumberg-law.com/

Gay, Jeremy, Barrister & Solicitor, Dartmouth, NS.
http://members.attcanada.ca/~gay/jeremy.html

Geraghty, George, Barrister & Solicitor, Vancouver, BC.
http://www.gglawcorp.com/

Giffen Lee, Kitchener, Ont.
http://www.giffenleelaw.com/

Gillman, Gary, Barrister & Solicitor, Toronto, Ont.
http://www.lawgill.com/

Gold, Doron, Barrister & Solicitor, North York, Ont.

http://www3.sympatico.ca/doron/doron.html

Goldberg, Shinder & Kronick, Ottawa, Ont.
http://www.gsgk.com/

Golish, Kenneth, Barrister & Solicitor, Windsor, Ont.
http://www.golishlaw.com

Goodman and Carr, Toronto, Ont. This site features an extensive library of articles and publications on legal developments; library is searchable.
http://www.goodmancarr.com/

Gordon & Velletta, Victoria, BC.
http://victorialaw.bc.ca/

Gottlieb, Gary Lloyd, Barrister and Solicitor, Toronto, Ont.
http://www.interlog.com/~glgqc/

Gowling, Strathy & Henderson, Ottawa and Toronto, Ont/Vancouver BC.
http://www.gowlings.com

Grosman, Grosman, & Gale, Toronto, Ont. Information on employment law and human rights.
http://www.grosman.com/

Guberman, Garson, Toronto, Ont. Materials and links relating to immigration law, as well as an online immigration questionnaire.
http://www.gubermangarson.com/

Guiste & Southcott, Toronto, Ont. An association of lawyers with "a creative, unconventional and results oriented approach to advocacy and problem solving." Focusing on employment law, human rights, criminal law, and *Charter* matters.

http://www.interlog.com/~southgui/

Harris, Lesley Ellen, Barrister & Solicitor. The site for Lesley Ellen Harris' book *Canadian Copyright Law* includes articles on Internet copyright issues and links to copyright legislation and treaties.
http://www.mcgrawhill.ca/copyrightlaw/

Heenan Blaikie, Toronto, Ont/Montréal, Que/Vancouver, BC. One of Canada's national law firms features legal news and newsletters, as well as articles on corporate/commercial, labour/employment, and litigation topics.
http://www.heenanblaikie.com/

Henderson, Bill, Barrister & Solicitor, Toronto, Ont. Articles and links relating to Aboriginal law, as well as an extensive collection of links to other Canadian legal resources.
http://www.bloorstreet.com/lawoff.htm

Hicken, Mark, Barrister & Solicitor, Vancouver, BC. Host to ElectricLawyer.com and legaldocument.com.
http://www.legaldocument.com/

Horn, Richard, Barrister & Solicitor, Burnaby, BC.
http://www.infoserve.net/horn/index.html

Hughes, Amys, Toronto, Ont. Noteworthy and the OIC Note, on Financial Services Commission developments, are newsletters featured at this firm's site.
http://www.hughesamys.com/

Jamieson Bains, Saskatoon, Sask. Information on the conduct of personal injury actions and estate matters in Saskatchewan.

http://www.jblawyers.com/

Johnston, Lewis & Franklin, Nanaimo, BC.
http://www.jlf.bc.ca/

Jones, Peter, Barrister & Solicitor, Toronto, Ont. The "Translink Website" features articles and links relating to electronic commerce.
http://www.webcom.com/~pjones/
welcome.html

Jourard, Ron, Barrister & Solicitor, Toronto, Ont. Information on defending impaired driving charges from this Toronto criminal lawyer.
http://www.defencelaw.com/

Karas & Associates, Toronto, Ont.
http://www.karas.ca/

Kepes, Robert, Barrister & Solicitor, North York, Ont.
http://www.mintzca.com/

Kerr, Philip, Barrister & Solicitor, Ottawa, Ont. Articles and links relating to intellectual property.
http://www.trytel.com/~pbkerr/

Kirby, Eades, Gale, Baker, Ottawa, Ont. Articles and links relating to intellectual property.
http://www.kirbyeades.com/

Lackman, Firestone, Toronto, Ont.
http://www.pathcom.com/~lflaw/

Lafleur Brown, Montréal, Que.
http://www.lafleurbrown.ca/

Lancaster, Mix & Welch, St. Catharines, Ont.
http://www.lmw.com/

Lang Michener Lawrence & Shaw, Vancouver, BC.
http://www.lmls.com/

Lathrop, Thomas, Barrister & Solicitor, Victoria, BC.
http://members.home.net/tlathrop/

Lavery, de Billy, Montréal, Que. Articles and publications organized by practice area.
http://www.laverydebilly.com/
homeen.htm

Lawson Lundell, Vancouver, BC. A virtual tour shows off this downtown Vancouver firm's stylish offices.
http://www.lawsonlundell.com/

Levine Associates, Toronto, Ont.
http://www.interlog.com/~levlaw/

Lienaux, Charles, Barrister & Solicitor, Halifax, NS.
http://fox.nstn.ca/~clienaux/

Linde, Carey, Barrister & Solicitor, Vancouver, BC. Hosts "The Surfing Lawyer," a site that links to law-related sites, and "Divorce for Men."
http://www.netlegal.com/

Lindsay Kenney, Vancouver, BC.
http://www.lindsaykenney.bc.ca/

Lowe & Co., Vancouver, BC. Articles on immigration law issues, as well as an online immigration assessment form.
http://www.lowe-co.com/lowe/

Lytle Fisher, Calgary, Alta.
http://www.ironclad.com/maclyfi/
home.html

Macaulay McColl, Vancouver, BC.
http://www.macaulay.com/

MacIsaac Group of Law Firms, Victoria, BC.
http://vvv.com/macvic/index.html

MacLean Nicol, Vancouver, BC. Information about divorce law and a "Child Support Guideline Calculator" from this boutique family law firm.
http://www.divorce.bc.ca/

MacMillan, S.G.R., Barrister & Solicitor, Toronto, Ont.
http://www.sgrm.com/

Mann & Associates, Ottawa, Ont.
http://www.ggmlaw.com/

Martin, Calvin, Barrister & Solicitor, Toronto, Ont.
http://www.calvinmartinqc.com/

McCarthy Tetrault, Toronto, Ont/Vancouver, BC. Features a searchable library of articles written by firm lawyers.
http://www.mccarthy.ca/

McCourt Law Offices, Edmonton, Alta. Edmonton, Alberta accident attorneys with, shall we say, a somewhat unconventional website.
http://plaza.powersurfr.com/mccourtlaw/

McLaughlin, Michael J., Barrister & Solicitor, Ottawa, Ont. Real estate and business law, wills and estates.
http://www.geocities.com/
michaeljmclaughlin/

McMaster, William A., Barrister & Solicitor, Toronto, Ont. Plaintiffs' personal injury and insurance litigation.
http://www.interlog.com/~wmlaw/

McMillan Binch, Toronto, Ont. An extensive (and searchable) collection of articles and publications organized by practice area.

http://www.mcbinch.com/

McNamee, John, Barrister & Solicitor, Burnaby, BC.
http://www.mcnamee-law.com/

Miller, Joel, Barrister & Solicitor, Toronto, Ont. Host to the Family Law Centre, a smartly designed collection of materials relating to family law.
http://www.familylawcentre.com/

Miller Thomson, Toronto, Ont/Calgary, Alta/Vancouver, BC.
http://www.millerthomson.ca/

Morahan & Aujla, Victoria, BC.
http://www.victorialaw.com

Morrie Sacks Law Corporation, Vancouver, BC. Divorce and family law site.
http://www.sackslaw.bc.ca/

Murphy Collette Murphy, Moncton, NB. *Law Notes*, a bimonthly newsletter to corporate clients, can be found here.
http://www.discribe.ca/murco/
profile.htm

Nickerson Roberts, Edmonton, Alta.
http://www.tgx.com/nickrob/

Ollek, Sucha S., Barrister & Solicitor, Nanaimo, BC. Articles on wills and estates and commercial issues at E-law, the site of this Nanaimo lawyer and mediator.
http://www.e-law.bc.ca/

Oscapella, Eugene, Barrister & Solicitor, Ottawa, Ont.
http://fox.nstn.ca/~eoscapel/

Osler, Hoskin & Harcourt LLP, Toronto, Ont. This well-designed site features an outstanding collection of articles and commentaries on recent legal developments.

http://www.osler.com/

Owen Bird, Vancouver, BC.
http://www.owenbird.com/

Oyen Wiggs Green & Mutala, Vancouver, BC. Articles and materials on intellectual property issues. Featured is information about filing requirements for patent, trademark and industrial design applications.
http://www.patentable.com/

Peterson Stark, Vancouver, BC.
http://www.petersonstark.bc.ca/

Pink Murray Graham, Halifax, NS.
http://www.criminaldefence.com/

Pope, William H., Barrister & Solicitor, Dawson Creek, BC. Home to PowerSoft Innovations, a legal technology company.
http://www.powerinn.com/

Pushor Mitchell, Lawyers, Kelowna, BC. The website of one of the largest law firms in BC's interior includes over 120 free legal information articles and alerts.
http://www.pushormitchell.com

Racioppo Zuber Coetzee Dionne, Mississauga, Ont.
http://www.rz-law.com/

Ramsay Thompson Lampman, Nanaimo, BC.
http://www.rtl-law.com/

Reid, McNaughton, St. Catharines, Ont.
http://www.vaxxine.com/lawyers/

Reynolds, Mirth, Richards & Farmer, Edmonton, Alta.
http://www.rmrf.ab.ca/

Richards Buell Sutton, Vancouver, BC. This site features "briefs" on legal issues.

http://www.rbs.com/

Riley, Bill, Barrister & Solicitor, Ottawa, Ont.
http://www.travel-net.com/~billr/

Robertson Stromberg, Saskatoon, Sask. Newsletters and materials on Saskatchewan law.
http://www.robertsonstromberg.com/

Rodrigues, Roger D., Law Offices of, Toronto, Ont. Materials relating to immigration law.
http://www.interlog.com/~rdrlaw/

Rogers, Moore, Toronto, Ont.
http://www.rogersmoore.com/

Rotenberg, Lawrence, Barrister & Solicitor, Dundas, Ont.
http://www.netaccess.on.ca/~roenberg/

Salloum Doak, Kelowna, BC.
http://www.awinc.com/salloum/

Saucier & Company, Burnaby, BC.
http://members.tripod.com/sauciercompany/index.html

Saxe, Dianne, Barrister & Solicitor, Toronto, Ont. *Faxletters*, a monthly newsletter on environmental law developments, is available here, as is the Environmental Resources page, a listing of links to environmental law sites around the globe.
http://www.envirolaw.com/

Shiller Layton Arbuck , Toronto, Ont.
http://www.shillers.com/

Sim, Peter, Barrister & Solicitor, Winnipeg, Man. Home to Canadian Legal Resources on the WWW, a comprehensive index to Canadian law sites on the web, organized

by resource type and by province, and also searchable.
http://www.mbnet.mb.ca/~psim/index.html

Singer, Colin, Barrister & Solicitor, Montréal, Que. A collection of materials on Canadian immigration law can be searched at this site.
http://www.singer.ca/

Singleton Urquhart Scott, Vancouver, BC. Articles and client alerts on environmental and construction law, among other practice areas, are featured at this site.
http://www.singleton.com/

Sklar, Murray, Barrister & Solicitor, Montréal, Que.
http://www.netaxis.qc.ca/fia/law.html

Smart & Biggar - Fetherstonhaugh & Co., Vancouver, BC/Ottawa, Ont. Patent and trademark agents. http://www.smart-biggar.ca/

Smith Lyons, Toronto, Ont. Featured at this site is an extensive and well organized set of links to Canadian law and other resources. Also here are legal commentaries, articles on doing business in Canada, and an extensive Information Technology Law page, with articles about and links to Internet legal issues.
http://www.smithlyons.ca/

Solomon, Grosberg, Toronto, Ont.
http://www.solgro.com/

Sorenson, Gary, Barrister & Solicitor, Kitchener, Ont. Materials and links relating to Canadian tax law.
http://members.home.com/gsorenson/taxlaw/

Sotos Associates, Toronto, Ont.
http://www.sotoskarvanis.com/

Steinberg, Morton, Frymer, North York, Ont.
http://www.smflaw.com/

Stewart McKelvey Stirling Scales, Saint John, NB.
http://www.smss.com/

Stitt Feld Handy Houston, Toronto, Ont. Articles, workshops, and links relating to alternative dispute resolution.
http://www.sfhh.com/

Sutherland, Mark, Bumstead, Flemming, Waterloo, Ont.
http://www.solicitors.com/

Swetsky, Eric, Barrister & Solicitor, Toronto, Ont.
http://advertisinglawyer.wld.com/

Torys, Toronto, Ont. Business Law Guides and Client Memoranda are featured at the website of one of Canada's largest firms.
http://www.torytory.ca/

Tremblay, Gabriel, Barrister & Solicitor, Montréal, Que.
http://gtavocat.cjb.net/

Weiler, Todd, Ottawa, Ont. Articles and links relating to international trade and regulatory reform.
http://www.cyberus.ca/~tweiler/

Weinman, Joyce, Barrister & Solicitor, Toronto, Ont. This site includes *Dental Legal News*, a newsletter "written for dentists, lawyers, dental hygienists, and patients."
http://www.inforamp.net/~gardblum/

Weir & Foulds, Toronto, Ont. Featured here is an extensive section on Doing Business

in Canada; also here are other firm articles and publications.
http://www.weirfoulds.com/

White, Ottenheimer & Baker, St. John's, NF. Articles and links relating to Newfoundland law.
http://www.wob.nf.ca/

Witten, Edmonton, Alta.
http://www.wittenlaw.com/

Woloshyn and Company, Regina and Saskatoon, Sask.
http://www.sasklaw.com/

COURTS

Alberta Courts. Information from the Alberta Court of Appeal, Court of Queen's Bench, and Provincial Court. Features full text cases from the Court of Appeal and Provincial Court since 1998. Searchable.
http://www.albertacourts.ab.ca/

British Columbia Provincial Court. BC Provincial Court Rules of Court, full text decisions, new judicial appointments, and information about the Court.
http://www.provincialcourt.bc.ca/

British Columbia Superior Courts. Website for the BC Supreme Court and Court of Appeal features full text cases from both levels of court. Cases are loaded the day of decision, archived since January 1996, and searchable. Also here are resources from both levels of court, including listings of judges, Notices and Practice Directions, addresses for court registries across BC, and Annual Reports.
http://www.courts.gov.bc.ca/

Federal Court of Canada. Decisions of the Federal Court are available in full text, beginning with cases from 1993, at the website of the Office of the Commissioner for Federal Judicial Affairs. Searchable by keyword or by drilling down through a subject listing. Also here are the Federal Court Rules and Forms, in several formats.
http://www.fja.gc.ca/en/cf/index.html

Manitoba Justice Court Registry System. A searchable record of all documents filed and hearings scheduled in the Manitoba Court of Appeal and the Manitoba Court of Queen's Bench. Contains Court of Queen's Bench records from 1984 and Court of Appeal records from 1991. Updated daily. Includes a court calendar.
http://www.jus.gov.mb.ca/registry/index.htm

Ontario Courts. Information from the Ontario Court of Appeal, Superior Court of Justice, and Ontario Court of Justice. Features the full text of Court of Appeal cases, dating from 1998.
http://www.ontariocourts.on.ca/

Prince Edward Island Supreme Court. Features the full text of PEI Supreme Court decisions since January 1, 1997 (in PDF format). Also here are PEI Rules of Civil Procedure, Supreme Court forms, and Practice Notes issued by the Chief Justice.
http://www.gov.pe.ca/courts/supreme/index.php3

Supreme Court of Canada. Website for the country's top court features full text of cases, dating from 1989, with an excellent search form (field searches are possible by case name, judge, abstract, cases considered, etc.). Also here is information about

the court and its members, a schedule of hearings, the full text of the Rules of the Supreme Court of Canada (including forms), Notices to the Profession, and instructions for filing an application for leave to appeal.
http://www.scc-csc.gc.ca/services.htm

GOVERNMENT

FINDING TOOLS

Canada's Government. The "Primary Internet Site" for the federal government, this is a key starting point when fishing for Canadian government material on the Internet. Links are available to all federal government Internet sites. Also featured are factsheets about Canada, a way to search for government information, and the Government Electronic Directory Services (GEDS), a searchable directory of phone numbers and email addresses for all federal public servants. From Public Works and Government Services.
http://canada.gc.ca

Canadian Government Information on the Internet. An outstanding collection of annotated links to government sites on the web, at federal, provincial, and municipal levels. Federal sites are organized by topic. Annotations are done by Anita Cannon and a host of contributors. Sponsored by Public Works and Government Services Canada. Searchable.

http://dsp-psd.pwgsc.gc.ca/dsp-psd/Reference/cgii_index-e.html

FEDERAL GOVERNMENT

Auditor General's Office. The full text of the Auditor General's reports can be found here.
http://www.oag-bvg.gc.ca/

Canada Customs and Revenue Agency (formerly Revenue Canada). Tax guides and forms, and such Revenue Canada publications as advance income tax rulings (ATRs), income tax information circulars (ICs), income tax interpretation bulletins (ITs), GST technical information bulletins, and GST notices.
http://www.ccra-adrc.gc.ca/

Canada's Government. The "Primary Internet Site" for the feds, including links to all other federal Internet sites. Includes a way to search over all documents at Canada Government sites.
http://canada.gc.ca/

Canadian Environmental Assessment Agency. Featured is a searchable "public registry system," a master list of all environmental assessments carried out under the *Canadian Environmental Assessment Act* (*CEEA*). Also available is the full text of the *CEEA* and regulations, as well as guides on environmental assessment policy and procedure to assist parties in complying with environmental regulations.
http://www.ceaa.gc.ca/

Canadian Intellectual Property Office. Includes access to the Canadian Patent Database (a searchable archive of over 75 years of patent descriptions and images), a trade-

marks database, the text of intellectual property legislation (such as the Patent Rules and the Trademarks Regulations), and guides to copyright, patents, trademarks and industrial designs.
http://strategis.ic.gc.ca/sc_mrksv/cipo/welcome/datb-e.html#cipologo

Citizenship and Immigration Canada. A very deep site featuring application kits and forms, policy documents and fact sheets, and Ministry Manuals and Operational Memoranda for Citizenship Policy, Legislation, Port of Entry Processing, and more.
http://www.cic.gc.ca

Environment Canada. A wealth of material relating to the environment.
http://www.ec.gc.ca/

Finance Canada. Federal budget documents and extensive body of background economic and tax material.
http://www.fin.gc.ca/

Fisheries & Oceans Canada. Available here are DFO news releases, newsletters and informational documents, the full text of fisheries acts, orders, and regulations, and links to regional fisheries-related sites.
http://www.ncr.dfo.ca

Health Canada. Extensive resources relating to health care and its regulation, including fact sheets and background material on diseases and health issues, as well as the full text of health regulations and guidelines.
http://www.hwc.ca

Immigration and Refugee Board of Canada. Features a searchable "Legislation Guide for the Immigration Appeal Division," and

RefLex, a searchable collection of digests of immigration and refugee law decisions since 1991.
http://www.cisr.gc.ca

Justice Canada. A searchable database of the Consolidated Statutes of Canada and the Consolidated Regulations of Canada. Also extensive materials on recent initiatives and other Justice publications.
http://canada.justice.gc.ca/

Industry Canada. Ministry news releases, speeches, newsletters, discussion papers, and annual reports.
http://info.ic.gc.ca/

National Archives. ArchiviaNet allows access a vast amount of information from various National Archives databases and resources.
http://www.archives.ca/

Natural Resources Canada. In addition to Ministry news releases, speeches, and newsletters, this site offers statistics on natural resources, a link to the searchable online catalogue of the Ministry Library, and links to other natural resources collections on the Internet.
http://www.nrcan.gc.ca/

Parliamentary Internet. The full text of bills on the order paper, Hansard from both the House of Commons and the Senate, Committee proceedings, and more. Searchable.
http://www.parl.gc.ca/36/main-e.htm

Statistics Canada. This site provides a searchable archive of StatsCan daily reports, the latest social and economic indicators (an excellent resource), and access to several statistical databases (for a fee). Links

are provided to other statistical offices around the globe.
http://www.statcan.ca

Strategis, Industry Canada's Business Information Site. A very deep site, Strategis offers such useful resources as a Database of Federally Incorporated Companies, where corporate data can be searched, trade and investment statistics and data, and extensive information on industry performance.
http://strategis.ic.gc.ca

Transport Canada. Featured here are consolidations of dozens of acts and regulations relating to Transport Canada programs, from the *Canada Shipping Act* and Regulations to the *Transportation of Dangerous Goods Act* and Regulations. Also here are extensive sections devoted to safety, aviation, marine transportation, land transportation, and dangerous goods.
http://www.tc.gc.ca/

PROVINCIAL GOVERNMENT

Alberta Government. Includes budget information, daily news releases, materials from government departments.
http://www.gov.ab.ca/

British Columbia Government. Government news releases, material from government departments, searchable directory of government employees. Includes a search tool that can search over many BC government websites.
http://www.gov.bc.ca/

Manitoba Government. Legislative proceedings, selected Ministry information, budget documents.
http://www.gov.mb.ca/

New Brunswick Government. Ministry information, budget documents, and legislative materials (bill tracking section and Hansard). A searchable site.
http://www.gov.nb.ca/

Newfoundland Government. Information on selected departments and ministries, budget documents.
http://www.gov.nf.ca/

Northwest Territories Government. Weekly government news, an excellent status of bills section, and the text of Hansard are featured at the NWT government website.
http://www.gov.nt.ca/

Nova Scotia Government. Budget documents, legislative materials (including a bills tracking section and the full text of recent bills), and government department information.
http://www.gov.ns.ca/

Nunavut Government. The website of Canada's third territory can be read in Inuktitut by downloading the free Nunacom font.
http://www.gov.nu.ca/

Ontario Government. Ontario legislation, government forms, government telephone directory, budget information, and Ministry information. A searchable site.
http://www.gov.on.ca/

Prince Edward Island Government. Budget documents, a chart tracking the progress of bills, and daily transcripts of proceedings before the Legislative Assembly.
http://www.gov.pe.ca/

Québec Government. Government policy documents and speeches, and Ministry information.

http://www.gouv.qc.ca/

Saskatchewan Government. Daily government news releases and department information, as well as budget documents.
http://www.gov.sk.ca/

Yukon Government. Daily government news, Hansard.
http://www.gov.yk.ca/

LAWS

FINDING TOOLS

Continuing Legal Education Society of BC's Legal Links. Categories are based on a Yahoo-like structure that includes listings of cases, statutes, regulations, and tribunal rulings.
http://www.cle.bc.ca/resources/

FindLaw. A (searchable) directory of legal resources in the United States, Canada, and elsewhere.
http://www.findlaw.com/

Virtual Canadian Law Library. This directory to Canadian law includes pointers to legislation, case law, and tribunal rulings.
http://www.lexum.umontreal.ca/index_en.html

CASE LAW

Alberta Courts. Website for the Alberta Court of Appeal, Court of Queen's Bench, and Provincial Court features full text cases

from the Court of Appeal and Provincial Court since 1998. Searchable.
http://www.albertacourts.ab.ca/

British Columbia Superior Courts. Website for the BC Supreme Court and Court of Appeal features full text cases from both levels of court. Cases are loaded the day of decision, archived since January 1996, and searchable. Also here are Notices and Practice Directions from both levels of court.
http://www.courts.gov.bc.ca/

Federal Court of Canada. Decisions of the Federal Court are available in full text, beginning with cases from 1993, at the website of the Office of the Commissioner for Federal Judicial Affairs. Searchable by keyword or by drilling down through a subject listing. Also here are the Federal Court Rules and Forms, in several formats.
http://www.fja.gc.ca/en/cf/index.html

Ontario Courts. Website for the Ontario Court of Appeal, Superior Court of Justice, and Ontario Court of Justice features the full text of Court of Appeal cases, dating from 1998.
http://www.ontariocourts.on.ca/

Prince Edward Island Supreme Court. Features the full text of PEI Supreme Court decisions since January 1, 1997 (in PDF format). Also here are PEI *Rules of Civil Procedure*, Supreme Court forms, and Practice Notes issued by the Chief Justice.
http://www.gov.pe.ca/courts/supreme/index.php3

Supreme Court of Canada. Full text of cases from the country's top court, dating from 1989. Available in web, text, RTF, and WordPerfect for Windows formats. Loaded the day of release. Searchable; field searches possible by case name, judge, abstract, cases considered, etc. A topical directory (search by concept) also allows you to drill down by subject listings to find cases. http://www.lexum.umontreal.ca/csc-scc/en/index.html

STATUTES & REGULATIONS

Alberta Statutes and Regulations. The full text of Alberta statutes and regulations, updated to July 2000.
http://www.gov.ab.ca/qp/indiv.html

British Columbia Statutes. The full text of the R.S.B.C. 1996, consolidated to November 1999, in a format that is easy to browse or download. From the BC Queen's Printer.
http://www.qp.gov.bc.ca/bcstats/index.htm

Canada Gazette. The official news bulletin of the Government of Canada, publishing public notices and proposed regulations (Part I), regulations and other statutory instruments (Part II), and the most recent Public Acts of Parliament and their enactment proclamations (Part III). Note that all Parts are in PDF format.
http://canada.gc.ca/gazette/gazette_e.html

Canada Statutes and Regulations. Full text of Statutes and Regulations of Canada, consolidated to April 30, 2000. Available in two formats: FolioViews for searching and text for easier downloading.
http://canada.justice.gc.ca/Loireg/index_en.html

Manitoba Statutes. Statutes of Manitoba consolidated to September 1999 (in pdf format).

http://www.gov.mb.ca/chc/statpub/free/index.html

New Brunswick Statutes. Full text of New Brunswick statutes, consolidated to March 31, 2000. Searchable.
http://www.gov.nb.ca/justice/asrlste.htm

Northwest Territories Statutes and Regulations. Statutes and Regulations of the Northwest Territories, current to September 2000, from the Access to Justice Network.
http://legis.acjnet.org/TNO/index_en.html

Nova Scotia Statutes. Statutes of Nova Scotia, consolidated to April 15, 1999, and searchable. From the Office of the Legislative Counsel, Nova Scotia House of Assembly.
http://www.gov.ns.ca/legi/legc/index.htm

Nunavut Statutes and Regulations. Statutes and regulations of Canada's newest territory, consolidated to April 1, 1999. Hosted by the Access to Justice Network.
http://legis.acjnet.org/nunavut/index_en.html

Ontario Statutes and Regulations. Ontario statutes and regulations consolidated to July 1, 1999. Searchable using the powerful (but not always easy to use) Folio web search engine. From Publications Ontario and onto the web via Libraxus, Inc.
http://209.195.107.57/en/index.html

Yukon Statues and Regulations. Statutes (including 1999 Statutes) and regulations (consolidated to December 31, 1997) of Yukon.
http://legis.acjnet.org/Yukon/index_en.html

LEGISLATIVE MATERIALS

Alberta's Legislative Assembly. The full text of bills, Hansard, and an excellent status of bills section. Searchable.
http://www.assembly.ab.ca/

British Columbia Legislative Assembly. Full text of first and third reading bills, dating from 1992. Progress of bills section tracks status of bills. Hansard, votes, and orders of the day are also available. A searchable site.
http://www.legis.gov.bc.ca/

Manitoba Legislative Assembly. Legislative materials include a status of legislation section, the full text of bills (in PDF format), the Legislative Assembly Rule Book, and (when using Real Player software), live broadcasts of Question Period.
http://www.gov.mb.ca/leg-asmb/
index.html

New Brunswick Legislative Assembly. The text of first reading bills, a status of legislation section, Journals of the Legislative Assembly, and Committee reports.
http://www.gov.nb.ca/legis/index.htm

Newfoundland House of Assembly. Hansard and background information.
http://www.gov.nf.ca/house/

Nova Scotia House of Assembly. Text of first reading and assented to bills, progress of bills section, Hansard, consolidated statutes, and more at this excellent site.
http://www.gov.ns.ca/legi/index.htm

Ontario Legislative Assembly. Bill tracking section, full text of first reading bills, Hansard, orders and notices paper, votes and proceedings.
http://www.ontla.on.ca/

Parliamentary Internet. The full text of bills on the order paper, Hansard from both the House of Commons and the Senate, Committee proceedings, and more. Searchable.
http://www.parl.gc.ca/36/main-e.htm

Prince Edward Island Legislative Assembly. A progress of bills section, text of first reading bills (in PDF format), Hansard (available three days after each sitting day), and broadcasts of proceedings via RealAudio.
http://www.gov.pe.ca/leg/index.php3

Quebec National Assembly. Full text of bills, transcripts of debates before National Assembly (Hansard). Order paper and notices, votes and proceedings. Keyword searchable.
http://www.assnat.qc.ca/eng/Publications
/index.html

Saskatchewan Legislative Assembly. Bill tracking section, full text of bills, Hansard, daily votes and proceedings.
http://www.legassembly.sk.ca/

TRIBUNAL DECISIONS

Alberta Labour Relations Board. Recent decisions of the Alberta LRB are available here until published in the Alberta Labour Relations Board Reports and entered into QL's database. Also here are the Board's Rules of Procedure, Voting Rules, Information Bulletins, and newsletters, as well as a guide to the *Labour Relations Code* and the *Public Service Employee Relations Act*.
http://www.gov.ab.ca/alrb/

British Columbia Environmental Appeal Board. Available here are the full text and summaries of decisions of the Environmental Appeal Board, the EAB Procedure Man-

ual, and information on filing appeals under BC environmental legislation.
http://www.eab.gov.bc.ca/

British Columbia Human Rights Tribunal. The full text of Tribunal decisions since 1997, a schedule of hearings, the full text of the *Human Rights Code,* and information on Tribunal procedure.
http://www.bchrt.gov.bc.ca/

British Columbia Labour Relations Board. Features recent Board decisions (in PDF format), LRB Rules, the Labour Relations Regulation, LRB guidelines and bulletins, and relevant forms.
http://www.lrb.bc.ca/

British Columbia Office of the Information and Privacy Commissioner. Full text of orders and other decisions made by the Commissioner, investigation and site visit reports, and links to other resources dealing with freedom of information and protection of privacy.
http://www.oipcbc.org/

British Columbia Securities Commission. Features a full text (and searchable) archive of policy documents, including National and Local Policy Statements, Notices & Interpretation Notes, Blanket Orders & Rulings, news releases, and forms. Also available are recent Commission decisions, a schedule of hearings (updated weekly), a searchable database of registered dealers and advisers, and SEDAR updates (in PDF format).
http://www.bcsc.bc.ca/

British Columbia Workers' Compensation Board. WorkSafe online features WCB news releases, newsletters, publications on occupational safety and health, regulations, forms, decisions of the Appeal Division (taken from the *Workers' Compensation Reporter*), and such policy documents and manuals as the *Rehabilitation Services and Claims Manual* and the *Prevention Manual* (Bill 14 Policies).
http://www.wcb.bc.ca/

Canadian Human Rights Tribunal. The text of all the decisions rendered by the Tribunal since 1990, as well as a consolidated *Canadian Human Rights Act.*
http://www.chrt-tcdp.gc.ca/

Canadian International Trade Tribunal. The CITT, an administrative tribunal that conducts inquiries into trade disputes, includes at its website the full text of the Tribunal's decisions and investigations. Also here are the Tribunal's guidelines, practice notes, and other publications, and links to other trade-related sites.
http://www.citt.gc.ca/menu_e.htm

Canadian Radio-television and Telecommunications Commission. The full text of CRTC decisions, notices, and orders, made available within a day of their release. Also here is telecommunications legislation and CRTC news releases.
http://www.crtc.gc.ca/

Competition Tribunal. Summary information on all applications filed with the Tribunal, and the full text of selected decisions issued by the Tribunal after 1990.
http://www.ct-tc.gc.ca/

Copyright Board Canada. Decisions of the Copyright Board, certified and proposed tariffs issued by the Board, and the full text of the *Copyright Act* and regulations.

http://www.cb-cda.gc.ca/

Ontario Human Rights Commission. Available here is the text of the *Ontario Human Rights Code*, summaries of recent decisions from the Human Rights Board of Inquiry and the courts relating to human rights issues, and Ontario Human Rights Commission policy documents.
http://www.ohrc.on.ca/

Ontario Securities Commission. Includes enforcement decisions of the Commission since 1997, the text of Commission orders and rulings, investor information, and lists of all reporting issuers and all companies registered to sell securities in Ontario.
http://www.osc.gov.on.ca/

LEGAL EDUCATION

FINDING TOOLS

Canadian Law Schools. From the Council of Canadian Law Deans, this site provides links to the websites of all Canadian law schools, with contact information.
http://www.canadalawschools.org/

CONTINUING LEGAL EDUCATION

Continuing Legal Education Society of BC. Features legal news and commentary including digests of recent BC court cases, practice directions from the courts, and links to legal resources elsewhere. A course calendar and publications catalogue offer information about courses and practice manuals, in every area of law, for lawyers and legal support staff.
http://www.cle.bc.ca

Continuing Legal Education Society of Nova Scotia. Information about CLE of Nova Scotia courses and publications, and links to resources elsewhere.
http://www.cle.ns.ca/

Legal Education Society of Alberta. Includes a schedule of upcoming LESA courses, information about and an application form for the Alberta Bar Admission Course, and the LESA research guide, a searchable index to papers published by LESA. A searchable site.
http://www.lesa.org/

Federation of Law Societies of Canada National CLE Programs. Information about the National Criminal and Family Law Programs put on by the Federation of Law Societies of Canada.
http://www.flsc.ca/english/
nationalcleprograms/education.htm

LAW REFORM

Alberta Law Reform Institute. ALRI papers and reports, as well as updates on work in progress.
http://www.law.ualberta.ca/alri/

British Columbia Law Institute. Text of Institute papers, constitutional documents, databases, and links to other law reform bodies around the world. An outstanding resource.
http://www.lawreform.gov.bc.ca/

Law Commission of Canada. Papers, projects, and news releases from the law re-

form agency responsible to the Parliament of Canada.
http://www.lcc.gc.ca/

Nova Scotia Law Reform Commission. Text of Commission discussion papers and reports.
http://www.chebucto.ns.ca/Law/LRC/LRC-Home.html

LAW SCHOOLS

Dalhousie Law School. Available at the website is an online version of the Law School's Calendar, faculty profiles and email addresses, as well as a link to Novanet, a searchable database of the collections of several Nova Scotia libraries, including the Law School's. http://is.dal.ca/~wwwlaw/index.html

McGill University – Faculty of Law. Registration materials, information about the faculty, course materials, and the *McGill Law Journal* are among the offerings at this well designed site.
http://www.law.mcgill.ca/

Osgoode Hall Law School. Program and school information, as well as CLE programs, the *Osgoode Hall Law Journal*, and (on the School "Intranet"), course schedules, websites, contact info and more. http://www.osgoode.yorku.ca

Queen's University Faculty of Law. In addition to information about the Law School, its programs and faculty, this site offers electronic course materials, an index to the *Queen's Law Journal*, and aids to conducting legal research.
http://qsilver.queensu.ca/law/

Université de Moncton – École de droit. Information about the Law School and its programs is available here.
http://www.umoncton.ca/droit/

Université de Montréal – Faculté de droit. The Centre for Public Law Research (CRDP) has been a leader in providing legal information on the Internet. The CRDP's website hosts the outstanding Supreme Court of Canada decisions database. Other resources include a version of the *Quebec Civil Code* (in French), and the Directory of the Canadian Association of Law Teachers (a searchable archive containing biographies and contact addresses of law teachers in Canada).
http://www.droit.umontreal.ca/

Université de Sherbrooke – Faculté de droit. Program and school information.
http://www.usherb.ca/droit/

Université du Québec à Montréal – Département des sciences juridiques. Available at this site is information about the school and its programs, electronic course materials, abstracts of articles in the *Canadian Journal of Law and Society*, and such institutes as Centre d'études sur le droit international et la mondialisation.
http://www.juris.uqam.ca/

Université Laval – Faculté de droit. Program and school information.
http://www.ulaval.ca/fd/

University of Alberta – Faculty of Law. Beyond information about the Law School and its programs are several valuable resources, including a host of research centres, such as the Alberta Law Reform Institute and the Health Law Institute.
http://www.law.ualberta.ca/

University of British Columbia – Faculty of Law. Information about the Law School and its programs mingles with a series of valuable documents and links at this site. Among the research centres hosted by this site are the FLAIR Project (Faculty of Law Artificial Intelligence Research Project), which develops expert systems for researching case law, and the International Centre for Criminal Law Reform and Criminal Justice Policy, which offers conference papers and articles on such topics as domestic violence and international corrections, as well as links to related sites, from Amnesty International to the United Nations Criminal Justice Information Network.
http://www.law.ubc.ca/

University of Calgary – Faculty of Law. In addition to information about the Law School and its programs, this site provides a home for the Canadian Institute of Resources Law. The Law Library section offers helpful "research guides" and a deep and well organized collection of links to other Canadian law sites on the Internet.
http://www.ucalgary.ca/UofC/faculties/LAW/

University of Manitoba – Faculty of Law. School information includes a faculty email directory. Also here is information about the *Manitoba Law Journal,* the Legal Research Institute publications catalogue, and a link to the collections catalogue at the E.K. Williams Law Library.
http://www.umanitoba.ca/faculties/law/

University of New Brunswick – Faculty of Law. Beyond school and program information are links to legal resources on the Internet, and a way to search over the catalogue of the New Brunswick Law Society Library.
http://www.unb.ca/web/law/UNBLAW.html

University of Ottawa, Faculty of Common Law. Program and school information, as well as material from the Human Rights Research and Education Centre and the Centre for Trade Policy and Law. http://www.uottawa.ca/academic/commonlaw/

University of Saskatchewan – College of Law. Information for prospective and current students, a faculty directory, and from the Law Library site, links to law sites on the Internet and a link to the Law Library catalogue.
http://law.usask.ca/

University of Toronto Faculty of Law. Information about the school, its programs, and the faculty is available, as well as a directory of faculty publications, the Constitutional Studies page, a comprehensive guide to Canadian and international law on the web, and a link to the U of T Library Catalogue database, which can perform searches over the collections in close to 50 libraries at the University, including the Bora Laskin Law Library.
http://www.law.utoronto.ca

University of Victoria – Faculty of Law. Law School and program information is here, including an admissions package. Also here is a directory of faculty publications, such institutes as the Environmental Law Centre and the UVic Institute for Dispute Resolution, UVic Law News and an alumni update section (memo to alumni: it's never been so easy to stay in touch with the Alma Mater).

http://www.law.uvic.ca

University of Western Ontario – Faculty of Law. School and program information.
http://www.uwo.ca/law/

University of Windsor – Faculty of Law. School and program information.
http://www.uwindsor.ca/law/

LEGAL ORGANIZATIONS

FINDING TOOLS

Federation of Law Societies of Canada. This site provides information about and contact numbers for law societies in each province, as well as links to those law societies with websites. Also here is material about Federation committees and activities, and the text of the By-laws of the Federation.
http://www.flsc.ca/

BAR ASSOCIATIONS & OTHER LAW ASSOCIATIONS

American Bar Association. Information on ABA events, entities and publications.
http://www.abanet.org/

Canadian Association of Law Libraries. CALL membership info, as well as news, activities, and publication information.
http://www.callacbd.ca/

Canadian Association of Law Teachers. CALT information, and a searchable directory of Canadian law teachers.
http://www2.lexum.umontreal.ca/acpd/index.cfm?Lan=AN

Canadian Bar Association. CBA membership info, publications, initiatives, and meetings.
http://www.cba.org/

Canadian Bar Association - British Columbia Branch. News releases, issue alerts, legislative updates, section information, and an events calendar highlight the BC section of the CBA website.
http://www.bccba.org/gate.asp

Canadian Bar Association - Ontario Branch. A schedule of upcoming section meetings and CLE seminars, an index to CLE materials, and information about CBA programmes and resources.
http://www.cbao.org/gate.asp

Canadian Society for the Advancement of Legal Technology. CSALT news, events, and a catalogue of law office technology products.
http://www.csalt.on.ca/

Legal Research Network. LRN events, updates, and membership info.
http://notinprint.com/lrn/

Ontario Trial Lawyers Association. OTLA conferences and events, and (for members only) searchable databases of expert witnesses and OTLA publications.
http://www.otla.com/

Trial Lawyers Association of BC. The TLABC site features a calendar of upcoming

events, section news, and (for members only) issues of *The Verdict* and *TLABC Update*.
http://www.tlabc.org/

Victoria Bar Association. Features upcoming events of the local bar association in Victoria.
http://www.vicbar.com/

West Coast Women's Legal Education and Action Fund (LEAF). Extensive resources on the litigation, law reform and public legal education activities of West Coast LEAF. Includes Leaflet newsletters, legal updates, and a FAQ on equality rights.
http://www.westcoastleaf.org/

LAW SOCIETIES

Law Society of British Columbia. The Resource Library includes the *Legal Profession Act*, the *Law Society Rules*, the *Professional Conduct Handbook*, Practice Checklists, and Benchers newsletters. Also here are notices to the profession, services for lawyers, and a calendar of Law Society meetings and events.
http://www.lawsociety.bc.ca/

Federation of Law Societies of Canada. Information about and contact numbers for law societies in each province, as well as links to law society websites. Also FLSC news, activities, publications, and CLE programs.
http://www.flsc.ca/

Law Society of Alberta. Features the full text of the *Legal Profession Act of Alberta*, the *Rules of the Law Society of Alberta*, Law Society forms, the *Code of Professional Conduct*

for the Legal Profession, and Benchers Advisories.
http://www.lawsocietyalberta.com/

Law Society of Manitoba. Information about Law Society activities and publications.
http://www.lawsociety.mb.ca/

Law Society of Saskatchewan. Features a searchable catalogue of all Law Society libraries in Saskatchewan, as well as (for pay) databases of Saskatchewan case digests, judgments, and bills.
http://www.lawsociety.sk.ca/

Law Society of Upper Canada. Features legislation and rules governing lawyers in Ontario, notices to the profession, and issues of the *Ontario Lawyers Gazette*.
http://www.lsuc.on.ca/

Nova Scotia Barristers' Society. Features issues of the Society Record, email and web addresses for Nova Scotia lawyers, and links to sites relating to Nova Scotia law.
http://www.nsbs.ns.ca/index.html

LEGAL-RELATED BUSINESSES

FINDING TOOLS

Hieros Gamos. Maintained by Lex Mundi, a global association of over 100 law firms, this searchable site has exhaustive listings

of law-related businesses around the world, both on the Internet and off.
http://www.hg.org/

LAW PUBLISHERS

Butterworths Canada. A publications catalogue and excerpts from the current edition of the *Lawyers Weekly* are featured here.
http://www.butterworths.ca/

Canada Law Book. A publications catalogue and CD ROM demonstration page are featured at CLB's website.
http://www.canadalawbook.ca

Carswell Professional Publishing. This site includes a searchable publications catalogue, product samplers, and the most recent issue of *Law Book News*.
http://www.carswell.com

CCH Canadian. Featured here is a searchable publications catalogue, free information samplers for downloading, and links to law and business-related sites.
http://www.ca.cch.com

Maritime Law Book. This site features the National Reporter System Online, a searchable database of MLB reporter series.
http://www.mlb.nb.ca/

McGraw-Hill Ryerson. A searchable publications catalogue is available here.
http://www.mcgrawhill.ca/

Micromedia. Featured is an online catalogue and product samples for downloading.
http://www.mmltd.com/

Western Legal Publications. A publications catalogue is featured at WLP's website.
http://www.westernlegal.com/

LEGAL SUPPORT SERVICES

CCNS - The Information Place. A public records searching and filing service.
http://www.ccnsinfo.com/

The Counsel Network. Lawyer recruitment and career services.
http://www.headhunt.com/

Dye & Durham. Legal office products & search services.
http://www.dyedurham.ca/

Harcourts. Robemakers & tailors.
http://www.harcourts.com/

Litigation Management Inc. This site includes a guide to managing complex litigation.
http://www.litigate.com/

Marshall Research Corporation. Computer software.
http://www.marshallresearch.com/

Sands & Associates. This site, from a firm of bankruptcy trustees, includes extensive materials relating to bankruptcies in Canada.

ONLINE DATABASE PROVIDERS

DIALOG. This sophisticated site features search tips and information about the company's databases, including a searchable database catalogue.
http://www.dialog.com

eCARSWELL. The website for Carswell's Internet-based online services available in several practice areas (law.pro, securities.pro, bankruptcy.pro and family.pro). Also here is a gateway for accessing Westlaw.

http://www.ecarswell.com/

INFOMART. Featured at Infomart's website are daily front page news clippings from the *Montreal Gazette*, the *Ottawa Citizen*, the *Calgary Herald*, and the *Vancouver Sun and Province*. Also here is a searchable list of databases.
http://www.infomart.ca

LEXIS-NEXIS. The website of the United States-based online legal database provider includes a database listing, a technical manual, search tips, and all the product information you could possibly want.
http://www.lexis-nexis.com

QUICKLAW. The website of this online legal database provider features timely summaries of Canada's hottest new cases and legal documents, including most Supreme Court of Canada decisions within a day of their release. Also here is a customer service page, a listing of QL databases, and Quicklink software for downloading.
http://www.quicklaw.com/

GLOSSARY

ADSL. Asymmetric Digital Subscriber Line. The latest trend in high-speed Internet access, ADSL is a high-speed data service that works over copper telephone lines that can support downstream bandwidths of up to 8 Mbps and upstream bandwidths of 1.5 Mbps.

ANSI. American National Standards Institute. The body responsible for standards like ASCII.

ARPA. Advance Research Projects Agency, sponsored by the US Department of Defense.

ARPANET. ARPA Network (see ARPA). An early experiment in networking computers, ARPANET was based on the TCP/IP protocol and was specifically intended to withstand partial collapse due to nuclear war. It is commonly viewed as the genesis of the Internet.

ASCII. American Standard Code for Information Interchange. A standard for representing computer characters that allows for data to be transferred between different computer systems.

ASCII art. The sometimes artistic practice of making designs from the ASCII character set. These are encountered most frequently appended to Internet correspondence. ASCII art can be elaborate and creative, using the character set to represent people or other images.

Bandwidth. The size of the data pipeline, typically described in terms of the amount of data that can be transferred over a particular line in a given period of time. The higher the bandwidth, the faster the data flows. Bandwidth is commonly measured in bits per second (bps).

Baud. The Baud Rating is named after a 19th century French scientist named Baudot who used it to compare the speeds of Morse code transmission. In common parlance Baud Rate refers to the number of bits a modem can send or receive per second.

BBS. Bulletin Board System. Usually refers to a small, dial-up computer system designed for local users, although many BBSes are now more broadly accessible via the Internet.

Bit. A Binary Digit (zero or one). The smallest unit of data handled by computers.

BITNET. An academic network providing email and file transfer services. BITNET also carries mailing lists on various subjects.

Bookmark. A navigational aid used by World Wide Web browsers. Bookmarks allow the user to return directly to the location of a particular Internet resource, even in a subsequent online session, without searching or committing the resource address to memory.

Boolean Search Logic. The use of the logical operators "and," "or" and "not" to modify and focus a search query, giving it more accuracy than a basic keyword search.

Browser. A piece of client software used to navigate the World Wide Web. AOL's Netscape Navigator and Microsoft's Internet Explorer are two leading web browsers.

BTW. Abbreviation for By The Way. Commonly used in Internet correspondence.

CA*Net. The network that once formed the backbone of the Internet in Canada.

Cancelbot. A software program first developed by Norwegian programmer Arnt Gulbrandsen, which can be used to automatically erase targeted postings from a newsgroup server.

Client. Software that requests services from another computer (called the server). One half of the client/server model of computing.

Compression. A utility function which allows a given file to be stored and transmitted in compacted form, thus saving time and storage space. Such a file must be decompressed before reading or running.

Cryptography. The study of encoding messages or data for transmission using a cypher, or code (see encryption).

Daemon. Despite its name, a benign UNIX program that, among other things, handles Internet email deliveries that do not reach their intended recipient. If your email can not for some reason reach your correspondent, you will get back your original message plus a message from a "mailer daemon."

Directory. An Internet information resource that organizes Internet resources into some kind of logical structure, usually based on subject topic or geographic location.

DNS. Domain Name System. The system that locates the IP addresses corresponding to named computers and domains (see Domain Name).

Domain Name. A unique description of a computer having host status on the Internet. The name takes the form of words separated into segments by dots (periods). The segments increase in specificity moving from right to left, from country or organization type, to site name, to computer name.

Download. The operation of copying a file from a remote computer "down" to a local computer.

Electronic signature. A small block of encrypted text attached by the author to the bottom of a document. The signature is encrypted by the author, and can be decrypted by recipients to verify the document's origin (see encryption).

Email. Electronic mail. The central communications service on the Internet, and on networks in general. Email takes the form of typewritten notes, exchanged between any two users with email addresses on the same network.

Emoticon. Symbols, or emotional constructs, used as punctuation in Internet correspondence to remind the reader of inended humour or other emotion. :-) is the most common emoticon, so much so that emoticons are often referred to as smileys.

Encryption. The practice of encoding data for transmission. The sender and recipient must share a common decryption program, or key, in order to participate in encrypted communication.

Ethernet. A common networking standard for Local Area Networks.

F2F. Abbreviation for Face to Face. When you actually meet those people you have been corresponding with over the Internet.

FAQ. A Frequently Asked Questions list is a document covering basic information relating to a given topic, newsgroup or mailing list.

Finger. A protocol used for locating people on the Internet. Finger servers maintain information about the individual users on a given network. They may be set up to respond to public enquiries (from Finger clients) regarding a local user's identity or email address.

Firewall. A software/hardware barrier that controls access to a network from outside the network. A firewall is a particularly important precaution when linking an existing network to the Internet. Without a firewall between an office LAN and the Internet, for example, unauthorized traffic from the public Internet can access the private resources on the LAN.

Flame. Colloquial term for an argumentative, even hostile, posting or email note. Flames exchanged between two or more participants are called collectively Flame Wars.

Freenet. Free Internet Service Providers, generally set up by community non-profit organizations to provide free dial-up access to the Internet.

Freeware. Software that the author makes available for public use without the expectation of payment. Many such programs are available for download from Internet host computers.

FTP. File Transfer Protocol. One of the Internet's original information retrieval services. FTP allows you to visit a remote host computer and to take data and other public files home with you.

GIF. Graphics Interchange Format. A format developed in the mid-1980s by CompuServe to store photo-quality graphic images in electronic form. Now commonly used everywhere online.

Gopher. A sophisticated information retrieval service developed at the University of Minnesota, now largely superceded by the World Wide Web. Gopher is built on thousands of linked menus maintained by universities and other institutions. The menus provide access to a range of resources, including text, graphics, and links to other Internet services such as FTP and telnet.

Gopherspace. Colloquial name for the total of all linked gopher menus, which collectively provide the user with a navigable virtual "space" containing information.

Host. A computer on a network providing services to other computers. In the case of the Internet, these services might include, for example, email, FTP, and the World Wide Web.

HTML. HyperText Markup Language. The language used to create hypertext documents for the World Wide Web. HTML is a simple implementation of Standard Generalized Markup Language (SGML), an international standard for the description of marked-up electronic text (see also Hypertext).

HTTP. HyperText Transfer Protocol, which governs the transfer of hypertext files on the Internet. HTTP is built on the client-server model of computing. The World Wide Web is built in large part on the HTTP protocol.

Hypertext. 1. Highlighted words (or links) within a document that can be selected in order to access another document, which is typically related topically to the highlighted word. 2. Documents containing such links.

IANAL. Abbreviation for I Am Not A Lawyer. Employed by some Internet users when debating legal matters, especially preceding statements for which they wish to take no responsibility.

IMHO. Abbreviation for In My Humble Opinion. An expression used in Internet correspondence, usually signifying that the thoughts that follow will be anything but humble.

Internet. A worldwide system of interconnected computer networks operating on an agreed set of protocols called collectively TCP/IP (see TCP/IP).

InterNIC. A US-based registrar of Internet Domain Names.

IP address. A unique numeric Internet address that is assigned to each Internet host computer. Like the Domain Name, the IP (for Internet Protocol) address comprises segments separated by dots (periods). An IP address always has four parts that identify the precise location and name of the computer in concern.

IRC. Internet Relay Chat. The Internet's version of the party phone-line. The IRC protocol permits real-time discussion with other participants, by typing comments on-screen in turn. IRC conversations take place on "channels" that can be created, joined or left freely by participants.

IRL. Abbreviation for In Real Life. A phrase acknowledging that reality does exist outside the cyber-confines of the Internet.

ISDN. Integrated Services Digital Network. A mechanism to exact more transmission speed out of existing phone lines, from 64 Kbps and up.

ISP. Internet Service Provider. Usually a commercial operation providing dial-up access to the Internet to individuals not directly connected themselves.

Killfile. A file created in a news reader software program that allows the user to filter newsgroup postings to some extent, by excluding messages on certain topics or from certain people.

LAN. Local Area Network. A network of computers located in the same physical area.

LISTSERV. A popular mailing list management software program, also referred to as a remailing program. The term LISTSERV is also often used interchangeably with the term mailing lists (see Mailing list).

Lurk. What Internet users call hanging out in a newsgroup or mailing list, reading the postings and not actually posting anything. Not pejorative normally, lurking is actually recommended for newcomers, to give them time to pick up the flavour of the discussion and get up to speed on the topic.

Mailing list. Mailing lists permit users to post messages via a remailing program, which duplicates the messages and re-mails them to every subscriber on the given mailing list. Mailing lists exist on a very wide range of topics and are often moderated, which lends to a high quality of information exchange.

MIME. Multi-purpose Internet Mail Extensions. An extension of the Internet mail protocol that enables sending of 8-bit email messages, i.e., to support extended character sets, voice mail, fax images, etc.

Modem. Hardware allowing a personal computer user to receive and transmit data over phone lines.

Mosaic. The first very widespread web browser (a software program used to view the World Wide Web).

Net.god. Someone who has been on the Internet since the Precambrian era (i.e., since before 1990), who has seen it all and knows how to use UNIX.

Net.police. Internet users who zealously impose on others their interpretation of Internet culture and protocol. The more tactful of these users are sometimes referred to as Net.citizens; the more combative are at times known as Net.nazis.

Netiquette. The total of all rules and conventions, written and unwritten, governing interaction on the Internet.

Netscape. A software program used to view the World Wide Web. The leading web browser before it was surpassed by Microsoft's Internet Explorer.

Network. Any hardware/software configuration of multiple computers (or one computer and one or more terminals) designed to allow the sharing of data resources between multiple users.

Newbie. Someone who is new to the Internet. This term is usually used with a derogatory edge by experienced Internet users who have forgotten that they, too, were once newbies who didn't know the answer to everything.

Newsgroups. Venues on the Internet for lively discussion along highly topical lines.

Newsgroups resemble electronic bulletin boards, where users post messages to a common site, and read and respond to those postings that are of interest to them.

NSFNet. A high-speed network that once formed the backbone of the Internet in the United States, and was funded by the National Science Foundation.

PGP. Pretty Good Privacy. A popular encryption program (see encryption).

PPP. Point to Point Protocol (see SLIP).

Protocol. The set of rules that governs how different computers can communicate and work together without confusion. On the Internet, a protocol is the standard governing a given service.

RFC. Request For Comments. A series of documents available on the Internet that describe technical aspects of the Internet.

ROT13. A simple encoding scheme in which each letter in a message is replaced by the letter 13 spaces away from it in the alphabet. As you might expect, not used for high-level encoding.

ROTFL. Abbreviation for Rolling on the Floor Laughing. An expression used in Internet correspondence to indicate just how amusing another's comment was.

Router. A special piece of hardware that handles communications between two networks. Between an office LAN and the Internet (along with a Firewall, see above) will typically stand a router.

RSA Public Key Encryption. A class of encryption program named for its inventors Rivest, Shamir and Adelman. When first activated, an RSA Public Key Encryption program will create two keys. One is the sender's private key. The other is a public key, which the sender distributes to intended recipients. Any two network users can exchange encrypted messages as long as they have exchanged their public keys.

RSN. Abbreviation for Real Soon Now. A somewhat ironic version of ASAP.

RTFM. Abbreviation for Read the F -ing Manual. A rather harsh expression used in Internet correspondence to suggest that the recipient should spend time reading a FAQ list or a manual before asking what the writer perceives to be an elementary question. Sometimes collapsed to the more polite RTM.

Search Engine. A software tool allowing you to perform keyword or subject searches over all, or a portion of, the Internet.

Server. A computer running a software package (or the software package itself) that provides a particular service to clients (see Client). The server is the other half of the client/server model of computing.

Shareware. Software that the author makes available for public use on the basis that eventually they will receive payment for it. Usually, shareware is offered for no initial charge, and payment is made on the honour system after a trial period. Many such programs are available for download from Internet host computers.

.Sig file. A short message appended to Internet correspondence, typically containing information about the author. Also known as a signature file. ASCII art frequently shows up in .sig files (see ASCII art).

Signal to noise ratio. Signal (useful information on a site or in a discussion) expressed as "high" or "low" relative to Noise (useless, distracting information in the same discussion or site)—e.g., "There are so many flame wars going on, this newsgroup has a real low signal to noise ratio."

SLIP. Serial Line Internet Protocol. This protocol, like PPP (see PPP above), allows the dial-up Internet user to enjoy the full possibilities of a TCP/IP connection. Instead of merely logging into someone else's host computer and looking at the Internet through that host's shell, SLIP and PPP allow the user to temporarily become a host on the Internet.

Snail mail. Internet colloquialism for the postal service, which, as the term suggests, is considered agonizingly slow by most Internet users.

Spam. To post the same message individually to a wide number of newsgroups or mailing lists without considering the suitability of the posting to the discussions in progress. Spam is also used as a noun—e.g., "Canter and Siegel perpetrated one of the biggest spams in the history of the Internet."

Sysadmin. A system administrator. Someone who runs a host system or public access site.

Sysop. A system operator. Someone who runs a Bulletin Board System.

T1 link. A leased phone line offering 1.544 Mbps transmission speed.

T3 link. A leased phone line offering an even better 45 Mbps transmission speed.

TANSTAAFL. Abbreviation for There Ain't No Such Thing as a Free Lunch. Some Internet users actually do use this complex acronym in their correspondence.

TCP/IP. Transmission Control Protocol/Internet Protocol. Used to refer to the total set of protocols that govern every operation performed on the Internet. TCP and IP are actually two specific protocols that govern two particular Internet operations (although arguably the most important ones). TCP breaks down and re-assembles data into packets for transmission between computers. IP expedites delivery of the packets by routing them in transit.

Telnet. An early Internet service that allows you to login to a remote host computer as a terminal. Once logged on through telnet, you can operate the host machine in the way it was intended: exploring an online catalogue for example.

Terminal emulation. The process whereby a computer acts like a terminal for the purposes of a given operation.

Terminal. A device that allows you to send commands to a remote computer (a host).

TIA. Abbreviation for Thanks In Advance.

UNIX. An operating system specifically intended for multi-user use. UNIX has the TCP/IP protocol built in.

URL. Uniform Resource Locator. The address of a given Internet resource. It provides the user with information on the precise location of the resource (country, host computer, filename) as well as the service that can be used to access the resource (email, the World Wide Web etc.).

Usenet. A world wide system of news-groups, Usenet is available via the Internet and features many of the most popular newsgroups on the Internet.

UUCP. UNIX to UNIX CoPy. A method for transferring email and newsgroup postings that requires fewer resources than TCP/IP, but which can result in much slower transfer times.

Virus. A program developed by a programmer and run by a user (albeit an unwitting user). A virus program is typically replicating; i.e., it copies itself to any new disk or diskette it comes in contact with, and causes variable damage to the host system, from minor performance impairment to total system collapse.

VT100. A terminal emulation standard based on the Digital Equipment Corporation's VT100 terminal, the industry standard in the 1970s.

W3C. The parent body in the World Wide Web maturation process.

WAIS. Wide Area Information Servers. An information retrieval and publishing tool conceived in 1991 by Brewster Kahle at Thinking Machines Inc. WAIS servers contain databases over which full text searches can be run, returning hits ordered by relevance.

Web browser. A piece of client software used to navigate the World Wide Web. Netscape Navigator and Internet Explorer are two leading web browsers.

Web. The World Wide Web. The dominant service of the Internet. The web, as it is commonly called, is built on a figurative web of linked multimedia documents containing combinations of text, graphics, sound, and moving images.

Webmaster. Someone who runs a World Wide Web site.

Website. A site on the World Wide Web.

WWW. The World Wide Web (see Web).

YMMV. An abbreviation for Your Mileage May Vary. An expression used in Internet correspondence to suggest the variable quality of many Internet software programs, features, and experiences.

INDEX